Con cope

2025

Monthly astrological forecasts for 2025

TATIANA BORSCH

Translated from Russian by Sonja Swenson and Alexander Viner
Edited by Alexander Viner

AstraArt Books is an imprint of Coinflow limited, Cyprus
Published by Coinflow Limited, Cyprus
For queries please contact: tatianaborsch@yahoo.com

ISBN: 978-9925-609-58-1 (print)
ISBN: 978-9925-609-59-8 (ebook)

Contents

Astrological Insights into 2025: A Year of Challenges and Opportunities

The year 2025 will continue the challenging period that began in 2020 with the onset of the Age of Aquarius, as I mentioned in my 2020 forecast. The year can be roughly divided into two very different phases. The first half of 2025 will be marked by instability, struggles, and crises, both economically and politically. However, the second half of the year promises to be more positive and stable, with many problems gradually being resolved, the economy beginning to recover, and political issues starting to be addressed.

Starting in January, Jupiter, the most powerful planet in our solar system, will be in the sign of Gemini and will form several unfavorable aspects with Saturn during the first half of the year. Jupiter symbolizes new trends, while Saturn represents outdated state and economic systems. Their conflict signifies a battle between the old and the new. The old system has run its course and must give way to the new. However, obsolete political and economic structures rarely surrender without a fight, leading to fierce confrontations worldwide. This struggle is not confined to politics—new, often revolutionary trends will impact many areas of life. In 2025, we will witness changes in the political landscape of most countries, as well as in the lives of many individuals. Old politicians will be replaced by new ones, a process that will benefit the world as a whole.

The most challenging months of 2025 will be January, February, and March, when the conflict between Jupiter and Saturn will be compounded by retrograde Mars, moving backward from December 6, 2024, to February 24, 2025. This could lead to unrest in many regions, particularly in England, the USA, and EU countries. We can expect large-scale demonstrations, political strife, and conflicts rooted in religious differences. These trends may begin as early as November-December 2024 and continue into the first months of 2025. During this same period, military conflicts in global hotspots may reach a critical phase.

However, from mid-March to June, a period of realization and stabilization will emerge—politicians and society will start to recognize the need for change. The second half of the year will be more favorable: although changes won't happen overnight and not in every area, the situation will begin to stabilize and improve.

I would like to note that from 2021 to 2030, many planetary alignments will mirror those of the 1940s and 1950s, a time that profoundly changed the world.

Economy

In the first half of 2025, the economic situation is expected to deteriorate significantly. A large-scale financial crisis that may have already started in the second half of 2024 is likely to continue, affecting all countries worldwide. The second half of 2025, however, is expected to be much calmer, with the gradual recovery of the global economy from the crisis.

China will continue to be one of the world's economic leaders, with its influence on global processes growing noticeably. Domestically, the popularity of Chinese leader Xi Jinping will increase. However, the economic rivalry between the United States, Europe, and China will intensify, with China continuing to outmaneuver its competitors in the trade war.

India is set to undergo a year of restructuring. Measures will be taken to optimize the economy, and construction efforts will ramp up, yielding tangible results within two years, propelling the country into the future. Over the next three years, India will make significant strides in addressing issues such as poverty, and by 2030, it is expected to become one of the world's leading economies.

In the second half of 2025, businesses related to agriculture and food production will experience significant growth. Those involved in the dairy industry are particularly likely to achieve notable success.

United States

The United States will continue to face internal divisions. Pluto periodically returns to its position in the natal chart of the United States, a planet that is highly significant for the country as it governs the financial state and moral outlook of the population. Pluto symbolizes purification and renewal, but before it renews a system, it first destroys the old one. The 2024 elections will occur during a very tense time. In 2024, transiting Uranus will enter Gemini in the U.S. chart, and by 2027, it will occupy the same position it held during the Civil War. This suggests that societal polarization will deepen.

The 2024 presidential election in the United States will be extremely challenging. As I predicted in last year's forecast, Biden has exited the race: 'It is hard to imagine Joe Biden hanging onto the presidency. He will leave. I believe that Donald Trump will win, as Kamala Harris's horoscope appears weaker. This victory will lead to internal divisions within the country. (I am writing this prediction in July 2024, before my book is published, so the election results are still unknown.) However, I want to emphasize that the election period will be difficult for Trump as well, with many unpleasant surprises.

In 2025, the United States will continue to lose its standing on the international stage. The trend of weakening influence will become increasingly apparent and is likely to persist. This decline could result from failures on many fronts, where the resources to maintain the role of global hegemon are insufficient, and opponents will exploit this weakness.

United Kingdom

The United Kingdom will need to take decisive measures to stabilize its economy. Divergent opinions within the ruling circles may intensify the struggle between political parties, creating additional tension in society. A surge in public dissatisfaction, driven by the current political direction of the country, is also possible. However, thanks to Jupiter, the planet of luck, which will be in the financial sector of the UK's horoscope, significant progress in overcoming accumulated economic problems is expected in 2025.

The horoscope of the United Kingdom is based on several key dates. If we consider the founding date of the United Kingdom—January 1, 1801, when the union of Great Britain and Ireland took place—then in the next five years, we might see trends toward the disintegration of the United Kingdom.

European Union

The political and economic situation in Germany and France will be the most challenging within the European Union. Germany is still going through one of the most difficult periods, known as Sade Sati in Indian astrology. For Germany, this period primarily signifies economic decline and internal political strife. Conflicts based on national and religious grounds are also possible. This difficult period began in 2022 and will last for another 2-3 years.

Emmanuel Macron and his party will lose their position in France. However, even under Marine Le Pen's party in 2025 and 2026, neither prosperity nor even stabilization of the internal situation can be expected. External forces may actively hinder these developments. The economic situation in Italy also remains weak.

Russia

As I predicted in 2024, Putin remained in power after the presidential elections in Russia and began reshuffling the government.

In the first half of 2025, significant military conflicts are expected in Russia, which may involve countries beyond Ukraine, possibly including Europe and the United States. The Russian leadership will continue to change many people responsible for the country's economic and political development.

The West will continue to pressure Russia. The escalation of the conflict in Ukraine will continue in the first half of 2025, potentially reaching a more alarming level. Since this prediction is being written in the summer of 2024, it is possible to foresee that in the summer and fall of 2024, as well as in the winter of 2025, direct confrontation between Russia and NATO is not out of the question. The situation could become critical. However, a large-scale war could be prevented by factors unrelated to Ukraine, such as internal political struggles in Europe and the United States or major natural disasters affecting many regions worldwide, including the United States. It is possible that both scenarios could occur.

For Putin, the first half of 2025 will be extremely challenging due to unprecedented confrontation with the West. However, by spring 2025, it will become clear that defeating Russia on the battlefield is impossible. In the second half of 2025, Ukraine will be forced to cede Russian-speaking territories to Russia, and negotiations will proceed on terms set by Russia. These negotiations may continue into the first half of 2026.

Negotiations may also take place before this time, but without real results. The West will continue to demand territorial concessions and intensify sanctions and economic pressure, but this will not change the situation on the ground. Ultimately, some territories will be ceded to Russia, and this process may not always be peaceful.

Overall, the second half of 2025 will be more stable for Russia than the first. It will be a relatively good time for the country. Sanctions will, of course, remain, but events will slowly but surely begin to unfold in favor of the Russian Federation as the influence of the United States weakens under the pressure of its political and economic problems.

National policy in the Russian Federation will change, possibly necessitating the adoption of strict laws related to migration. This may occur due to terrorist attacks. December 2024, January, and February 2025 are particularly challenging in this regard.

Ukraine

It appears that by 2025, Zelensky may no longer be in Ukraine. What exactly will happen to him is difficult to say, but his situation will be extremely challenging. The period from December 2024 to February 2025 is particularly critical for him. It's hard to predict his fate, but he may be forced to flee the country due to numerous accusations, both from within Ukraine and from international sponsors.

In 2025, Poland may openly assert its claim over Lviv and other western territories, potentially deploying troops to these areas. My forecast suggests that Ukraine will be divided into spheres of influence, and I believe this division could begin as early as 2025. Hungary might claim Transcarpathia, possibly through a voluntary process like a referendum.

In the eastern territories that Russia has captured, the country will continue significant restoration efforts, rebuilding cities and infrastructure.

Middle East

As I predicted in my 2024 forecast, this year saw the outbreak of war in the Middle East. The situation in the Middle East, as well as in other "hot spots" around the world, is likely to escalate further. In the second half of 2024 and the first half of 2025, real conflicts may occur, not only along Israel's borders but also involving other countries. My prediction is that a ceasefire or peace agreement will be reached closer to the second half of 2025, but only after the situation reaches a critical point. In other words, things will get worse before they get better.

Technology

With Pluto entering the sign of Aquarius, which happened last year in 2023, various innovative technologies, neural networks, and artificial intelligence have gained significant momentum. It's worth noting that Aquarius is ruled by Uranus, which is associated with progress and unexpected changes, and artificial intelligence can be seen as one expression of this energy. We are also witnessing significant transformations in finance—mobile applications and electronic currencies are becoming increasingly widespread. Since Pluto will remain in Aquarius for about 20 years, the world will undergo profound changes during this period, and 2024–2025 will bring many unexpected technological breakthroughs. Naturally, this will impact space exploration, and we can expect significant advancements in this field in the coming years, potentially revealing much more about life beyond our planet.

Weather

The weather in 2025 will continue to deliver unpleasant surprises. In regions that have already suffered from floods, there is a likelihood of similar situations recurring, but on an even larger scale.

In the spring and summer of 2025, major wildfires are expected, so it's wise to prepare in advance. Saturn and Neptune will be in the fire sign of Aries throughout the summer, leading to an increase in the scale of fires compared to previous years.

In seismically active areas of the planet, earthquakes are possible.

Family

When it comes to people's lives, it can be said that the challenging planetary alignments in the first half of 2025 will affect everyone. How these aspects will manifest depends on individual horoscopes. For some, it could mean divorce; for others, professional troubles—each person will experience something unique.

The second half of 2025 looks more stable from an astrological perspective. The planets will calm down, and life will gradually return to normal. The second half of 2025 is a good time for marriage, childbirth, and acquiring property. People will begin to return to a proper understanding of family values, taking more care of their parents and elder family members.

Health

In terms of health, the first half of 2025 could also bring several unpleasant surprises.

Infections related to respiratory issues may reappear, as well as neurological disorders that could be difficult to diagnose. Those with chronic leg conditions may also face various flare-ups. Summer 2025 could bring exacerbations of cardiovascular diseases, migraines, and strokes. So take care of yourself if you have any predispositions to these conditions.

The second half of the year will bring new advancements—significant progress in technologies related to cancer treatment and various tumor diseases is expected.

During this period, people may become more concerned with various diets, leading to an increase in the production of organic foods, which will become more sought after.

Fashion

In the first half of 2025, fashion will be dominated by youthful trends and extravagant outfits. There may be some chaos, with a mix of styles that were once considered incompatible.

Since Jupiter is in the air sign of Gemini, lightweight, transparent fabrics, mesh, chiffon, and comfortable knitwear will be in demand. Colors will range from greenish-gray and bluish-gray to soft pastel shades.

In the second half of the year, as Jupiter moves into the sign of Cancer and forms a friendly aspect with Saturn, a return to classic styles is expected. Leather in various forms will become popular again, and denim will see a resurgence in various styles. Colors will include all shades of blue, black, and gray.

Travel

In the first half of 2025, I would not recommend long-distance travel or making important decisions regarding relocation.

In this regard, the second half of the year will be more successful.

For more detailed information, check out my forecast for the zodiac signs.

Good luck in 2025!
Astrologer Tatiana Borsch

2025 Overview for all Zodiac signs

ARIES

In 2025, your journey forward continues, but the road is challenging. Overcoming obstacles, stay true to yourself, and everything will turn out well.

Business. The most difficult time in 2025 is the first half of the year. The opposition of Jupiter and Saturn, which shapes the year's events, means major problems with colleagues from other cities or countries. This news is not very good, but there is a plus! This situation is familiar to you, so you know how to work and live with it.

Legal issues that began in the past year, 2024, are likely to continue. The most challenging months of the first half of 2025 are January, February, and March. During this period, your ruler Mars is moving backward, making it difficult to act boldly and openly as you are used to. April and May are relatively calm, and you will be able to partially catch up on what was missed. Starting in July, the situation changes dramatically. The movement of Jupiter into the sign of Cancer changes both the overall mood and your priorities.

Entrepreneurs and managers will be concerned with expanding their business and will begin active work in this direction. Various operations with real estate, land, and large-scale construction are possible. Perhaps a foundation is being prepared for a new stage in business, and the stars will support this idea. Work in this direction will continue into 2026.

Employees may face intrigues within the team in the first half of the year, as well as changes in the organization. All of this will prompt thoughts of joining a family business or starting their own venture. A solution will be found, as the saying goes: 'Whatever happens, happens for the best,' and remember that the sky is always fair.

Money. The first half of the year is financially challenging. Excessive expenses are possible, related to business in one case and personal life in another. In the second half of the year, the situation will significantly improve; entrepreneurs can count on support from partners, sponsorship, and favorable loans. Alternatively, help may come from a spouse, parents, or a close person.

Love and Family. In the first half of 2025, relations with relatives will significantly complicate: in one case, a prolonged quarrel is likely, and in another, you will have to solve family problems, helping with words, deeds, and possibly money.

With children, problems are likely in the first months of the year, leading to disagreements and significant expenses. The second half of the year is more peaceful; the problems that have arisen will be resolved, and peace will reign in families. Parents and close people will provide great support in all matters.

Most representatives of your sign are planning new acquisitions. For example, they may start building a new house or a major renovation of the old one. These household activities will take up not only the second half of 2025 but also the first half of 2026.

Health. In the first half of 2025, your energy potential is quite high. However, during this period, travel poses a danger, whether short or long distances. Stars recommend refraining from traveling to other countries entirely, as the likelihood of various problems is very high.

Drivers should be more attentive on the road in the first half of the year. The probability of accidents and unpleasant incidents on the road is quite high.

In the second half of the year, your energy potential will slightly decrease; states of lethargy, fatigue, and a tendency to gain weight are possible. During this time, don't forget about sports and remember that "moving is living."

TAURUS

The main task for 2025 is to assess your strengths realistically and avoid taking on unmanageable tasks. Take care of yourself and cherish what you already have!

Business. The first half of 2025 is quite challenging for all professional activities. The opposition of the two giant planets, Jupiter and Saturn, means problems with some friends or people who have influence and power. The reason may be financial matters or some unfulfilled obligations. This problem is not new to you, as you have already faced it in the fall of 2024—this is just its logical continuation.

In another scenario, there may be changes in business, such as expansion or transformation, which will also require a lot of funds. Everything will proceed with great difficulty, and your task is to calculate expenses in advance to avoid a financial crisis.

In the second half of the year, the situation will significantly improve. Old connections will be restored, and contacts with colleagues from other cities or countries will become noticeably more active. Many of your sign will have the opportunity to start a business in distant places, and these plans will come to fruition at different times in 2025 or already in 2026.

The second half of the year is good for learning, gaining new knowledge, as well as restoring lost connections and seeking new contacts.

Money. The first half of 2025 will be financially draining. Money will be going out constantly, and in one case, this is related to unresolved professional matters, and in another—to personal life. Many will have to pay off debts, settle loans, and fulfill obligations. However, you will not be entirely out of money, so you will be able to resolve the problems.

The second half of the year is more stable financially. Expenses will decrease significantly, and income will increase.

Love and Family. Personal life in the first half of the year will be uneven and restless. Many families will focus on improving their homes, which could involve repairing the old or acquiring new property. In both cases, you will face substantial expenses, more than initially expected.

Relationships for lovers are complex, and in some cases, there may be talks of separation. Redefining the rules of the relationship while in it is not easy and may not be successful. You clearly know the changes you want to make, and it seems simple, but reality may be different. Thus, the entire first half of 2025 may pass in disputes and disagreements.

In the second half of the year, much will change. Perhaps both parties will realize that there is something fundamental in the relationship worth preserving. Hold on to that feeling, and everything will gradually settle down.

Singles can expect an interesting meeting and a passionate romance.

In the second half of the year, many of your sign will renew relationships with old friends and close ones living in other cities or countries. Frequent trips or relocations are possible. Relationships with relatives will become much warmer; some of your close family members will thrive and be ready to share their luck, both morally and financially.

The influence of relatives in the second half of the year will be felt in all matters, both personal and professional.

Health. In the first half of 2025, your energy levels will be low, and the nervous atmosphere at home and work will take a toll. Take care of yourself and remember that health is paramount, everything else will follow. In the second half of the year, the planetary pressure will ease, your lost vitality will return, and you will regain confidence in yourself.

GEMINI

The upcoming year is bright and astonishing, with positive celestial influences intricately intertwined with negative ones. However, the positive influences will prevail, so forge ahead boldly!

Business. Positives this year include an exceptionally high energy level, determination, and unwavering confidence in yourself and the correctness of your decisions. Negatives include harshness and an all-or-nothing mentality—"if you're not with us, you're against us." This will lead to both significant successes and tough conflicts. In this regard, the first half of

2025 is especially indicative, when entrepreneurs and bosses will have to face people with influence and power, and employees may encounter problems with their superiors.

The first months of the year—January, February, and March—are particularly challenging, with financial problems adding to the already mentioned difficulties.

Relationships with colleagues from other cities or countries will also become significantly more complicated, and it will be challenging to influence this process. The good news is that Jupiter, the planet of luck, is on your side, residing in your sign and ready to pull you out of any trouble.

In the second half of the year, the situation will change, partly because, despite obstacles, you will establish your own rules of the game. Difficult relationships with powerful figures will gradually resolve, and it will become clear that you were right in many, if not all, aspects. Financial freedom will emerge, allowing you to look to the future with more confidence and calm.

Employees may receive a new position within their current organization or an offer from a more promising company. In both cases, financial positions will improve. In other words, the professional sphere foresees a year of struggle that will undoubtedly end in your victory.

Money. The most challenging financial months are January and February. The entire second half of 2025, however, is an excellent time. During this period, the financial situation for most of your sign will noticeably improve, and you may even rise to a higher financial level and stay there for a long time.

Love and Family. Personal life in 2025 looks as interesting as professional. If you haven't met your partner in 2024, the chances of such a meeting are very high in the first half of 2025. Recently started relationships are developing well, and many families may welcome new children or grandchildren in the second half of the year.

One of the problems in 2025, especially in its first half, could be complicated relationships with parents or elder family members. Problems within the family circle are also likely.

Many of your sign will be involved in home improvements in the second half of the year. This may include renovations, buying furniture, or even acquiring new property.

Health. Throughout the year, your energy levels are quite high, and you are active, industrious, and very attractive to the opposite sex. Take advantage of these opportunities and keep looking forward!

CANCER

You will experience a transformation akin to a butterfly emerging from a caterpillar's cocoon. In the first half of the year, you may feel like a green caterpillar, but then you'll spread your wings and soar. Dare to take flight!

Business. The first half of the year is unfavorable for all professional endeavors. Problems that began in the second half of 2024 may continue. These could involve legal issues or prolonged inspections, and difficulties may also arise from partners in other cities or countries. Additionally, many of your sign will encounter intrigues and schemes from both hidden and overt enemies. Thus, the first half of the year can be summed up by the saying, "Every alley is a dead end."

However, in the second half of the year, the situation will drastically improve. Jupiter, the planet of luck, enters your sign, meaning closed doors will open, and things that didn't work out before will start coming to fruition. Such luck hasn't been seen for a long time, so take action!

Connections with colleagues from other cities or countries will begin to recover slowly, and legal issues, if present in the past, will also be resolved.

Entrepreneurs will find new projects, and employees have a good chance of getting a new, more prestigious job.

Money. The financial situation in the first half of the year leaves much to be desired, which is not surprising given the circumstances. January and February are particularly challenging, with a severe lack of funds.

Starting from mid-March, the situation will improve slightly and fully stabilize by the summer and fall of 2025. During this period, changes will begin that will later bring professional success and money, a process that will continue into the following year, 2026.

Love and Family. Personal life in the first half of the year is also not particularly uplifting. During this period, your flaws will be more visible to others than your virtues.

Protect your reputation, as there will be those eager to expose what you'd prefer to keep hidden. Lovers may experience a cooling period and possibly a breakup. If this happens to you, don't take it too hard. The world is vast, and there are many people in it; you'll find your match. By the second half of the year, this will become very clear. From July onwards, you'll notice a change in how others perceive you, and certainly for the better.

In the second half of 2025, single individuals may meet someone who will become their lifelong partner. The situation will significantly improve for married couples as well. In short, everything will fall into place.

Health. The negative influence of the planets in the first half of the year will also affect your health. Even the young and energetic may not feel very confident or lively. Older and weakened individuals are advised to monitor their health closely and seek medical help if necessary.

All Cancers should be more cautious when traveling and driving in the first half of the year. It is recommended to avoid long-distance trips altogether, as the risk of accidents and unpleasant incidents is quite high, especially in January and February.

In the second half of the year, these restrictions will be lifted, celestial energies will start to support you, and even those who are seriously ill will quickly recover.

LEO

In 2025, you need to learn to balance your desires with your capabilities. You know exactly what you want, but reality might differ. Remember, "A bird in the hand is worth two in the bush," and act accordingly!

Business. 2025 begins on a challenging note for you. Problems that started in the past year, 2024, will continue. According to the stars, these issues are likely to involve a group of influential and powerful people, with money, old debts, or other commitments being the root cause of the problems. Legal troubles might also arise, or, in a milder scenario, disagreements with friends over financial matters could occur.

The most difficult months in the first half of 2025 are January, February, and March. After this period, the situation will start to stabilize, and the second half of the year will be calmer and more predictable. During this time, many Leos might go behind the scenes to restructure their business, preparing for success that is expected to come in the latter half of 2026.

Employees may consider changing jobs due to dissatisfaction from their superiors making the work environment difficult, if not unbearable. If this happens, stay calm — by the second half of 2026, the situation will improve.

Money. Financially, the first half of the year is quite challenging. Money will be constantly going out, either due to professional difficulties or personal issues. The second half of the year will be more stable. Many will gain profits from real estate transactions, receive support from business partners, or secure favorable loans.

Love and Family. Significant events will also occur in your personal life. The first half of the year is tough for both lovers and married couples. Stern Pluto, firmly positioned in the sector of the sky governing marriage and long-term relationships, will test the strength of all existing connections. This could lead to separations or burdensome responsibilities concerning a loved one.

In the second half of the year, many Leos will begin major home renovations. This process can take various forms: building a new house, remodeling an existing one, or purchasing new property. These activities may extend into the early months of 2026.

Health. In the first half of the year, your energy levels will be quite high, allowing you to handle all of life's challenges effectively. In the second half of the year, your energy will significantly decrease, so make sure to dedicate more time to yourself. You will have opportunities to do so. The latter part of the year also suggests a need for seclusion, stepping back from the hustle and bustle, and philosophically reflecting on life.

VIRGO

2025 is a continuation of situations that arose in the recent past. Slowly but surely, you are finding your way out of the maze of problems you inadvertently found yourself in.

Business. The business landscape is entering a new but rather challenging phase. In the first half of the year, the main issue for many leaders and entrepreneurs will be their relationships with partners. In some cases, conflicts may arise related to the development of the business or possibly its division.

Employees will face stiff competition, significantly weakening their professional positions. While relations with superiors will remain relatively intact, career advancement may slow down. The most challenging months in the first half of the year are January, February, and March. After this period, the situation will slightly improve. It is worth noting that the problems in 2025 will not come as a surprise, as you have faced similar issues in 2023 and 2024.

The second half of 2025 is more stable and somewhat calmer. It will feel as though the stars have decided to support you. During this period, old friends or influential people may take an active role in your affairs. This will improve relationships with hostile partners, opening up the possibility for negotiations that could end in a favorable compromise.

Employees will also find support, strengthening their positions. While problems may still arise periodically, the second half of 2025 looks generally peaceful.

Money. Financially, 2025 is stable, though there won't be any windfalls or significant increases in income. The stars recommend living within your means, controlling your expenses, and realistically assessing your capabilities.

Love and Family. In your personal life, problems from the past will continue. Conflicts with a spouse or close person will logically continue, especially in the first half of 2025.

If money is the issue, it is unlikely that you will achieve your desired outcome in the first half of the year. However, positive dialogue is possible in the second half, potentially leading to full reconciliation at best. At worst, you may peacefully resolve past issues and part ways amicably. In any case, take advantage of the opportunities the universe provides and act according to the scenario fate has prepared.

Health. For most of the year, your energy levels are quite high. However, be mindful of your health in January, February, and March—these are the most challenging months of the year, when old chronic illnesses may flare up, and new ones might unexpectedly appear.

This is especially true for the elderly and those with weakened health. Young and robust individuals are advised to monitor mood swings, lead a healthy lifestyle, and avoid unnecessary stress and fuss.

LIBRA

A bright, challenging, and fruitful year lies ahead. You will achieve a lot, but it won't come easily. In short, through hardship to the stars!

Business. Professionally, the year can be roughly divided into two distinctly different periods. In the first period, most Libras will face a number of problems. Entrepreneurs and managers will continue to experience disagreements with colleagues from other cities or countries, with conflicts occasionally becoming quite severe. There may be a resurgence of old legal issues, as well as constant visits from regulatory bodies.

Additionally, leaders at all levels may encounter incompetence, hostility, or dishonesty from subordinates. These mistakes can lead to significant complications in important matters, so it's crucial to monitor what's happening and double-check all assignments.

Employees might face organizational changes and hostility from colleagues. The most challenging months in the first half of the year are January, February, and March.

The second half of 2025 is more successful. It seems you will handle all the challenges excellently and end up in a strong position. Businesspeople and managers can look forward to launching major projects and enjoying substantial profits. Employees might receive a promotion at their current job, along with a salary increase.

Hostility from distant colleagues will gradually fade. Your partners may have to acknowledge your strengths and victories, agreeing to the rules you set.

Money. The financial outlook is also promising in the second half of 2025, with noticeable increases in income for most Libras. The most challenging months for finances and other resources will likely be January and February.

Love and Family. Family and romantic relationships will not be particularly stable for much of the year. On one hand, this is due to heavy workloads and numerous professional problems. Your focus might be entirely on work, leaving little time for loved ones, leading to noticeable cooling in relationships.

The latter half of June, July, and early August will be particularly difficult, with conflicts potentially arising unexpectedly, even among the most harmonious couples. Pay close attention to these disputes, as they could signal unwanted changes in the future. If your partner is busy with household tasks, offer support both verbally and physically, benefiting both sides in the end.

In the first half of 2025, many Libras may encounter issues with relatives. The stars advise staying as far away from family intrigues as possible, as this is not a situation where truth will emerge from arguments. Ultimately, everything will resolve itself without your involvement, likely to your benefit.

Health. Your energy levels in 2025 will generally be high, but in the first half of the year, all Libras should be particularly careful when traveling and driving. It's advisable to avoid long trips and flights, as the risk of complications is quite high. These restrictions will ease in the second half of the year.

SCORPIO

The year 2025 opens up new horizons for you. To reach them, you will have to face obstacles, so be prepared to overcome various challenges. The motto of the year: "Constant dropping will wear away a stone."

Business. The first half of 2025 is openly not your time. Entrepreneurs and managers will have to fend off various problems, including organizational and financial issues. It is quite possible that this involves an expansion started in the recent past, large-scale construction, or various real estate transactions. Such activities will proceed with difficulties, delays, and problems.

Many Scorpios will also have to deal with inspections, legal issues, and hostility from various official bodies. Employees may face significantly strained relations with management and some colleagues. This may lead to a desire to change jobs, but such opportunities are unlikely to arise in the first half of 2025, which is worth keeping in mind.

The second half of the year is more promising. During this period, new horizons will open up, but they may look different for everyone. In one case, it could be a move or opening a business in another city or country. In another case, it could be the completion of a large-scale business expansion, major construction, and the beginning of new important ventures on this basis.

Employees can count on new job opportunities, and in some cases, these may involve relocation. All the changes that occur in the first half of 2025 and in 2026 can be positively assessed. Embrace them, hoping for the best. Everything will be fine!

Money. The first half of 2025 is a financially draining period. Money will be spent continuously, possibly even more than initially planned.

The second half of the year is much more stable financially. Expenses will significantly decrease, and income will increase, and this favorable trend will continue into the next year, 2026.

Love and Family. Personal life in the first half of the year is challenging for both lovers and spouses. Lovers may often quarrel, sometimes leading to separation. The causes of problems can vary – jealousy, different value systems, and even financial disputes.

Spouses will face issues with children. In one case, it could be a long separation, and in another, a serious quarrel. Many will have to invest large sums in the upbringing, development, and establishment of the younger generation.

The second half of the year is more peaceful. Quarreling couples might consider reconciliation, and the stars will surely offer them this opportunity. Parents will mend relationships with their children. Reunions with children living in other cities or countries are also possible.

Those planning renovations or real estate transactions will be able to complete these activities by the fall of 2025 and move into new housing.

Health. In the first half of 2025, your energy levels will be significantly reduced, leading to the exacerbation of old ailments and the unexpected appearance of new ones. In the second half of the year, the stars will change their stance and try to support you. You will gain more energy, noticeable to all Scorpios regardless of age. In the first half of the year, be cautious during trips and while driving.

SAGITTARIUS

In 2025, your ruler Jupiter is in the sector of the sky responsible for relationships, meaning connections are everything. To make the most of this year, remember that "two heads are better than one." Learn to build relationships, even though it will sometimes be quite challenging.

Business. The beginning of 2025 will bring various problems for many Sagittarians. These issues likely stem from the summer and autumn of 2024 and will now continue. In one scenario, there may be problems with colleagues from other cities or countries, leading to financial difficulties. In another, you might have to deal with legal issues that arose recently. Some Sagittarians may also face real estate problems. These issues will persist until about April, after which the situation will resolve.

In the first half of 2025, employees will face inspections, intrigues, and unhealthy competition. Organizational changes will cause uncertainty and anxiety, leading to a desire to change jobs or fields of activity. The most determined might decide to start their own business.

The second half of 2025 will be more stable and calm. Entrepreneurs and managers will focus on strengthening or expanding their businesses. This period will involve various real estate operations and a lot of administrative and organizational work. In the latter half of 2024, new people may have appeared on your horizon, with relationships developing in different ways. This trend will continue in 2025—some new partners will prove useful, while others might turn out to be disappointments. The stars advise evaluating people based on their actions rather than words to avoid mistakes.

Money. The financial situation in 2025 will vary. The first half of the year will involve many expenses related to professional issues and personal problems. The second half of the year will be more stable, with good support from colleagues and possibly help from friends or loved ones.

Love and Family. In your personal life, the planetary emphasis this year is on your partner, meaning most of the initiative will come from your significant other rather than you. This dependence on your partner will affect both lovers and spouses. Relationships started in 2024 will develop well, which is good for those long seeking a partner. However, for those already in a committed relationship, a new love will bring several problems. Sitting on two chairs won't work; you will have to make a choice, which will be quite difficult. In case of a divorce, dividing shared property will be a significant issue, and you'll deal with this in the first half of 2025. In the second half, a resolution will be found, unique to each situation.

The second half of the year is a time for resolving various housing issues. You might build a house, a summer home, or undertake major renovations. These activities will continue until the summer of 2026, so prepare for an extended period of home improvement.

Health. In 2025, your energy levels will be low, so carefully plan your workload and ensure you find time to rest. The saying "never do today what you can put off until tomorrow" might become very relevant for you this year.

CAPRICORN

The life rules you've become accustomed to may change without warning. What was once considered stable may no longer be. To maximize the benefits of this year, you need to navigate the turbulent waters of events and be ready to adapt to new rules.

Business. The first half of the year is both dynamic and challenging for career-related matters. Problems you've already encountered in the autumn and winter of 2024 will continue. These include exacerbating legal issues and significantly worsening relations with colleagues from other cities or countries. Ultimately, financial problems may arise, which will require daily attention.

Entrepreneurs and managers should prepare for inspections, which are rarely pleasant. There may be conflicts within the team, affecting both employees and entrepreneurs. The most difficult months are January and February, when serious conflicts with business partners, which also began in 2024, may occur. Despite these problems, there will still be plenty of work to do.

In the second half of the year, the situation will unexpectedly improve. It will seem as if the planets have decided to help you. Problems will be resolved one way or another, old connections will be restored, and opportunities for productive and stable work will arise. During this period, old partners, friends, and people from your past will play a significant role in your affairs. Communication with colleagues from other cities or countries will normalize, and although problems in this area may still arise, the situation will be much better than at the beginning of 2025.

Money. The financial situation will be turbulent, especially in the first months of the year, when expenses will be excessive. The second half of the year will be calmer, with fewer expenses, while income remains stable.

Love and Family. Personal relationships in the first half of the year will be filled with uncertainty and nervousness. Lovers may distance themselves from each other and even consider separation. However, there is still attraction and sexual desire in these relationships, which makes it hard to completely let go. Emotional instability may last until mid-summer, after which clarity and calm will arrive. The solution found will be decisive, but it will look different in each specific case. Those juggling two relationships will likely choose their previous partner and part with the new attachment. Estranged spouses will be able to reconcile.

Single people who are disillusioned with previous relationships will have the chance to meet their destiny in the second half of the year.

Relationships with relatives, which caused you many troubles in the second half of 2024 and the first half of 2025, will become less hostile. In short, if the planets put pressure on you in the first half of the year, you can look forward to the second half, when the sky will turn from wrath to mercy.

Health. The first half of the year is unfavorable for health. Special caution is advised for the elderly and those with weakened health, as there may be exacerbations of old illnesses and unexpected new ones. Additionally, there is a high risk of accidents and injuries in January and February. Be especially careful when traveling and driving; it might be better to stay home during these months. The second half of 2025 is more positive for health, likely because there will be fewer problems and you will be less stressed.

AQUARIUS

The year will bring changes to both your work and personal life. This is a wonderful yet turbulent time for taking decisive steps towards your goals in both professional and romantic relationships.

Business. The year 2025 can be divided into two halves. In the first half, financial matters will be the main issue. Planned activities will require much more funding than initially anticipated, so be prepared to calculate everything in advance.

It's possible that financial problems will lead to delays in your affairs, so balance your plans, desires, and capabilities. This advice is particularly aimed at entrepreneurs and managers involved in expanding their business. Additionally, they should pay more attention to their subordinates, who may occasionally behave inappropriately and aggressively, affecting the team atmosphere and the flow of work. Expect inspections, the reactivation of old legal problems, or the emergence of new ones.

Employees are advised to be friendly in their interactions with colleagues and avoid participating in intrigues. The most challenging months in this regard are January, February, and June. Overall, the atmosphere in the organization may be unstable in the first half of the year, so the best approach is to calmly perform your duties without getting caught up in the surrounding chaos.

The second half of the year is more stable. During this period, things will progress smoothly and quickly, likely because money will become available. Entrepreneurs and managers will be able to hire new, competent, and reliable employees. At the same time, the old staff who have proven themselves will remain. Employees will be given new responsibilities, benefiting them both morally and financially.

Money. The first half of the year looks particularly challenging financially, with many expenses and few incomes. Often, large expenditures will be related to personal life, household concerns, and children. The second half of the year is more stable financially. Income will increase, and expenses will decrease, allowing you to look to the future with confidence and implement your long-term plans.

Love and Family. The first half of the year in personal life looks turbulent. Storms are followed by calms, but the thunder may strike again. Lovers may experience extreme highs and lows in their relationships. The stars recommend distinguishing between important issues and trivial matters, making it easier to deal with problems. If a separation does occur, consider it a valuable lesson for the future. This advice is also relevant for spouses, as their relationships may also come under celestial pressure. Household issues will be resolved successfully, particularly in the first half of the year.

Parents will need to invest money, time, and nerves into their children.

Health. For most of the year, your energy levels will be low, so the stars recommend paying extra attention to your health, giving up bad habits, and adopting healthy ones.

Many Aquarians will need to care for their parents, elderly family members, or a close loved one. The first few months of the year, especially January and February, will be particularly challenging in this regard.

PISCES

Despite the pressure from Saturn, you are steadily moving forward. Don't stop, even if your path sometimes resembles a labyrinth. Your personal motto for this year is: "The road is made by walking!"

Business. In professional terms, this year can be described as difficult yet successful. Significant challenges are expected in the first few months, continuing the problems that arose in the fall and winter of 2024. Those engaged in expanding their business will face inspections, as well as stubbornness and incompetence from subordinates. Entrepreneurs and managers should closely monitor their surroundings, as there may be both covert and overt opposition. Employees need to be more attentive to their colleagues and superiors, as there will be those who want to take their positions. January and February are particularly challenging, but starting from March, the situation will stabilize somewhat.

It should also be noted that the first half of the year is chaotic, unstable, and full of surprises, mostly unpleasant. Influencing the situation will be difficult, so it's wise to review all weak points in your work and take necessary measures.

The second half of 2025 is calmer. During this period, it will become clear that you have successfully handled all the challenges posed by the stars and are steadily moving forward. The popularity of many representatives of your sign will noticeably increase—either within a narrow circle of specialists or with broader public recognition. The main benefits of the second half of 2025 will be stability and the restoration of previous connections.

During this period, relationships with colleagues from other cities or countries, which had significantly deteriorated in the fall and winter of 2024 and the first months of 2025, will be resolved. In the second half of 2025, everything will slowly but surely return to normal.

Money. Significant expenses are likely in the first half of 2025, related to work, business expansion, family problems, and household concerns. In the second half of the year, finances will improve, directly indicating success in business and stabilization in personal life.

Love and Family. For many Pisces, work will take a back seat, and significant developments can be expected in personal life. Various housing operations—construction, renovation, purchase of a new home—will occupy the entire first half of the year. Naturally, the atmosphere in many families will be tense and unstable, with financial and emotional difficulties disrupting peace at home.

In the second half of the year, the situation will improve significantly, and many families will welcome children or grandchildren. This period is favorable for lovers, with new romances and the potential for rekindling old connections. Those who quarreled in the past will realize that love still exists and forgive each other's grievances.

Health. In the first half of the year, the energy levels of most Pisces will be quite low. Therefore, maintain a healthy lifestyle and ensure you find time for rest. There may be a tendency to gain weight, so plan a diet, remember the benefits of exercise, and engage in moderate physical activity. In the second half of the year, energy will increase, along with your attractiveness, charm, and influence on others.

January

New York Time			London Time		
Calendar Day	Lunar Day	Lunar Day Start Time	Calendar Day	Lunar Day	Lunar Day Start Time
31/12/24	2	7:54:20 AM	31/12/24	2	8:32:59 AM
01/01/25	3	8:38:27 AM	01/01/25	3	9:12:32 AM
02/01/25	4	9:16:49 AM	02/01/25	4	9:44:09 AM
03/01/25	5	9:50:37 AM	03/01/25	5	10:10:00 AM
04/01/25	6	10:21:18 AM	04/01/25	6	10:32:08 AM
05/01/25	7	10:50:26 AM	05/01/25	7	10:52:20 AM
06/01/25	8	11:19:31 AM	06/01/25	8	11:12:10 AM
07/01/25	9	11:50:09 AM	07/01/25	9	11:33:09 AM
08/01/25	10	12:24:01 PM	08/01/25	10	11:57:02 AM
09/01/25	11	1:02:52 PM	09/01/25	11	12:25:58 PM
10/01/25	12	1:48:21 PM	10/01/25	12	1:02:33 PM
11/01/25	13	2:41:18 PM	11/01/25	13	1:49:18 PM
12/01/25	14	3:41:05 PM	12/01/25	14	2:47:15 PM
13/01/25	15	4:45:27 PM	13/01/25	15	3:54:35 PM
14/01/25	16	5:51:26 PM	14/01/25	16	5:07:10 PM
15/01/25	17	6:56:40 PM	15/01/25	17	6:20:52 PM
16/01/25	18	7:59:54 PM	16/01/25	18	7:33:09 PM
17/01/25	19	9:00:56 PM	17/01/25	19	8:43:09 PM
18/01/25	20	10:00:16 PM	18/01/25	20	9:51:07 PM
19/01/25	21	10:58:36 PM	19/01/25	21	10:57:47 PM
20/01/25	22	11:56:47 PM	21/01/25	22	12:04:04 AM
22/01/25	23	12:55:27 AM	22/01/25	23	1:10:39 AM
23/01/25	24	1:54:55 AM	23/01/25	24	2:17:49 AM
24/01/25	25	2:54:54 AM	24/01/25	25	3:24:57 AM
25/01/25	26	3:54:21 AM	25/01/25	26	4:30:17 AM
26/01/25	27	4:51:30 AM	26/01/25	27	5:30:59 AM
27/01/25	28	5:44:26 AM	27/01/25	28	6:24:05 AM
28/01/25	29	6:31:48 AM	28/01/25	29	7:08:08 AM
29/01/25	30	7:13:21 AM	29/01/25	30	7:43:37 AM
29/01/25	1	7:37:19 AM	29/01/25	1	12:37:19 PM
30/01/25	2	7:49:50 AM	30/01/25	2	8:12:21 AM
31/01/25	3	8:22:34 AM	31/01/25	3	8:36:29 AM

You can find the description of each lunar day in the chapter "A Guide to The Moon Cycle and Lunar Days"

ARIES

"All things are difficult before they are easy." This is your mantra for January. Remember, there are no unsolvable problems, even if you encounter difficulties.

Business. January promises a lot of opportunities. You can enhance your authority among colleagues, gain approval from superiors, and catch the attention of influential people, which is always beneficial. However, Mars, your ruler, is still retrograde, advising caution. Focus on thoroughness rather than speed in business matters. At the same time, avoid unnecessary delays—plan your steps carefully and progress steadily.

The main challenge this month might be complex relationships with colleagues from other cities or countries. For most Aries, this isn't new; you've dealt with similar issues before. Be cautious and prudent—the situation remains unresolved, but there's a chance to improve your position through intermediaries or allies. If they can't help, it's best to leave the matter for another time when the circumstances are more favorable.

Those involved in business or organizational matters, such as construction or office renovations, might revisit and resolve lingering issues this month.

Money. Financially, January is favorable. Funds will come in regularly, and the amounts will noticeably increase. Key dates for receiving significant income are January 4, 5, 8, 9, 17, 18, 27, and 28. However, expect significant expenses, most related to personal life or helping friends. If someone owes you money, don't expect repayment this month. In fact, conflicts with debtors are likely.

Love and Family. The romantic sphere might not bring much joy in January. Lovers could face disagreements, especially in the first week of the month. Spouses may deal with real problems involving children and substantial related expenses in the first ten days. However, personal matters should improve somewhat in the last ten days of the month.

Many families will continue activities related to home improvement, which may include minor repairs or finishing earlier projects. Some might also purchase decorative items for their homes.

If you have a trip planned, prepare thoroughly, and if you're unsure of its necessity, it might be better to cancel it altogether.

Ongoing issues with relatives will likely continue, as these problems began last year. Unfortunately, they may persist for at least another six months.

Health. You are energetic and healthy in January, with enough vitality to support others in need. However, exercise caution while traveling and driving throughout the month.

TAURUS

In January, don't overestimate your abilities—there's a risk of getting involved in risky relationships and projects. This advice applies to both your work and personal life.

Business. Many Taurus professionals will spend most of January addressing issues from last year. These often involve complex financial matters with old friends or influential figures. By the end of the month, some issues may seem resolved, but don't be fooled—they might resurface later.

Many of these problems will revolve around money, debt obligations, and unresolved financial matters. Some situations may even escalate to legal complications, so it's wise to be prepared in advance.

Relationships with colleagues from other cities or countries will become more active, and you may see both successes and challenges in this area. However, there is hope that the successes will outweigh the challenges.

Professionally, the best period of January is the last ten days when things noticeably improve. Significant help may come from old friends or even family members.

Money. Financially, January will be unpredictable. Significant expenses are likely in the first half of the month, but the situation will improve later. The largest sum of money will arrive in the last days of January.

Love and Family. The personal sphere looks uneven and tense. Many families will face issues with parents or older relatives, which could involve illness or other troubles, and in some cases, serious disagreements.

Relationships among spouses remain unstable, particularly for couples who've had ongoing issues in the past.

For those in love, this month is challenging. The first two weeks, in particular, will be emotionally charged. Sensitivity will be heightened, and offenses may arise unexpectedly. Keep your emotions in check, avoid suspicion and jealousy, and think carefully before speaking or acting. Diplomacy is essential, even when it's difficult. This advice applies to both work and personal life.

As January progresses, the tension will ease, and the end of the month looks much more favorable.

Health. Your energy levels are low in January, likely due to the tense atmosphere of the month. Avoid overexertion, be cautious while traveling and driving. Remember, any problem can be solved with the right approach.

GEMINI

In January, it's time to "lick your wounds" from last year, both in your professional life and in matters of love or lingering family issues.

Business. January isn't particularly productive for professional pursuits. A New Year's vacation might be exactly what you need right now. However, if work is unavoidable, focus on the essentials. The first half of the month seems less promising, while the last ten days offer the best opportunity to resolve professional issues. During this period, employees can address complex matters with their superiors, and entrepreneurs will tackle lingering issues with official entities, challenging partners, and other unresolved problems from the past year. As the saying goes, "Everyone tends to focus on their own concerns."

In the first half of the month, besides the mentioned challenges, you might face unexpected legal issues, problems with official paperwork, or complications with distant colleagues. There could also be the cancellation of a planned trip or difficulties with its execution.

Money. Financially, the first half of January is unstable. Expenses may continue to pile up, whether for holidays and vacations or home improvements and significant purchases to enhance your living space. The second half of the month looks more positive, with the largest sums expected to arrive on January 12, 13, 22, 23, 25, 26, and 31.

Love and Family. The tense personal situation begins to ease. After recent troubles, there comes an understanding that peace is better than a good quarrel. This might lead to reconciliation, or in cases of separation, to dignified and measured agreements. The latter is more likely if a new love has replaced an old attachment. Relationships with parents also become calmer and easier to manage.

Despite the relatively peaceful atmosphere in January, it's wise not to relax completely — some issues remain unresolved, leaving a residual concern.

Health. The energy levels in January are not stable. The stars advise against overestimating your strength and taking on heavy burdens. After January 20, your usual vitality and spirit will return. Be particularly cautious while traveling and driving in the first half of the month, as the risk of accidents and dangerous situations on the road is quite high during this time.

CANCER

In January, be cautious and avoid overestimating your strength. Remember the saying, "God helps those who help themselves," and act accordingly.

Business. The main task in January is to maintain good relationships with those around you, although this may be challenging at times. This is especially true for those dealing with longstanding legal issues, debt obligations, or resolving contentious matters with colleagues from other cities or countries.

After the stresses of the past year, January offers a chance to settle some of these issues. You may find people who can help lighten your load and take on some of your challenges. The second half of the month looks more promising, with a light at the end of the tunnel. The stars will take on much of the burden, but you must provide careful planning, patience, and diplomacy.

Money. Financially, January may not be very successful. Money might be spent continuously, either on work-related expenses or personal matters. Many will need to pay off old debts, settle loans, or fulfill previously made hasty promises. Alternatively, funds might need to be invested in construction or repairs, which could exceed initial budgets. Income in January may be insignificant or even nonexistent.

Love and Family. Personal life could take center stage this month, especially for singles. Pleasant surprises are possible—old acquaintances or friends may reappear, and relationships could take a romantic turn. Alternatively, a new person might appear among old friends, sparking an exciting romance. Therefore, make sure to be visible and always in good shape.

Those involved in home improvement projects might continue these demanding activities, investing time, nerves, and money. There's no end in sight yet, but as the saying goes, "the road will be mastered by the walking."

Health. For most of January, your energy levels may not be particularly high, so special caution is advised for those who are vulnerable or elderly. In the first few days of the month, the risk of accidents and injuries increases, so all Cancerians should be mindful. The "black days" are January 1 to 3, during which risky situations, arguments, financial losses, and other unforeseen problems may occur. Get through this period calmly, and the situation will noticeably improve afterward.

In the second half of January, pay attention to the period from the 26th to the 30th—this time also brings a decrease in energy and difficulties in your endeavors.

LEO

In January, it's crucial not to overestimate your strength—this applies to both your work and relationships with loved ones. Calmness, restraint, and caution will be your best strategies during this period.

Business. The first ten days of the month may feel nearly unproductive in terms of professional activities, possibly due to the lingering effects of the New Year's holidays disrupting your routine.

After January 8th, prospects improve, but many Leos will still need to address complex issues that originated in the previous year. These could involve financial disputes, unresolved claims from friends, like-minded individuals, or even high-ranking people. In the worst cases, these issues may escalate into legal problems. While the first half of the month may feel tense, the second half offers some "light at the end of the tunnel." By the end of January, you are likely to find a satisfactory resolution to these matters.

Additionally, managers should pay close attention to their subordinates, and employees should be mindful of their colleagues. Workplace intrigues, misunderstandings, and disruptions are possible.

Money. Financially, January is challenging. Many Leos will need to repay debts and settle loans, which may prove difficult. However, towards the end of the month, the financial situation is expected to improve somewhat, allowing the most pressing issues to be resolved one way or another.

Love and Family. Stability may also be lacking in your personal life. The most challenging days will be from January 1st to 6th. These are volatile days, so it's best to avoid conflicts, as they could escalate quickly. Alternatively, a close person might face difficulties that will require your direct involvement.

Many Leos will need to focus on their children, investing significant resources into their development, education, and other needs.

Health. Energetically, January is not your strongest month. Pay close attention to your own health as well as the well-being of your loved ones.

The most difficult days will be from January 12th to 15th, when there is an increased risk of colds, infections, and flare-ups of chronic conditions.

Throughout January, try to avoid overexertion and strive to maintain a healthy lifestyle. This advice is particularly important for all Leos, especially those who are more vulnerable or elderly.

VIRGO

Seasonal holidays may extend into January, and this could work to your advantage. This month is more conducive to rest, making the approach of "work can wait while you take your time" particularly fitting.

Business. If you need to work, try to limit your efforts during the first twenty days of January. You may find yourself lacking important information, and your decisions could be prone to errors. A challenging relationship with a certain business partner may persist—this is not a new issue, as it began last year in 2024 and continues now.

Entrepreneurs and managers may face disagreements with partners over joint ventures, with the possibility of further division. Difficulties with official authorities are also likely. Employees may experience serious competition and should practice politeness in their interactions with superiors and those in higher positions.

The latter part of January looks more promising. During this time, you can expect help from old friends or influential figures. This support will arrive at just the right moment, allowing some issues to be resolved by the end of the month, while others may need to be addressed later.

Money. Financially, January is challenging. Money will be continuously spent, whether for work, personal life, or the needs of children and close ones. Significant sums are expected around January 10th, 11th, 20th, 21st, 29th, and 30th. However, the money received may quickly be spent, leaving you with a neutral or potentially negative balance by the end of the month.

Love and Family. Your personal life raises many questions, affecting both those in love and those who are married. Virgos have been experiencing issues in their personal lives for over a year, and these problems vary widely.

Unfortunately, January will not bring anything new—past challenges remain unresolved and continue to demand attention.

Health. Your energy levels are generally high this month, but early January could bring unexpected health setbacks, accidents, or injuries. The most challenging days are from January 1st to 5th. The end of the month, particularly from January 28th to 31st, may also be unfavorable, so practice moderation and avoid overexertion.

LIBRA

In January, you'll find a brief respite from your usual activities, but this quiet period will be short-lived. As they say, "duty calls!"

Business. For those actively working under this sign, challenges will arise in the first ten days of January. Conflicts with friends, like-minded individuals, or high-profile contacts are possible during this time. These conflicts might be ideological or financial in nature and are likely to persist in the coming months. Additionally, you will need to address complex issues recently raised by partners or adversaries from other cities or countries.

If you manage to avoid these complications, you may still encounter developments in legal matters, particularly those stemming from past issues. The most difficult time will be in the first half of January, but after that, the situation should stabilize somewhat, giving you a chance to deal with the most pressing problems or at least outline possible solutions.

Employees may experience ongoing changes within their organization, making professional life feel uneven and unsettled, though no layoffs or other serious disruptions are expected.

Money. Financially, the second half of January is more favorable. The most significant sums are expected on January 12th to 14th, 22nd, 23rd, and 31st. However, the first half of the month will involve numerous expenses, mainly related to the holidays and the needs of loved ones.

Love and Family. If your focus is on your personal life, the situation may feel uneven and tense. Many families will encounter challenges with their children; in some cases, a sudden quarrel is possible, while in others, you may need to address emerging issues with one of your offspring. Relationships with close relatives could also feel strained. These issues likely originated last year, and you will now have to deal with their lingering effects in the near future.

For trips planned in January, it's wise to approach them pragmatically and cautiously. Carefully consider potential scenarios, and if doubts arise, it might be better to cancel the plans. This advice is especially relevant for long-distance travel.

Health. Throughout the month, you may feel less confident and energetic than usual. To counteract this, ensure you get enough rest and remember the benefits of morning exercise. Additionally, be cautious while traveling and driving.

SCORPIO

January will feel like a roller coaster ride, filled with challenges and unpredictability. Stay alert to what's happening around you and trust your intuition to help navigate the complexities you face.

Business. For professionally active Scorpios, this period is turbulent. Organizational changes are likely to continue for employees, and shifts in leadership may lead to instability in your position. However, these developments have been brewing for a while, so you are probably already aware of what might be discussed.

The primary difficulty during this time is uncertainty. Therefore, avoid making any drastic decisions and try to wait out the storm. This advice is especially important for those facing ambiguity in their current job or those who have recently become unemployed. In both situations, it's wise to carefully evaluate your options and strategically plan your next steps.

Entrepreneurs may encounter challenges with official institutions and regulatory bodies. Those involved in expanding their business or construction might find themselves exceeding their budget this month.

Money. Financially, January will be tough. Expenses will be ongoing, linked to both business activities and personal life.

Love and Family. The romantic front is complicated as well. Lovers may feel disappointed in each other for various reasons—ranging from trivial financial disagreements to deeper emotional differences and contrasting values. This situation began in the recent past and will continue into January.

The first half of the month will be particularly challenging, while the second half offers more optimism. During this time, tensions will ease, allowing you to view the situation more rationally, which is the right approach to resolution. If the love is still alive, take this opportunity to work things out. If not, it may be time to reassess.

Many families will encounter issues with children during the first half of January, with problems rooted in the recent past. These issues are unlikely to be resolved immediately, but that doesn't mean you should completely pause your efforts. Address challenges as they arise and remember that there are no unsolvable problems. Give it 4-5 months, and the situation should improve, with the groundwork being laid now.

In the second half of the month, there may be pleasant reunions with relatives or children living in another city or country.

During the first half of January, some families will also face challenges related to parents, whether concerning health issues or a major argument. It's important to assess potential risks and remember that peace at home is far better than even the kindest quarrel.

Health. Your energy levels are low this month, and this trend will continue until June. Therefore, maintaining a healthy lifestyle should become your priority. The stars also advise caution while driving.

SAGITTARIUS

January will be hectic and restless for you. Your attention will be pulled in many directions—children, parents, and work will all demand your focus. While escaping professional duties won't be easy, you'll manage to juggle everything.

Business. The first twenty days of the month may not go as planned. Your progress could be hindered by several factors beyond your control. In the first ten days of January, issues with colleagues from other cities or countries may arise, and a worsening international situation could also impact your business.

Another challenge this January is the ongoing disagreements with certain partners. For most Sagittarians, this isn't new—it all began back in 2024. January will bring a continuation of the contentious issues from the recent past. Resolutions will not come quickly, but if significant property or real estate is involved, there is hope that everything will be settled by the end of 2025. Some improvements can be expected in the second half of January.

Employees should prioritize diplomacy in their interactions with colleagues and superiors. Under these conditions, January should pass without significant issues.

Money. Financially, January is contradictory. Both expenses and income are expected, with the hope that income will prevail. The most favorable dates for receiving significant sums are the 8th, 9th, 12th, 13th, 22nd, 23rd, 27th, and 28th of January.

Love and Family. Personal life appears uneven and tense. In early January, many Sagittarians may face unexpected issues with relatives, particularly those living in other cities or countries.

Relationships in some families may be strained, with disputes over real estate being a possible source of conflict. If a new love has recently replaced an old attachment, discussions may also turn to divorce and its complications.

Harmonious families will need to focus on caring for parents or elderly family members.

Health. Your energy levels aren't particularly high in January, so take care of yourself. Avoid overexertion and be mindful of winter colds and infections. Exercise caution while traveling and driving, especially in the first half of the month, which could be particularly challenging in this regard.

CAPRICORN

January is an intense month for you. You might find yourself being particularly harsh in your words and actions, making it unpleasant for those who become the target of your criticism. Remember, patience is key — achievements can be made quietly and without fuss.

Business. The primary concern for many Capricorns continues to be strained relationships with colleagues from other cities or countries. These issues have been brewing in a challenging, negative mode for some time, and this month, you will need to address unresolved matters from the past year.

Entrepreneurs should pay close attention to their subordinates, and employees should tread carefully with colleagues, especially if conflicts have arisen recently. The most difficulties are expected in the first half of the month, after which the situation should improve somewhat. Difficult relationships with partners may become clearer, and it may be possible to find an acceptable compromise on contentious issues or at least outline a path toward one.

Those dealing with longstanding legal issues should prepare for these matters to remain on the agenda for another 4-5 months. Be ready to defend yourself and, at times, go on the offensive.

Money. The financial situation looks quite turbulent. Especially high expenses are anticipated in the first ten days of January, with some of these costs being unforeseen. Therefore, exercise caution with all matters related to money and material possessions, especially from January 1st to 3rd. However, it's not all bad; you won't be left without money. Significant financial inflows are likely around January 10th, 11th, 20th, 21st, 29th, and 30th.

Love and Family. Those focused on their personal lives will also face difficulties. Long-married couples may enter into another conflict, and if serious issues or divorce are involved, financial matters will also come to the surface.

Many Capricorns will continue to face problems with relatives. In one case, it may involve old grievances or a long-standing quarrel; in another, it could be issues your relatives are facing. In the latter case, you'll need to provide both moral and financial support.

The majority of personal issues will arise during the first 20 days of the month, while the last ten days look calmer, if not entirely positive.

Health. Your energy levels will improve slightly this month, but that's no reason to push yourself to the limit. Be cautious during the first week of January and avoid risky situations. Take extra care during trips and while driving. Special attention is needed for elderly people and those weakened by chronic cardiovascular and musculoskeletal conditions.

AQUARIUS

January is a month filled with emotional tension, so it's essential to keep your impulses in check to avoid rash words and actions. This advice applies equally to both your professional and personal life.

Business. The first half of January may present several challenges. Relationships with partners could significantly deteriorate, with a serious argument possible in the first week. Between January 10th and 20th, you may face complications with regulatory authorities or see the reemergence of an old legal issue. In such cases, proceed with caution and carefully consider each step to avoid missteps.

Employees may encounter team-related issues, such as office intrigue or the emergence of unwanted information. And business owners should closely monitor their subordinates to prevent professional or reputational setbacks.

Most of these challenges will likely arise during the first 20 days of the month, while the final third of January appears calmer, potentially offering a way out of the difficulties.

Money. Despite the turbulence in your professional life, financial concerns should not trouble you. Venus is securely positioned in the financial sector of your chart, ensuring that you won't be left without funds.

Key dates for financial inflows are January 4th, 12th, 13th, 22nd, 23rd, and 31st. Naturally, there will be expenses, but most will be related to leisure, children, and loved ones.

Love and Family. Dramatic scenarios may unfold in your personal life. The most challenging days will be during the festive period from January 1st to 5th. During this time, be attentive and diplomatic, especially if there are existing tensions in your relationships. Be mindful of your reputation as well, as mid-month could bring intrigue and the unexpected surfacing of undesirable, possibly distorted, information. If discussions about divorce arise, be prepared for potential legal complications.

Children will continue to be a focal point, with significant sums being directed toward their needs.

Relationships among lovers will be unstable, with disagreements and general dissatisfaction, often rooted in financial grievances. In some cases, lovers may realize their life views differ significantly.

Health. In January, your energy levels will be low—this is common in the lead-up to your birthday. Special caution is advised for the elderly and those with weakened health, as old ailments may flare up or new ones could arise unexpectedly. Those with cardiovascular, spinal, and musculoskeletal conditions should be particularly vigilant.

Young and healthy individuals should maintain a balanced lifestyle and avoid overburdening their bodies with excesses.

PISCES

This month will be filled with thrilling moments, both in business and in your personal life. As the saying goes, "Everyone has their cross to bear."

Business. For those who are professionally active, January will be productive yet somewhat unsettling. The best time for you will be from the 10th to the 30th of the month, during which you might receive good news from afar or embark on a successful trip. You can rely on valuable assistance from friends or gain favor from influential individuals.

However, the first ten days of January might present challenges. During this period, managers may face significant issues with subordinates or unexpected disruptions in workflow. The situation may seem critical, so it's essential to review all possible options and take necessary actions when possible.

Workplace complications may also arise for employees, including hostility from colleagues and organizational difficulties. Many of you will need to address issues that originated in the past year, 2024. These might include disputes with partners over real estate and various financial matters. Resolving these issues will be a slow process, with improvements expected only in the second half of 2025. For now, tackle problems step by step, keeping in mind the wisdom of the saying, "A journey of a thousand miles begins with a single step."

Money. Financially, January can be described as turbulent. Expenses will alternate with income, but expenses may slightly outweigh earnings. Most spending will likely be related to personal life, family matters, and children.

Love and Family. Personal life might take center stage this month, bringing a number of challenges. Couples with longstanding difficulties may continue to address complex issues that originated in 2024 or even earlier. Real estate could become a major irritant and a source of disputes among struggling couples. In the most difficult cases, divorce, property division, and disagreements over child-rearing are possible. If litigation is anticipated, be prepared for the likelihood of a complex outcome and consider seeking a reasonable compromise.

For lovers and those who have just started family life, the situation looks more promising. However, they will still face various issues involving parents and older family members.

Health. In terms of health, both the first and last weeks of January look particularly challenging. The period from the 1st to the 6th may be prone to accidents and conflicts, while the days from the 28th to the 30th could bring a significant weakening of energy, as well as the likelihood of colds and infections.

Those suffering from cardiovascular, spinal, and musculoskeletal conditions should be especially mindful of unexpected complications during this time. Take care of yourself and prioritize your well-being.

February

New York Time		
Calendar Day	Lunar Day	Lunar Day Start Time
01/02/25	4	8:53:02 AM
02/02/25	5	9:22:45 AM
03/02/25	6	9:53:17 AM
04/02/25	7	10:26:12 AM
05/02/25	8	11:03:11 AM
06/02/25	9	11:45:49 AM
07/02/25	10	12:35:12 PM
08/02/25	11	1:31:20 PM
09/02/25	12	2:32:46 PM
10/02/25	13	3:37:06 PM
11/02/25	14	4:41:55 PM
12/02/25	15	5:45:37 PM
13/02/25	16	6:47:32 PM
14/02/25	17	7:47:46 PM
15/02/25	18	8:46:47 PM
16/02/25	19	9:45:14 PM
17/02/25	20	10:43:42 PM
18/02/25	21	11:42:34 PM
20/02/25	22	12:41:45 AM
21/02/25	23	1:40:37 AM
22/02/25	24	2:37:53 AM
23/02/25	25	3:31:54 AM
24/02/25	26	4:21:14 AM
25/02/25	27	5:05:13 AM
26/02/25	28	5:44:08 AM
27/02/25	29	6:18:58 AM
27/02/25	1	7:46:43 PM
28/02/25	2	6:51:05 AM

London Time		
Calendar Day	Lunar Day	Lunar Day Start Time
01/02/25	4	8:57:54 AM
02/02/25	5	9:18:17 AM
03/02/25	6	9:39:10 AM
04/02/25	7	10:02:12 AM
05/02/25	8	10:29:18 AM
06/02/25	9	11:02:48 AM
07/02/25	10	11:45:09 AM
08/02/25	11	12:37:57 PM
09/02/25	12	1:40:38 PM
10/02/25	13	2:50:10 PM
11/02/25	14	4:02:40 PM
12/02/25	15	5:15:06 PM
13/02/25	16	6:25:58 PM
14/02/25	17	7:34:57 PM
15/02/25	18	8:42:28 PM
16/02/25	19	9:49:11 PM
17/02/25	20	10:55:43 PM
19/02/25	21	12:02:25 AM
20/02/25	22	1:09:02 AM
21/02/25	23	2:14:24 AM
22/02/25	24	3:16:20 AM
23/02/25	25	4:12:06 AM
24/02/25	26	4:59:43 AM
25/02/25	27	5:38:49 AM
26/02/25	28	6:10:37 AM
27/02/25	29	6:37:03 AM
28/02/25	1	12:46:43 AM
28/02/25	2	7:00:04 AM

You can find the description of each lunar day in the chapter "A Guide to The Moon Cycle and Lunar Days"

ARIES

Your ruling planet, Mars, remains in retrograde motion. For those who may have forgotten, this retrograde began on December 6 and will end on February 26. As a result, certain initiatives may encounter delays.

Business. February brings a calmer professional atmosphere compared to January. Relations with colleagues from other cities or countries may slightly improve, possibly because new friends and like-minded individuals emerge who could play an important role in resolving ongoing issues. This doesn't mean all previous problems are fully behind you—there's still more work ahead. However, now is the perfect time to lay the groundwork for future success.

Entrepreneurs and managers face considerable work in expanding their business, potentially involving real estate, housing, renovations, or major construction projects. This area is challenging, requiring revisiting the same issues, correcting mistakes, and refining plans. While this demands additional resources, the investment will ultimately strengthen the business.

For employees, the month remains fairly neutral. On the plus side, workplace intrigue and problems seem to be diminishing.

Money. Significant expenses are anticipated between February 10 and 13, related to both professional activities and personal matters.

Love and Family. Many Aries will find themselves deeply involved in domestic responsibilities. Changes at home, such as renovations, ongoing major construction, or acquiring decorative items, will align with your goals and capabilities. Some of these activities may even carry over from last year, 2024.

Domestic tasks will intensify after February 20 and extend into March. Financial disagreements with friends could also surface during this time.

Family relationships remain steady, with spouses working together on complex household tasks. Minor disagreements or squabbles are quickly resolved. A considerable portion of your resources will continue to go toward raising children or addressing their needs.

For those in romantic relationships, a cooling-off period or temporary separation could occur.

Health. Your energy levels will stay strong throughout most of the month. However, be mindful of a slight dip in vitality around the New Moon on February 27 and 28.

TAURUS

Your time to celebrate has finally arrived – many issues that once seemed impossible to resolve no longer appear so daunting. Slowly but surely, you are on your way to achieving your goals. The stars advise: don't stray from this path!

Business. In February, your professional activity will be at its peak, allowing you to tackle tasks that have troubled you in the past. Financially, things are also looking up, which helps ease a complex situation that may have arisen with someone in your circle or with influential figures. However, the problem may not be fully resolved just yet. Between the 9th and 12th, you might face demands from official authorities that require careful handling. Be diplomatic and composed, no matter the circumstances. Ambition and conflict won't lead to favorable outcomes. This advice also applies to employees who may face challenges with management.

Relations with partners from other cities or countries will stabilize, potentially with help from old partners or loyal allies. Difficult negotiations are possible, and the stars recommend that you stick firmly to your position. Distant partners may have weak or unstable positions, so while final agreements may not be reached in February, there is still an opportunity to improve the situation.

Money. Your financial situation will improve significantly, making it one of February's best rewards. Although expenses remain high, this time they will be fully offset by income.

Love and Family. The personal front may be less favorable than your professional life. This could be because work is currently taking priority.

As a result, you might find it difficult to spend enough time with your family and loved ones, potentially leading to distance or disagreements.

However, relationships with relatives show some improvement, and they might be more willing to compromise on certain issues. Some topics may need to be discussed repeatedly, but as the saying goes, "a bad peace is better than a good quarrel." Try to meet reconciled relatives halfway while still protecting your own interests.

Many of you will reconnect with old friends or past loves, possibly from another city or country. A trip is also highly likely.

Health. In February, your energy levels are high, and illnesses are unlikely to trouble you.

GEMINI

The favorable winds from late January continue into February, bringing improvements in both business and family life.

Business. This month, many professionally active Geminis will start or continue negotiations on new projects or job opportunities, which should enhance their professional standing and propel them forward. However, it's not all smooth sailing—financial matters remain uncertain until the end of February. Rest assured, these issues are expected to resolve favorably in March.

Connections with colleagues and friends from different cities or countries are looking up, and a successful trip may be on the horizon. Any unexpected complications that may arise between the 9th and 12th of February are likely to be sorted out by the end of the month.

Money. February is fairly good financially. Funds will flow in consistently, with the largest sums expected on the 1st, 9th, 10th, 18th, 19th, and 28th. However, expenses are also significant. Aggressive Mars has been in your financial sector for a while and is moving retrograde now, which means not all financial issues will be resolved as quickly as you'd like. Impulsive purchases may not work out as well as expected.

The stars advise thinking carefully before spending, avoiding rash financial commitments, and being cautious about lending money.

Love and Family. February uniquely blends practicality, business sense, and a romantic mood. Singles might meet a partner, likely during a trip or through friends visiting from afar.

Couples with a history together might consider marriage more seriously and even discuss it openly. Married life is smooth and harmonious, potentially highlighted by a trip that brings fresh energy into the relationship.

Health. Your energy levels are high throughout February, keeping illnesses at bay. The stars also encourage you not to be lazy; keep active with sports or simply walk more. Use your ample energy for peaceful purposes.

The only days to be cautious are from the 9th to the 12th—be careful while driving and avoid planning any trips, whether short or long.

CANCER

February might not be your month, so it's time to slow down! Now is not the time for bold actions but for undertakings that require patience, discipline, and modesty.

Business. Aggressive Mars has lingered in your sign for a while, but unfortunately, it is still in retrograde. This could make you more aggressive, intolerant, and prone to conflict.

While past problems continue to surface, opportunities for resolution are gradually maturing. Colleagues from different cities or countries are more cooperative, and towards the end of the month, you may find opportunities for more peaceful negotiations than in recent times. Those with long-standing legal issues might also find opportunities for resolution. A reasonable compromise is quite possible.

Those who have lost their jobs might find opportunities for negotiation, possibly leading to a return to a previous position or a new organization and role. Positive trends will become more apparent towards the end of

February and will definitely continue into March. The process is slow, but progress is being made, and that's what counts.

Money. Your financial situation will improve somewhat. The most significant sums are likely to come in on the 3rd, 4th, 21st, and 22nd of February.

In mid-February, you may encounter conflicts with friends, allies, or someone from your circle of patrons, primarily concerning money or other financial obligations. In such cases, it might be wise to concede, if not fully, then at least partially. The most challenging days in this regard are from the 9th to the 13th of February, which may bring large unforeseen expenses.

Love and Family. Personal life appears quite restless. Those involved in construction or renovation are striving for perfection, but achieving it won't be easy. You may need to redo some work, seek additional funds, and delve into the complex processes involved with this demanding undertaking. But as the saying goes, "A journey of a thousand miles begins with a single step," so you are on the right track. The same can be said for those who are linked to construction at work.

Family relationships aren't particularly stable. Mars's influence might make you prone to sarcasm and criticism. Pay attention to your behavior, resist aggressive impulses, mood swings, and other whims of a fluctuating nervous system. These recommendations also apply to those who are not bound by family ties but have a steady partner.

Health. Throughout February, your energy potential isn't stable. Protect your body from winter colds, infections, and the exacerbation of old chronic conditions.

From the 9th to the 12th of February, be mindful of injuries, accidents, and conflicts that might flare up unexpectedly. Exercise caution when driving throughout the month, particularly during the 9th to the 12th.

LEO

This month, your ambitions may not be backed by real opportunities. It's not the best time for grand ventures, and individual efforts may not bring you closer to your desired goals. The stars advise you to act like a hiker ascending a mountain: proceed cautiously, wisely, and don't neglect to rest and take breaks.

Business. The focus this month is on relationships with partners and people in positions of influence and power. After conflicts in the recent past, there will be opportunities to settle matters peacefully or through an acceptable compromise. You may need to involve mediators or loyal allies. With collective efforts, things will gradually improve. Looking ahead, the journey might be long and slow, but the most important thing is that there is light at the end of the tunnel, and it is towards this light that you must continue.

For employees, it's advisable to be mindful of your superiors and generally stay modest. You're not the leader now, but a team player, so try to collaborate with your colleagues and take their opinions into account. If you disagree with something, it's better to keep your thoughts to yourself for now.

Those involved in various domestic concerns, such as renovations or construction, might experience delays and the need for rework. Sometimes that's just how it goes, so do what the current situation demands.

Money. The financial situation remains unstable, but you can expect some funds on the 5th, 6th, 13th, 14th, 23rd, and 24th of February. However, expenses will likely exceed income, so try to be frugal and economize where possible.

Love and Family. Personal life unfolds with various scenarios. Spouses who get along well might focus intensely on domestic activities such as building or renovating, and this topic will definitely continue into the future. These busy activities will create a restless backdrop, so disagreements and arguments are sometimes possible. Real issues may also arise with children, especially due to financial-related concerns..

Young people might face issues with parents or elder family members. The most challenging days in this regard are from the 9th to the 12th of February.

The stars advise being cautious with those around you to avoid the likelihood of intrigues. This can be challenging, but it is possible. Remember that many events in February and March might occur behind your back, so try not to give any reason for gossip, insinuations, or intrigues. These recommendations are also suitable for those whose lives are primarily focused on work.

Health. Your energy potential is low this month, largely due to Mars, which has settled into a sector of the sky associated with decreased energy.

Maintain a healthy lifestyle, ensure you get enough sleep, and take preventive measures against old chronic diseases. Particularly difficult days for health are the 1st, 9th to 12th, 19th, 20th, and the days of the New Moon on the 27th and 28th of February.

VIRGO

Traditionally, February is one of the most labor-intensive months of the year for you. As the saying goes, "Feel the fear and do it anyway."

Business. For professionally active Virgos, February is quite favorable. Entrepreneurs can achieve a lot for their businesses and earn well. Relationships with business partners may improve, possibly due to the influential role of friends or high-ranking individuals. Take this chance as any improvement in complex issues reduces the likelihood of future conflicts. While the problem may not be fully resolved and could reemerge, if there's an opportunity to ease tensions, it's worth pursuing.

Unexpected deterioration in relationships with colleagues from other cities or countries could be another issue in February, particularly between the 9th and 12th. However, by the end of the month, most problems should be resolved. Those with legal issues might also face unexpected complications during this period, so review all possible options and take preventative measures.

Money. Financially, February is quite favorable. Funds will flow continuously, and the amounts will noticeably increase. Tentative dates for receiving significant sums are the 6th-8th, 16th, 17th, 25th, and 26th of February. There will be expenses, of course, but they will be necessary and manageable.

Love and Family. Those focused on their personal lives may continue to resolve complex issues related to a marital partner or close person. In some cases, their partner's position may soften, and friends or mutual acquaintances could play an important role in this. However, don't expect the situation to improve drastically; there are still many problems that require patience and tact, qualities your partner may not possess.

If there was a separation or divorce in the recent past, but issues related to finances or children remain, it's better to resolve them peacefully as opportunities for this should arise in February.

On the horizon for many Virgos, old acquaintances and friends may reappear. Singles might suddenly see more than just a friendly connection in someone from their past. Love is entirely possible, so why not? Especially since it could help ease the complex emotional atmosphere that has developed recently and continues now.

Health. This month, those who are weakened or elderly should pay close attention to their health. Young and healthy individuals just need to maintain a healthy lifestyle and remember the benefits of good sleep.

LIBRA

The stars promise an energetic and very responsible month for you. Any endeavors aimed at achieving recognition and fame are destined to succeed.

Business. This month, professionally active Libras will be able to complete complex tasks related to restructuring their businesses. Entrepreneurs will smooth out internal relations within the team and may attract new employees. Additionally, there will be an opportunity to mend relationships with some long-standing colleagues. Another piece of pleasant news in February is the possibility of constructive negotiations with colleagues from other cities or countries. The issue is not entirely resolved—rather, it's a matter for the future—but positive steps can already be taken now.

For employees, organizational changes are ongoing, but everything will turn out for the best. Thus, your positions are quite stable and may even strengthen in the near future.

Money. Despite a generally favorable professional situation, financial matters are not so bright. Many Libras may face significant expenses in mid-month, related to children or close ones. However, money will continue flowing in regularly, and by the end of the month, your balance will still be positive.

Love and Family. When it comes to your personal life, this month looks promising. Relationships between lovers and spouses will noticeably improve, and a joint trip that promises to go well is possible. The combined influence of Venus and Jupiter will also positively affect those whose relationships may have dimmed.

In many families, issues with children leading to major expenses could emerge mid-month. Alternatively, there may be a need to offer support and invest a substantial amount of money in their education, development, and upbringing.

Health. In February, your energy potential is quite high and illnesses are not a threat.

SCORPIO

February is a homey, cozy, and family-oriented month. Its main motto is "My home is my fortress."

Business. Professionally active Scorpios can take this calm period to tackle organizational tasks that are often postponed for later. It's a good time to tidy up business matters, improve relations with partners and colleagues, including those from other cities or countries. There's also an opportunity to rekindle old connections, particularly with distant partners. A productive trip may also be on the horizon.

Entrepreneurs can continue significant activities related to business expansion. This includes constructing new production facilities, major renovations, and other real estate operations. The month's steady and productive pace might be disrupted by some disagreements with partners, likely between February 9 and 12. However, these shouldn't have serious consequences and will be amicably resolved.

Additionally, February presents a good opportunity to take a short break and dedicate time to personal matters.

Money. No significant income is expected, but there won't be any major losses either. Many Scorpios can profit from various real estate transactions, whether through renting or selling. Profits from savings and various types of investments are also possible. Those not involved in business can expect financial support from family members, such as parents, a spouse, or a close person.

Love and Family. Many Scorpios will dedicate February to personal and family matters. Those planning to improve their living conditions can make decisive steps in this direction. This might include continuing construction, undertaking major renovations, or simply acquiring furniture or items that facilitate daily living.

Parents and close relatives will play an important role in all activities this month. Meetings with children living in other cities or countries are possible. The month is also good for renewing old connections; expect to encounter people from the past, including friends and former flames, perhaps even from faraway places.

Health. In February, your energy potential is slightly reduced, so pay attention to your body, stay active, remember the benefits of sports and getting enough sleep. Many Scorpios may notice a tendency to gain weight, so consider devising a diet that will benefit your body both now and in the future.

SAGITTARIUS

February is a dynamic and positive month for you. Your ability to juggle multiple projects at once is your ace in the hole, and you'll find it particularly useful right now.

Business. The month brings a significant improvement in relationships with partners, particularly those that might have been strained recently. This could be due to active involvement from colleagues abroad, legal professionals, or influential friends. If it involves disputed properties or other material assets, there's a good chance to make some headway on these issues and turn the situation to your advantage.

Connections with international colleagues may strengthen, possibly culminating in a successful trip.

Despite the overall favorable backdrop, mid-month may bring some complications in negotiations or professional setbacks for both employees and entrepreneurs. These challenges are temporary, and the situation is likely to stabilize by the end of the month.

Money. Your financial situation this month is stable. No significant profits are anticipated, but losses aren't expected either. Everything is proceeding in a calm, predictable manner.

Love and Family. On the personal front, things are looking up as well. If there were any conflicts over shared assets or real estate with your spouse recently, the atmosphere is likely to shift. You might realize that a cold peace is better than a warm fight, or perhaps a family member will help mediate a resolution.

Alternatively, couples may tackle complex property issues together, making significant strides towards their goals.

Lovers could find themselves united against parental pressures, bringing about harmony at home by month's end. Many of you may find travel rewarding this month, especially if you avoid the conflict-prone and accident-prone days of February 9-11.

Health. This month, your energy levels are high, keeping illnesses at bay. However, be cautious while driving and traveling from February 9-11, and steer clear of risky situations.

CAPRICORN

February is a month where "Labor weekdays are holidays for us!" This optimistic line from old Russian song could very well be your motto for the chilly month.

Business. The month looks promising professionally. You may achieve significant successes and even breakthroughs in business, career, and financial matters. Those involved in legal disputes will also see opportunities to turn situations in their favor—not completely, but significantly, which is better than nothing.

Your connections with colleagues from different cities or countries will notably improve. Old business partners and friends might come through for you on this front. There's still a long road and many challenges ahead, but as they say, "The journey of a thousand miles begins with a single step." You are on the right track, and that's what counts.

Employees can expect improved standing at work, perhaps reaching a new level of understanding with colleagues and management.

Money. Your financial situation is quite favorable. Money will flow in regularly, and you'll see a noticeable increase. Key dates for receiving significant sums are the 6th–8th, 15th–17th, and 25th–26th of February.

Major expenses are likely around the middle of the month, from the 9th to the 12th, probably related to personal matters or children.

Love and Family. Personal life also stabilizes. Troublesome relationships with relatives become clearer and more manageable. A spouse or a close person might play a crucial role in this, trying to mediate with stubborn family members and addressing past issues. While these problems won't disappear overnight, it's important to start making progress. Once the ice is broken, everything will seem easier.

Many families will face challenges with their children mid-month, including potential significant expenses. In other cases, you might find yourself investing in your children's upbringing and education.

Health. Your energy levels are not at their peak this month, particularly noticeable during the Full Moon from the 11th to the 13th. These days are also prone to conflicts and accidents. Take care of yourself and remember, "A sound mind in a sound body."

AQUARIUS

The stars advise you not to stop halfway to your goal. Even if your path sometimes resembles a labyrinth, don't despair. Remember, everything happens for the best, and time will tell.

Business. Changes continue for professionally active Aquarians. Managers and entrepreneurs will keep forming their teams, possibly rehiring former employees. Discussions on this will take up most of February and will continue into March.

Employees may try to stabilize relationships with colleagues and may even attempt to return to a previous job. With determination, this can be achieved. Relationships with distant colleagues will somewhat improve. Fruitful negotiations and a successful trip are possible.

All processes that start in February will carry on into March. If anything drags on, there is no need to rush. March will be the month when many complex issues will likely be resolved.

Money. The financial situation in February is quite stable. Funds will flow in as usual, with significant amounts expected on the 1st, 2nd, 9th, 10th, and 18th-20th of February. Besides regular earnings, some Aquarians might recover old debts.

Love and Family. Personal life this month is no less important than work. Parents continue to invest heavily in the upbringing and education of their children. If there were financial disagreements with your children recently, this month might bring partial resolutions. Relationships between spouses could be complex, possibly over issues related to home improvements or, in more severe cases, property division. The outcome depends on past situations and future plans.

Many families will face ongoing issues with parents or elderly family members. Mid-February, especially from the 9th to the 12th, will be the most challenging time, potentially filled with conflicts and unpleasant incidents.

Health. In February, your energy levels are low, which may exacerbate old ailments, infections, and colds. Many Aquarians will be prone to winter blues and mood swings; remember, maintaining internal balance is key to stability in both work and relationships.

PISCES

February presents a mix of success and challenges—essentially, just normal life.

Business. February is more suited for handling calm organizational tasks and personal affairs. Hardworking Pisces might tackle long-delayed projects. It's an ideal time to organize, plan for the future, or take a brief break to focus on personal matters.

Entrepreneurs and managers may continue expanding their businesses, possibly involving renovations or acquiring production spaces. Issues related to real estate are gradually being resolved, and you can expect some breakthroughs in this area.

Money. The financial situation is stable. With Venus, the planet of fortune, in your financial sector for most of February, you won't be short on funds. Expect earnings from both regular and unofficial sources. Some may receive financial support from family or secure a favorable loan. Profits from successful real estate transactions or banking savings are likely. Your expenses will be few and primarily personal.

Love and Family. Personal life will take center stage for many Pisces this month.

For those in relationships, it's a complex but interesting period. Old relationships may rekindle; partners who parted ways or fought might return apologetically. Whether reconciliation happens depends on your response. If you aren't too harsh, you can avoid further problems. The outcome hinges on past situations and the extent of transgressions on both sides.

Parents will devote time to their children, whose needs may require special attention and involvement. Another major theme is managing real estate matters—continuing renovations, buying new property, or selling the old, ensuring plenty of family responsibilities.

Health. Typically, the last month before your birthday is not great health-wise. You might experience a dip in energy, increasing the risk of infections, colds, and flare-ups of chronic conditions. Exercise particular caution with travel and driving from the 9th to the 12th. These days are also prone to conflicts and accidents.

March

New York Time		
Calendar Day	Lunar Day	Lunar Day Start Time
01/03/25	3	7:21:59 AM
02/03/25	4	7:53:09 AM
03/03/25	5	8:26:13 AM
04/03/25	6	9:02:46 AM
05/03/25	7	9:44:24 AM
06/03/25	8	10:32:14 AM
07/03/25	9	11:26:30 AM
08/03/25	10	12:26:05 PM
09/03/25	11	2:28:53 PM
10/03/25	12	3:32:40 PM
11/03/25	13	4:35:49 PM
12/03/25	14	5:37:34 PM
13/03/25	15	6:37:51 PM
14/03/25	16	7:37:02 PM
15/03/25	17	8:35:37 PM
16/03/25	18	9:34:07 PM
17/03/25	19	10:32:51 PM
18/03/25	20	11:31:47 PM
20/03/25	21	12:30:21 AM
21/03/25	22	1:27:31 AM
22/03/25	23	2:21:51 AM
23/03/25	24	3:11:57 AM
24/03/25	25	3:57:03 AM
25/03/25	26	4:37:13 AM
26/03/25	27	5:13:10 AM
27/03/25	28	5:46:09 AM
28/03/25	29	6:17:32 AM
29/03/25	30	6:48:51 AM
29/03/25	1	7:00:07 AM
30/03/25	2	7:21:39 AM
31/03/25	3	7:57:39 AM

London Time		
Calendar Day	Lunar Day	Lunar Day Start Time
01/03/25	3	7:21:26 AM
02/03/25	4	7:42:45 AM
03/03/25	5	8:05:38 AM
04/03/25	6	8:31:58 AM
05/03/25	7	9:03:55 AM
06/03/25	8	9:43:54 AM
07/03/25	9	10:33:41 AM
08/03/25	10	11:33:16 AM
09/03/25	11	12:40:12 PM
10/03/25	12	1:50:56 PM
11/03/25	13	3:02:25 PM
12/03/25	14	4:12:55 PM
13/03/25	15	5:21:54 PM
14/03/25	16	6:29:35 PM
15/03/25	17	7:36:28 PM
16/03/25	18	8:43:06 PM
17/03/25	19	9:49:49 PM
18/03/25	20	10:56:24 PM
20/03/25	21	12:01:56 AM
21/03/25	22	1:04:36 AM
22/03/25	23	2:01:57 AM
23/03/25	24	2:51:52 AM
24/03/25	25	3:33:30 AM
25/03/25	26	4:07:36 AM
26/03/25	27	4:35:49 AM
27/03/25	28	5:00:02 AM
28/03/25	29	5:22:02 AM
29/03/25	30	5:43:27 AM
29/03/25	1	11:00:07 AM
30/03/25	2	7:05:54 AM
31/03/25	3	7:31:14 AM

You can find the description of each lunar day in the chapter "A Guide to The Moon Cycle and Lunar Days"

ARIES

March doesn't promise exceptional success for you. The stars advise you to pause, reflect, and identify any shortcomings in your upcoming tasks, correcting them where possible.

Business. Professionally active Aries may face challenges, especially in the latter half of March when many projects will likely slow down. This pace may frustrate those accustomed to speed, but it also offers a chance to critically assess and amend potential mistakes. This period could involve various real estate operations, repairs, or construction. While there won't be any critical problems, some revisions and adjustments will be necessary.

Relationships with colleagues from different cities or countries might not be particularly satisfying. Distant partners could be pursuing their agendas, requiring your efforts to steer things favorably. This month's issues need your vigilant oversight, not relying too much on others. Success depends on your initiative.

Money. Despite some disarray in business, you won't be left without financial resources. Funds will come from both official and unofficial sources, including support from a spouse or close person, as well as profits from real estate transactions. Notable dates for receiving significant sums include March 4, 5, 12, 13, 23, 24, and 31.

Love and Family. Many Aries will devote most of their time to personal and family matters. Home improvements such as renovations or acquiring decorative items might be on the agenda. Be cautious with major purchases, especially as Venus goes retrograde from March 2 to April 13, with Mercury retrograde starting on April 15. If the purchase isn't essential, consider postponing it until a more favorable time.

Family relationships might experience tensions, likely a continuation of old issues, so you'll know what you're dealing with and how to handle it. Spousal relationships remain harmonious as they tackle the month's challenges together.

Health. In March, your energy levels are typically lower as the month before your birthday approaches. Take care of yourself and be particularly cautious around the Full Moon and Eclipse on March 13 and 14.

TAURUS

Don't rush into battle. March may not be your most favorable month, as Venus, your ruling planet, is in retrograde. The stars suggest working steadily and carefully, taking your time to fortify your position.

Business. The main challenge this month will be the intrigues within your circle. Many events may unfold behind your back rather than out in the open. You might also opt for a more behind-the-scenes approach to avoid direct confrontation with opponents. Another potential issue in March could be unresolved financial disagreements with friends or influential figures. This is a long-term problem that will resurface periodically. However, that doesn't mean you should sit idly by. On the contrary, pay close attention to this matter, addressing it step by step.

Amidst these challenges, a silver lining may appear in the form of improved relations with colleagues from other cities or countries. While full resolution is not yet in sight, progress has been made, which is better than nothing.

Entrepreneurs and managers may find themselves under the watchful eye of regulatory authorities. If this scrutiny began recently, expect it to intensify this month. Those with long-standing legal issues may face obstacles, both overt and covert, in March. Looking ahead, it's likely that March's challenges will carry over into next month.

Money. Financial stability is hard to come by in March. Expenses are expected to outpace income, and by the end of the month, your financial balance could be in the red. In some cases, this will be due to business matters, while in others, it will be linked to home and family needs.

Love and Family. In your personal life, challenges will vary depending on past events and your future plans. Many families will encounter or continue to face issues related to children, leading to significant expenses. Relationships with relatives will become more active, and support from them—both moral and financial—may be forthcoming. Financial help, in particular, will be welcome given the many expenses in March. A trip or a visit from distant relatives may also be on the horizon. Relationships between lovers and spouses appear tense, with misunderstandings and conflicts likely. Everyone has their skeletons in the closet, and they might surface at the most inconvenient time.

Health. The stressful atmosphere of March will take a toll on your health. Remember, nerves are often the root cause of many problems. Avoid unnecessary stress, get plenty of sleep, and keep in mind that, in the end, "this too shall pass."

GEMINI

Despite the obstacles that keep cropping up, you are confidently moving toward your goals. A calm life isn't in the cards just yet, but your efforts will soon pay off.

Business. March is an active and dynamic month for your professional life. Although opposition to your initiatives continues, the strength is on your side, and others will eventually realize it. Victory doesn't come without a fight, and this month, you will need to face another battle.

For entrepreneurs, opponents may come in the form of various official institutions, while employees might find themselves in conflict with their superiors.

Throughout March, expect lengthy negotiations with friends and influential figures. While these talks will generally go well, the outcomes may be delayed. Mercury, your ruling planet, is retrograde, and Venus joins it in reverse motion. This will slow down progress and create challenges in communication. In some cases, discussions may revolve around new jobs or projects, which you will achieve in time.

Relations with colleagues from other cities or countries are developing well overall, with meetings, negotiations, and a positive trip on the horizon.

Money. Financially, March looks promising. Money will come in steadily, and your income will noticeably increase. The most likely dates for receiving significant sums are March 8, 9, 17, 18, 27, and 28.

Love and Family. March is heavily focused on your professional life, leaving little time for personal affairs. You may encounter misunderstandings, so it's important to explain your busy schedule to loved ones to avoid any hurt feelings. This advice is especially relevant for those in new relationships or newly married. However, strong and stable couples will understand each other without lengthy explanations.

Health. Your energy levels in March are quite high, which will help you tackle all the challenges of this intense but contradictory month. The stars strongly advise you to stay calm, avoid unnecessary stress, and trust in yourself and your guiding star. Keep a planner at hand, clearly outline your plans, and stick to your timelines.

CANCER

The upcoming month will feel like an obstacle course, where reaching the finish line won't be easy. Move slowly, pay close attention to the path ahead, and carefully calculate each step.

Business. You will be active, energetic, and enterprising in your professional life. Discussions about a new job or project are possible, although they might take longer than expected, eventually yielding positive results.

Connections with colleagues from other cities or countries will progress with mixed success—some things will work out, while others will require more effort. All the positive outcomes this month will be the result of your efforts alone. Only you can overcome past disagreements and steer events in the right direction.

Those dealing with long-standing legal issues may also see some improvement in their positions, though full victory is still a way off. Although the outlook is generally positive, progress may be slow. Venus and Mercury will both be in retrograde for most of March, so it's best not to expect quick results. Still, everything you achieve this month will bring you closer to a highly successful period starting in the summer of 2025.

For now, pay attention to details and don't overlook the small things.

Money. The financial situation is stable, but no more than that. Significant successes are not expected, but neither are losses. The estimated dates for receiving the largest sums are March 1, 2, 10, 11, 20, 21, 29, and 30. Expenses will be few, predictable, and reasonable.

Love and Family. No major events are expected in your personal life. However, couples who have drifted apart may reassess their relationships. The initiative may need to come from you, as your partner may not show much enthusiasm. If you take the initiative, your partner's response may pleasantly surprise you.

A trip or meetings with old friends and acquaintances are possible.

Health. Your energy levels in March will be quite high, and you won't need to worry about illnesses.

LEO

March will be both challenging and significant for you. You will need to consider the circumstances while also standing firm on your point of view, which won't be easy.

Business. Most professionally active Leos will face important problems to solve. One of them will be financial negotiations, which may drag on for various reasons, delaying any immediate agreement. You'll have to negotiate, revisit the same issues, and involve mediators and allies. The final result will likely come later—by the end of April or in May. For now, prepare the necessary documents and back them up with facts. This advice also applies to legal matters. You may find yourself in negotiations related to finances, and it's best not to dig in your heels. The ideal outcome is a reasonable compromise, so that's what you should aim for.

Partners from other cities or countries may seem friendly and calm, but this could be a façade hiding ulterior motives. Most likely, they are trying to lull you into a false sense of security and turn the situation to their advantage. Therefore, stay alert, avoid rushing decisions, and if partners seem evasive or slow to act, simply wait them out.

With Mercury and Venus in retrograde for most of the month, it's a bad time for making important decisions or signing significant agreements.

Money. Finances will dominate your focus in March, and for good reason. You'll be able to secure more favorable terms and may even see some profits this month.

For those not involved in business, it's wise to rely on parents, a close loved one, or a spouse. Negotiations about loans or sponsorship are possible, and you might also receive income from unofficial sources.

Love and Family. Those focused on personal life can successfully address household matters throughout March, both for themselves and for their loved ones. Renovations or real estate dealings may involve the whole family, and support from your surroundings is likely. At least part of the funds for household needs will likely come from a family member.

Divorced couples will continue to handle contentious property issues, repeatedly returning to the same problems. Although this is not new territory for you, unpleasant surprises may still arise.

Treat any trips planned for this month with caution and care. It's better to choose destinations where you've been before to avoid unpleasant surprises. This is the advice of retrograde Mercury and Venus, which also warn that any new people who enter your life in March and the first half of April may prove to be unreliable partners, both in business and in love.

Health. Your energy levels will be traditionally low in March, so make sure to lead a healthy lifestyle and take good care of yourself. You may also need to care for a family member's health, and if there are signs of this, it's best to take preventive measures.

VIRGO

Your main goal this month is to find common ground with those around you without compromising your own interests. It's a challenging task, but one you are capable of handling.

Business. Changes are possible in partnerships. After recent tensions and serious conflicts, there are now signs of a peaceful resolution to the issues that have arisen.

For independent entrepreneurs, this might involve business matters, possibly even dividing the business. For employees, it could mean dealing with competition or conflicts with management. However, now third parties are entering the conflict—these might be old friends or influential figures. They can play the role of peacemakers and help ease tensions between the opposing sides.

There will be many discussions around financial matters and the monetary aspects of an ongoing dispute. Although both sides will have the sense to act prudently, it's unlikely that an agreement will be reached this month. The process will drag on, and resistance is futile. As Mercury and Venus remind us, "Slow and steady wins the race," especially since both are retrograde for most of March.

Relations with colleagues from other cities or countries are generally developing well. Continued negotiations and a successful trip are likely.

Money. The financial outlook for the month is uncertain. Much of the money you were counting on may be delayed, but some funds will still come in. Estimated dates for the arrival of significant sums are March 6, 7, 15, 16, 25, and 26.

Love and Family. Those focused on their personal lives may resolve a number of difficult issues in March. Divorced or divorcing individuals may continue to negotiate favorable financial terms.

Those juggling multiple relationships will face the challenging task of deciding how to proceed. The moment of truth is approaching, and you will have to decide what to do and with whom you want to be.

In March, old acquaintances and friends may reappear on your horizon, and perhaps even former lovers will reach out. Someone from your past will likely help you find a way out of the maze of problems you've unintentionally found yourself in.

If you have travel plans this month, it's best to visit familiar places to avoid unpleasant surprises.

Health. Your energy levels are low this month, but if you maintain a healthy lifestyle, you should be able to avoid any serious health problems.

LIBRA

This month, you'll need to work hard without expecting immediate recognition or gratitude. Rest assured, though — they will find their way to you later.

Business. March is a challenging month, but it's not without success. 'Challenging success' might be the best way to describe it.

Leaders and entrepreneurs will need to work closely with their teams, and much will depend on their subordinates. Old, reliable colleagues will be especially valuable, as their experience will be more relevant than ever.

Among your partners, there is discord and uncertainty. They may be evasive and inconsistent, which could delay negotiations. You might have to revisit the same topics and discuss different terms of cooperation multiple times. This includes partners from other cities or countries, with whom relations remain somewhat unstable.

Despite your efforts and those of your team, you might not reach agreements this month. However, there's no need to rush—very soon, it will become clear that time is on your side, and success will be yours.

Employees will work diligently, and their efforts will be recognized by both colleagues and management.

Money. Financially, March is quite good. Money will come in regularly, and you may see a slight increase. The most likely dates for significant sums are March 8, 9, 17–19, 27, and 28.

Love and Family. In your personal life, things are moving along as usual. While Cupid's arrow may not strike this month, your dependence on your partner will be more noticeable.

The overall tension this month could lead to misunderstandings, even in harmonious relationships. You may find yourself being inconsistent and overly critical, while your partner may also be short on patience. This could result in a lack of understanding, especially on domestic matters.

Alternatively, a lack of time and a heavy workload could also affect the atmosphere at home. However, your charm and ability to smooth over rough edges will come to your rescue. Rely on these talents, and things will turn out fine.

Lovers may start contemplating the future of their relationship, but now is not the time to make any major decisions, even if something is bothering you. Venus, the planet of love, is retrograde, and by mid-March, retrograde Mercury will join it, increasing the likelihood of mistakes.

If you have trips planned for March, be sure to prepare carefully. It's better to choose familiar places to avoid disappointment.

Health. Many Libras may feel tired and drained in March. The heavy workload, responsibility in all areas of life, and relationship difficulties will take a toll on your health, which could start to rebel. To get through this period more easily, balance work with rest, and remember that health is the most important thing—everything else will follow.

SCORPIO

This month is well-suited for charitable activities and for showing care and involvement. You may choose to focus on a small circle of close people, or consider a broader audience—it's all up to your desire and resources.

Business. The professional sphere looks somewhat unsettled this month.

Leaders and entrepreneurs will focus on their teams, where there may be unrest and mutual misunderstandings. Many will start considering restructuring their workforce, and later on, these plans may come to fruition. Take this time to reflect on the changes you'd like to make and how best to implement them.

Your relationships with colleagues from other cities or countries are becoming smoother and more predictable, and you may soon reach a new level of understanding and trust. Old connections are especially important right now, and you may find yourself negotiating with former partners and planning to renew past collaborations.

For employees, changes within the organization continue, and this time, they involve shifts within the team planned by management. You might find yourself with additional responsibilities on top of your current duties. For now, these are just plans, discussions, and preliminary ideas, but in time, they will likely become reality.

Money. Financially, March is stable, with nothing unusual on the horizon. The most likely dates for receiving significant sums are March 2, 3, 10, 11, 20, 21, 29, and 30.

Love and Family. This month, your personal life could be just as important as your career. Many will focus on matters related to their children, and meetings with children who live in other cities or countries are possible.

You may find yourself needing to offer support, both moral and financial, to someone from the younger generation.

Home improvement projects continue, and you might need to address some issues that could drag out longer than expected. With Venus and Mercury both retrograde for most of March, it's not the best time to make major purchases or experiment with your home's interior. However, this is an ideal time to review what's been done and address any shortcomings.

Long-term couples will have the opportunity to strengthen their relationships, and there may be reunions with past loves who live in other cities or countries. A joint trip is also possible.

Health. In March, your energy levels are high, and you'll be resilient to illness.

SAGITTARIUS

March is a month of responsibility, practicality, and taking care of business. Most Sagittarians will channel these qualities into their personal and family lives, dedicating only about 10-15% of their attention to work.

Business. Professionally active Sagittarians will dedicate this month to resolving past issues, particularly those related to real estate, which may have caused significant conflicts in the recent past. While the situation is improving, it's still far from stable. Negotiations will continue in the same vein, pushing both sides toward a resolution, though progress will be slow. The primary challenge of March is the retrograde motion of Venus and Mercury for most of the month, causing delays and misalignments. However, the caravan keeps moving forward, though not as quickly as one might hope.

Relationships with colleagues from other cities or countries are developing well, and those interested in collaboration can continue their work at a measured pace.

For employees, balancing professional duties with home and family matters may be a challenge. If family matters take precedence, it might be wise to take time off and focus on your loved ones.

Money. March presents a turbulent financial picture. Money will come in, but it will go out just as quickly, often due to personal and family-related expenses.

Love and Family. As the stars suggest, many events in March will take place within the home and family.

Real estate issues may take center stage this month, triggered by various factors. In cases of divorce, spouses may continue dividing property, especially the home. "However, this time, a resolution may be near.

Harmonious couples will work together on household matters.

In the best-case scenario, this month could involve purchasing property for yourself or for someone close, possibly for your children. However, delays and challenges are likely to arise.

Many Sagittarians will find time to devote to their children, and significant expenses related to the younger generation may be on the horizon.

For singles, it's wise to be cautious with new acquaintances. March is not an ideal time for forming new relationships, as the combined retrograde influence of Venus and Mercury does not favor fresh connections. However, old acquaintances and long-time friends may prove to be valuable.

Health. Your energy levels are low this month, and you may often feel lethargic, tired, and unmotivated. It's important to keep these tendencies in check, as there could be a risk of weight gain and general sluggishness.

Remember the famous saying, "Movement is life," and act accordingly.

CAPRICORN

In March, it's wise to rein in your ambitions and be more attentive to those around you. Now, more than ever, the saying "One man is not a warrior in the field" applies.

Business. This month, the challenging situations in your affairs will finally start moving in the right direction. However, this progress will be slow, with delays and endless discussions. In some cases, this will involve real estate, land, and related debts; in others, it will be about resolving issues with colleagues from other cities or countries and negotiating future agreements. Another possibility is normalizing relationships with employees or subordinates who have become difficult to manage. Since these problems are not new to you, and you've faced them before, you'll easily recognize what's at stake. In some cases, these issues may even be interconnected.

Intermediaries, such as supportive partners, friends, or, in the case of legal disputes, skilled lawyers, can provide valuable assistance in resolving these matters.

Organizational changes will continue at work, but they won't cause you any personal difficulties.

The stars advise you to get along with those around you, resolve issues peacefully, and avoid rushing. Pushing things too quickly now will only harm you. Throughout most of March, both Mercury and Venus are retrograde, making it an unfavorable time for making final decisions or signing important documents.

Money. Financially, this month can be considered neutral. No major achievements are expected, but there won't be any major setbacks either.

Love and Family. Those focused on their personal lives will also face the challenging task of resolving issues related to family, children, and a close person. Complex problems concerning close relatives may be resolved with the help of your spouse or a loved one. Their efforts to reconcile feuding parties may bring results, if not immediately, then a bit later.

Couples going through tough times or those who have been through a divorce may bring up real estate matters this month, but the solution will come later. For now, you can discuss the most contentious topics and outline ways to resolve them.

Harmonious couples can tackle problems with relatives together, as well as various real estate-related matters. Lovers, on the other hand, will need to overcome resistance from parents and older relatives and solve various household issues related to living together.

Many Capricorns will embark on a trip in March, and in this case, the stars recommend choosing only familiar places to avoid unexpected disappointments.

Health. Your energy levels will be quite high in March, although some issues may arise at the beginning of the month, particularly from March 1 to March 8. Those who are weakened or elderly may struggle more, while the young and strong will handle this period with ease.

AQUARIUS

March might turn out to be a challenging month for you. But there's good news — despite the difficulties, you'll manage to take control of the situation and steer events in the right direction.

Business. There will be plenty of work this month, along with financial concerns. Many Aquarians will be focused on material and financial problems and will make significant progress in resolving them. For some, financial issues may be closely linked to partners from other cities or countries. Distant colleagues may enter negotiations but could delay decisions, which might drag the situation out for a month or even longer.

Alternatively, financial matters could be delayed due to missing documents or previous errors, so extra work on paperwork might be required. In all professional matters, entrepreneurs and managers can rely on their subordinates, who will prove to be responsible and dependable this time. Employees can expect support from colleagues and goodwill from their superiors.

If you're involved in business expansion, construction, or renovation, it's essential to approach this complex process with caution. Don't rush things; the best strategy now is to carefully check every step along the way.

Money. Financially, March looks quite favorable. Most monetary matters will be resolved this month, and any remaining issues will be handled later. However, the foundation for future success is being laid right now. Employees will receive additional assignments, which will lead to an increase in earnings. Many Aquarians will have old debts repaid, and some will profit from real estate transactions.

Love and Family. Those focused on personal life may spend considerable time with their children, and at the beginning of March, they will be able to help them both emotionally and financially. Many Aquarians may visit relatives living in another city or country this month. Alternatively, you might invite your parents or other relatives to visit you.

If you're engaged in renovation or construction projects, these efforts will continue, requiring patience, wisdom, and love to see them through. Couples in love will have the opportunity to improve their relationships, as it seems that the worst arguments are now behind you.

March is a good time for reflection, analyzing mistakes, and planning how to correct them. And if there's nothing more to be done, remember that the world is vast, full of people, and a new partner will come along for you. The stars also remind you that March is better suited for rekindling old friendships and romances, while new acquaintances may prove unreliable. This is signaled by Mercury and Venus, both retrograde for most of the month.

When planning trips in March, it's best to choose familiar destinations to avoid disappointment.

Health. In March, your energy levels may be low, but if you lead a healthy lifestyle and protect yourself from spring colds, you'll be able to avoid any major issues.

PISCES

March may not be the best time to achieve outstanding results in either your professional or personal life. So, just go with the flow, and eventually, it will lead you somewhere.

Business. Entrepreneurs and managers at all levels will need to focus on financial matters — tracking expenses, recording income, and planning budgets.

Relationships with partners from other cities or countries are going well, particularly with long-established connections. Negotiations, trips, and plans to resume cooperation are possible.

For employees, things are steady, with everything moving along as usual, albeit perhaps a bit more slowly than normal. In fact, this slow pace may be noticeable for professionals across the board. Planned activities might be canceled or postponed, and key people may be unavailable for various reasons. This is because Mercury and Venus will be retrograde for most of the month, which usually leads to misunderstandings and delays in both business and communications.

Creative professionals, such as musicians, singers, and journalists, are likely to fare well, with plenty of work and decent pay on the horizon.

Money. Finances will take up much of your time and energy, but the effort will be worthwhile. Many Pisces will see an increase in income. The most likely dates for receiving significant sums are March 2, 3, 10, 11, 20, 21, 29, and 30.

Love and Family. For most Pisces, the key events in March will center around personal life. Parents will have more time to spend with their children, who will bring them some joy. Many Pisces will continue to focus on home improvements, and the stars advise approaching these tasks with great care, as the risk of mistakes is high this month.

Couples in love may strengthen their relationships and may even consider taking a trip together. March also holds the potential for rekindling old romances — an old flame might unexpectedly reappear, reigniting a past love with renewed passion.

Health. Your energy levels will be strong this month, and health concerns shouldn't trouble you.

One more thing — March is perfect for a break. Remember, the world won't collapse if you take a week or two off from work to indulge yourself!

Trips planned for the first half of April should be to familiar places. During this period, with Mercury and Venus still retrograde, new destinations and acquaintances may bring disappointment. These restrictions will lift in the second half of the month.

Health. This month, you'll feel more confident, with your old energy and spirit returning. The stars recommend paying attention to your diet, especially if you have longstanding gastrointestinal issues.

TAURUS

This month, it's crucial to establish a clear stance on key issues and ensure you have the support of others.

Business. In April, you may find yourself relying on friends, like-minded individuals, or influential figures. Gaining their support might require extensive discussions, a re-evaluation of positions, and negotiations to reach acceptable terms of cooperation or separation. These challenges can impact both high-ranking officials and independent entrepreneurs.

Connections with colleagues from other cities or countries are progressing well. Those planning collaborations should see positive results towards the end of the month.

Employees might use friendly or family connections to advance their careers or secure a new job. After prolonged negotiations, you'll be able to reach an agreement and achieve your desired outcome. The stars advise you to act delicately, resolve some issues unofficially, and avoid rushing. Venus, your ruler, is retrograde, supported by retrograde Mercury, a situation that will persist until mid-April. After that, the planets will calm down, and delays and misunderstandings in business will cease.

Money. Financially, April may bring mixed results. There will be many expenses, but you won't be left without funds. Financial inflows are possible from both official and unofficial sources. Those not involved in business can count on support from close relatives.

Love and Family. In April, many Taureans should focus on their closest circle of friends. An interesting process is unfolding, where a friendship may evolve into something more. This transition may have been building for some time, and now the decisive moment has arrived. With Venus and Mars in contact, it's time to make a decision.

Lovers separated by time and distance will happily reunite, and joint trips are likely. Positive developments apply to those with prior connections, while new acquaintances made between March 2 and April 13 may bring disappointment.

Stable, family-oriented individuals will be able to strengthen relationships with relatives and some old friends.

Health. In April, your energy levels may fluctuate like the capricious spring weather. There will be times when you feel excellent and others when your energy suddenly drops. The last days of the month, from April 29 to 31, will be particularly challenging. During this period, reduce your activity and take care of yourself.

GEMINI

April is an excellent month for you to stake your claim under the Sun. Go for it!

Business. An active and largely positive spring month lies ahead. Employees can engage in important negotiations for a new job or a significant promotion in their current position. Entrepreneurs may finalize a major deal or secure approval for further development of a large-scale project.

However, in the first half of the month, you may encounter delays and challenges. You might find yourself lacking necessary documents or the right people at critical moments. But in the second half of April, all obstacles will fall, and you will achieve your goals. This is because, in the first half of April, your ruling planet, Mercury, is retrograde, along with Venus. Delays and inconsistencies are to be expected, but the outcome will be worth it—that's the most important thing!

Many Geminis will receive help from friends or people in high positions. Through combined efforts, you'll eventually move mountains!

Money. Financially, this month looks very promising. Money will come in regularly and in increasing amounts. If you want to ask for a raise, April is the right time to do so. Key dates for receiving the largest sums are April 1, 8, 9, 17-19, 27, and 28. While expenses will be present, the stars suggest they will be predictable and reasonable.

Love and Family. Your personal life is also stable. Those who are single and disillusioned with past relationships may start a workplace romance. At some point, your relationship with a colleague may warm up, and the stars recommend approaching these feelings with the same seriousness as your work. This will help ensure the continuation of the love story.

Harmonious couples will be pleased with each other's professional successes and will support one another in all endeavors.

Children will bring joy, and this period is favorable for them as well. If you're considering expanding your family, the stars are supportive. It seems the time to act on all fronts has arrived.

Health. Jupiter, a powerful source of energy, is on your side, so you won't have health problems either.

CANCER

In the coming weeks, several opportunities will arise to improve your position. Without a doubt, you'll make the most of them.

Business. This month, professionally active Cancerians will focus on the future. Intense negotiations about new projects or jobs are possible, and these efforts are likely to be successful by the end of April or in May. Those with ambitious plans for collaboration with partners from other cities or countries will be close to realizing their goals.

Negotiations with distant colleagues might take some time, but they will ultimately yield positive results. A successful trip is also possible.

Those dealing with longstanding legal issues may find ways to address their causes and finally resolve them this month. This spring, everything will fall into place. Your task is to moderate your ambitions and be willing to compromise—this is the only way to truly solve many problems.

Those involved in business expansion or construction will be close to completing these labor-intensive activities. This could involve building projects, major renovations, or other efforts that could become the cornerstone of future business development.

Money. Financially, April is quite stable. While large profits might not materialize right now, the prospects are certainly there! Keep working hard, and the results will come. Key dates for receiving the largest sums are April 2, 3, 10, 11, 20, 21, 29, and 30.

Love and Family. Your personal life continues as usual. Harmonious couples and long-time lovers might go on a trip and have a great time together. However, if the trip is planned for the first half of April, the stars recommend choosing familiar places. Venus and Mercury are retrograde during this period, so it's better to avoid experimenting with new experiences.

For singles and those disillusioned with past attachments, a workplace romance is possible. Shared professional interests often bring people closer together. If you're genuinely interested in a colleague, take the risk—the relationship may move forward and develop in unexpected ways. Remember, from March 2 to April 13, the stars favor only old connections and relationships with people you already know. New acquaintances made during this period are likely to bring nothing but trouble.

Health. In April, your energy levels are quite high, and even past ailments will heal quickly.

LEO

It's time to focus — you'll have a great opportunity to address past issues and strengthen your foundations.

Business. Entrepreneurs and managers will enter an important phase in their business affairs this month. Organizational activities, such as restructuring the business and preparing for major construction projects, are likely on the horizon.

Connections with colleagues from other cities or countries can play a key role. With their help, you may resolve past conflicts. There's a strong chance of settling disputed financial matters with friends or influential people. At least some of your previous issues will definitely be resolved.

If there are legal matters, you can expect a partial resolution of long-standing disputes. Don't be discouraged if things don't work out on the first attempt. Mercury and Venus are retrograde in the first half of the month, which often causes delays and minor miscommunications in business and personal dealings.

Employees might find themselves at a crossroads—whether to take a vacation, attend to personal matters, or balance both. It's up to you, but in the first half of the month, it might be wise to step back from work temporarily. The world won't collapse if you spend some time away from the office.

Money. Finances should not be problematic; funds will come in regularly from both official and unofficial sources. Unofficial sources may include profits from real estate transactions, support from parents or loved ones, and possible unexpected gifts. While expenses will be significant, they are all well-planned and reasonable.

Love and Family. Many Leos might dedicate themselves to home and family matters in April. Major household renovations or preparations for moving to a new home are possible.

Marital relationships can be as unpredictable as a spring day—periods of peaceful coexistence may be followed by sudden outbursts of hostility or dissatisfaction with the current situation. The end of April, from the 20th to the 28th, may be particularly challenging, with unexpected problems arising. Lovers may face similar situations.

Health. Overall, your energy levels are quite high, but you might need to care for loved ones who may fall ill or go through difficult times.

VIRGO

Be modest—your expectations might be too high right now, and attempts to overreach will likely end in failure. Be content with less, and you will gain more.

Business. Throughout the month, professionally active Virgos will have meetings with partners and lengthy discussions about both operational and financial matters. In case of problems, support will come from old friends or people in high positions. They can act as intermediaries, significantly easing the protracted negotiations.

If you notice a slowdown in all matters during the first half of April, expect to reach concrete agreements that satisfy both parties in the second half. This is because from March 2 to April 13, Venus and your ruler Mercury are retrograde, which always leads to delays. During this challenging period, it's best not to rush things; the best tactic is to gather the necessary arguments and back them up with documents and facts.

Towards the end of the month, connections with colleagues from other cities or countries will become active, and a trip or preparation for one is possible. Employees may engage in lengthy negotiations about a new job or a promotion within their organization, with results coming a bit later.

Money. Financially, this month won't bring surprises—everything will go as usual. Income will be quite predictable, and expenses will be reasonable. A complicated situation with partners from the past might be resolved through an acceptable compromise, and you will get what you deserve by the end of this month or a bit later. This could relate to professional activities or personal life.

Love and Family. If personal and family life is your priority, the stars recommend being more diplomatic and cautious, especially if a separation occurred in the past and now involves the division of property or other financial claims. Negotiations on this topic might be long, and showing impatience and dissatisfaction won't improve your position. In the end, you will get what is rightfully yours—no more, no less.

Long-time lovers may discuss their future, especially the possibility of living together. Such plans might arise towards the end of April. Harmonious couples may also discuss various issues related to real estate. Those "sitting on two chairs," meaning having two different attachments, will have to navigate flexibly to please both sides.

Health. This month, your energy levels are low, and special caution is advised for the elderly and those with weakened health. Young and strong individuals should maintain a healthy lifestyle and remember the benefits of good sleep.

LIBRA

You are in for a bright, active, and somewhat adventurous month. Remember that any risk should be well thought out, so consider everything at least a hundred times.

Business. Professionally, this month is quite active. Entrepreneurs and managers will have significant work with subordinates who will be entrusted with important and responsible tasks. It may be necessary to change staff, keeping only those who are competent and reliable, and removing others from their duties.

Connections with colleagues from other cities or countries remain important, and this time, relationships with them will be calmer than they were recently. Negotiations are possible, bringing intermediate but quite acceptable results. However, on this front, it's still wise to follow the proverb "Trust, but verify."

Mercury and Venus are retrograde from March 2 to April 13. During this period, many matters may be delayed, there could be bureaucratic red tape, and the necessary people might be unavailable. However, this is a good time to rethink and perhaps improve certain aspects of projects and tasks.

The second half of the month is more productive, and the work done in the past will undoubtedly yield results. So, don't rush into things in the first half of the month; the second half will compensate for all the efforts.

Changes within the organization are concluding for employees, and in one case, this means strengthening positions in the current job, while in another, successful job searches.

Money. Financially, April is quite stable. Money will come in regularly, with the key dates for receiving the largest sums being April 1, 4, 5, 14, 15, 23, and 24. Expenses will also be significant, with most occurring between April 20 and 28.

Love and Family. Personal life becomes more interesting in the second half of April. During this period, singles and those disappointed in past relationships can look forward to new acquaintances, likely within a circle of friends.

Lovers will be able to strengthen their relationships and may even go on a trip. Spouses will be harmoniously engaged in domestic matters; important steps in home improvement will be taken at the end of April and into May.

Children will cause much concern, and a significant sum may be needed for their needs in the third week of the month.

Health. This month, your energy levels are low, and the stars recommend paying more attention to your body. Special caution is advised for the elderly and those with chronic illnesses. They need to plan treatment for potential exacerbations, which are quite likely this month. Young and healthy individuals might find themselves more tired than usual, and in such cases, a good rest and proper sleep will help.

SCORPIO

This month, you will excel in the role of a mentor. Your words will be weighty and wise, and your authority will be unquestionable. This applies equally to both work and love.

Business. Many Scorpios will continue to focus on resolving relationships with colleagues from other cities or countries. Significant improvements in this area are expected in the second half of the month, allowing you to tackle real tasks and possibly new projects. Entrepreneurs and managers at all levels can continue expanding their business, which may involve various operational activities such as construction or major repairs.

Employees can negotiate for a new job or a promotion at their current position, with the best time for this being the second half of April. Positive results are more than likely during this period. The first half of April is more challenging. Mercury and Venus are retrograde from March 2 to April 13, typically leading to delays, inconsistencies, and other problems.

Money. Financially, April is stable but no more than that. No major profits are expected, but there will also be no losses. Expenses are predictable and reasonable, while income is modest but steady.

Love and Family. For many Scorpios, personal life may take center stage. April is an excellent time for spending time with children, educating and nurturing them. Meetings with children living in another city or country are possible. Relationships for lovers are quite stable, and there may be plans related to a trip or a shared future.

Many Scorpios are still focused on improving their home, and these challenging activities seem to be nearing a successful conclusion.

Health. In April, you are healthy, but periods of vitality may alternate with sudden drops in energy. In such cases, listen to your body and avoid testing its limits with excessive activity.

SAGITTARIUS

April, especially its first half, favors systematic, methodical work. This applies equally to personal matters and work duties.

Business. Entrepreneurs and managers will continue the challenging work related to business expansion. This involves further steps to resolve long-standing disputes over real estate or land. This time, you will be able to find common ground with opponents and discuss a mutually acceptable compromise. Ahead lies even greater work to expand your holdings, so it's worth preparing now.

The first half of April is quite difficult. Mercury and Venus are retrograde from March 2 to April 13, which always leads to delays in business matters. However, everything done recently will undoubtedly come to fruition in the second half of April or in May.

The second half of the month is a good time to showcase your achievements to the public and to boost your popularity. You might start a blog or channel, or, if you already have one, increase your audience.

Employees may spend much of their time on family matters, and the stars recommend taking a full vacation or at least a few days off.

Money. Financially, April is a challenging month. There will be many expenses, some related to work and others to home and family matters. However, you won't be completely out of money; if necessary, parents or close relatives will come to your aid. Profits from various real estate transactions and loans are also possible.

Love and Family. Many Sagittarians will focus on their personal lives in April. Quarreling or divorced spouses may finally agree on disputed property and the future of their children. Harmonious couples might engage in various real estate transactions, with some facing major projects related to a significant move, often to another city or country.

Children bring joy, and meetings with children living in another city or country are possible. April, especially its second half, is a great time for lovers. You may want to strengthen your bond, live together, or decide to marry.

Now is also a time to fall head over heels in love, worry about it, and think about the consequences of a new romance. In short, your personal life is in full swing, which is good for you.

Health. In April, your energy levels are quite high, and illnesses won't be a concern. However, the stars strongly advise you to be more careful while traveling and driving! In this regard, the last ten days of the month, especially the final days, are particularly challenging.

CAPRICORN

April has a dual nature for you. On one hand, you will need to tackle challenging professional tasks, and on the other, you will be closely involved with home and family matters.

Business. Professionally active Capricorns will focus on resolving complex issues with colleagues from other cities or countries. After many difficulties, you will see a light at the end of the tunnel, signaling hope for a satisfactory compromise. In this regard, old friends or influential partners can provide real help.

In the first half of the month, many matters may face delays, and you might have to revisit the same issues multiple times, rework already completed tasks, and renegotiate agreements. This is because Venus and Mercury are retrograde from March 2 to April 13, a period often characterized by slow progress. However, this time is also good for refining ongoing projects and addressing ambiguities and errors.

In the second half of April, all obstacles will be overcome, allowing for constructive negotiations and real progress. This period is also favorable for various operational tasks and resolving real estate issues. Employees will be able to smooth relations with colleagues, while entrepreneurs and managers can address issues with subordinates. Those with longstanding legal problems may find opportunities for compromise solutions in April.

Money. Financially, this month is rather neutral. Income will be usual, and expenses will be modest. The financial situation becomes more complicated in the last ten days of April, when spending will increase significantly. In many cases, this will be due to the needs of children or a close person.

Love and Family. Those focused on personal life will have to address family-related issues. This is not a new topic for you, but now there will be an opportunity for partial resolution. This applies equally to those who have to deal with complex family matters and those who are in conflict with relatives. In all matters involving relatives, your spouse or someone close to you can play an important role.

In the second half of the month, many will deal with real estate issues, possibly in places far from home. In the last ten days of April, children will require a lot of attention, and a significant amount of the family budget may be spent on their needs. This period also challenging for many lovers, with potential conflicts arising over money, jealousy, and differing views on current events.

Health. In April, your energy levels are quite high, and illnesses won't be a concern. However, the stars strongly advise you to be cautious while traveling and driving.

If a trip is planned for the period from April 1 to 13, it's better to choose familiar places to avoid unpleasant surprises and disappointments.

AQUARIUS

The motto of this month is purely material: "Happiness is not in money, but in its quantity." At the moment, this is indeed the case.

Business. This month, there will be plenty of work. Changes in the organization are concluding for employees, affecting the direction of work, financial aspects, and the team you will work with. These changes pose no threat to you; on the contrary, they can improve your professional and financial positions.

Entrepreneurs and managers will have a lot of work forming a team and ensuring its financial stability. Many Aquarians will align their interests with partners from other cities or countries and, in the second half of April, will be able to agree on cooperation or resolve old problems, primarily financial ones.

In the first ten days of April, all professional matters may proceed at a slower pace. Delays are inevitable, as Mercury and Venus are retrograde from March 2 to April 13. Typically, these periods involve finalizing documents, correcting errors, and dealing with the absence of necessary people. Only in the second half of the month will you be able to address and resolve the arising problems.

Money. Financially, this month is quite favorable. Money will come in regularly, and the amount will noticeably increase. Many Aquarians will have old debts returned to them. The key dates for receiving the largest sums are April 4, 5, 9, 10, 14, 15, 23, and 24.

Love and Family. Personal life proceeds as usual. Relationships with children improve significantly, and if you had to deal with their problems in the past, most of them now seem to be resolved.

Relationships for couples and lovers resemble the capricious spring sun—it sometimes hides behind clouds, and then it shines brightly. The third ten days of April are particularly indicative in this regard, with possible unexpected quarrels over trivial matters. If this situation follows the saying "Lovers' tiffs are harmless," that's one thing, but if not, it's worth being more tactful and delicate.

Health. In April, your energy levels are low, so lead a healthy lifestyle and take care of yourself. Many Aquarians will still need to care for the health of a family member. The situation is not simple, but you will manage because you have plenty of diligence and ingenuity.

PISCES

April is a time of changes in your personal life. However, financial matters cannot be ignored either. Remember, it's important to balance work and personal life.

Business. Professionally active Pisceans will dedicate April to resolving old disputes with partners. This could involve real estate or other major assets. Additionally, the month, especially its second half, is suitable for negotiations with distant colleagues and investors.

However, in the first half of April, affairs and negotiations may be prolonged, and you must come to terms with this. Demonstrating impatience and dissatisfaction will yield no results and won't improve your position. Mercury and Venus are retrograde from March 2 to April 13, making delays inevitable. But this is a good time to identify and correct errors in your work.

In the second half of April or in May, the work you've done will undoubtedly bear fruit. During this period, a trip or preparation for one is also possible. Those staying home can negotiate with former partners from distant places and restore previously lost connections.

Money. Financially, April is quite stable. Money will come in as usual, and in addition to official income, you can expect additional profits. Some will receive help from parents or a close person, while others may gain money from successful real estate transactions.

Love and Family. In many cases, the main events of April will occur in your personal life. Parents will have the opportunity to focus closely on their children's affairs, and they will bring some joy. Meetings with children living in another city or country are possible. Many Pisceans may change their place of residence — some to a new home, others to another city or country. In some cases, a return to a previous residence is planned.

Many families may welcome new children or grandchildren. Relationships for lovers may stabilize after some hesitation and doubts. There will be a realization that "an old friend is better than two new ones," and the decision to renew relationships or possibly take them to a new level will likely be mutual.

Health. In April, your energy levels are somewhat weakened, but by leading a healthy lifestyle, you can avoid troubles. The last ten days of the month are challenging, conflict-prone, and injury-prone. During this period, be more cautious in contacts, and attentive while traveling and driving.

May

New York Time			London Time		
Calendar Day	Lunar Day	Lunar Day Start Time	Calendar Day	Lunar Day	Lunar Day Start Time
01/05/25	5	9:05:19 AM	01/05/25	5	8:11:11 AM
02/05/25	6	10:09:26 AM	02/05/25	6	9:16:40 AM
03/05/25	7	11:15:16 AM	03/05/25	7	10:28:08 AM
04/05/25	8	12:20:22 PM	04/05/25	8	11:41:15 AM
05/05/25	9	1:23:31 PM	05/05/25	9	12:53:14 PM
06/05/25	10	2:24:30 PM	06/05/25	10	2:03:05 PM
07/05/25	11	3:23:48 PM	07/05/25	11	3:11:00 PM
08/05/25	12	4:22:07 PM	08/05/25	12	4:17:39 PM
09/05/25	13	5:20:12 PM	09/05/25	13	5:23:51 PM
10/05/25	14	6:18:36 PM	10/05/25	14	6:30:15 PM
11/05/25	15	7:17:32 PM	11/05/25	15	7:37:03 PM
12/05/25	16	8:16:41 PM	12/05/25	16	8:43:42 PM
13/05/25	17	9:15:07 PM	13/05/25	17	9:48:45 PM
14/05/25	18	10:11:20 PM	14/05/25	18	10:49:50 PM
15/05/25	19	11:03:44 PM	15/05/25	19	11:44:18 PM
16/05/25	20	11:51:04 PM	17/05/25	20	12:30:30 AM
18/05/25	21	12:32:59 AM	18/05/25	21	1:08:20 AM
19/05/25	22	1:09:56 AM	19/05/25	22	1:39:05 AM
20/05/25	23	1:43:01 AM	20/05/25	23	2:04:37 AM
21/05/25	24	2:13:30 AM	21/05/25	24	2:26:46 AM
22/05/25	25	2:42:50 AM	22/05/25	25	2:47:10 AM
23/05/25	26	3:12:29 AM	23/05/25	26	3:07:20 AM
24/05/25	27	3:44:07 AM	24/05/25	27	3:28:51 AM
25/05/25	28	4:19:32 AM	25/05/25	28	3:53:37 AM
26/05/25	29	5:00:45 AM	26/05/25	29	4:24:00 AM
26/05/25	1	11:04:26 PM	27/05/25	1	4:04:26 AM
27/05/25	2	5:49:31 AM	27/05/25	2	5:03:00 AM
28/05/25	3	6:46:27 AM	28/05/25	3	5:53:21 AM
29/05/25	4	7:50:12 AM	29/05/25	4	6:55:42 AM
30/05/25	5	8:57:40 AM	30/05/25	5	8:07:03 AM
31/05/25	6	10:05:27 AM	31/05/25	6	9:22:16 AM

You can find the description of each lunar day in the chapter "A Guide to The Moon Cycle and Lunar Days"

ARIES

Finally, your ruling planet, Mars, is in a strong position, which means you will feel more confident and able to manage events as you see fit.

Business. The primary concern for most professionally active Aries will be financial matters. In this regard, you can confidently expect success.

Relationships with colleagues from other cities or countries are improving; after a period of opposition and challenging crises, you're emerging from many past dead-end situations. Clear trends towards this positive process will continue in the future. Trips planned for May will be very successful.

Challenges this month may include conflicts with friends or people with power and influence. While these are currently short-lived, they could be early warning signs that require your attention. Relationships are changing, and this process will be long and complex. Over the next five to six years, only the most loyal and devoted friends will remain by your side. And for now, the first days of the month, the period from May 4th to 6th, and the Full Moon days—May 11 and 12 — could be particularly challenging.

Money. Financially, May is looks promising. Money will come in regularly and the amount will increase slightly. Expenses this month may still be related to children and close ones, but they are natural and won't be particularly burdensome. Key dates for receiving the largest sums: May 6th, 7th, 16th, and 17th.

Love and Family. Spousal and romantic relationships are warm and trusting, with your significant other ready to support you in all your endeavors. A joint trip or preparation for one is possible. Children bring joy, and the older and younger generations will live in harmony this month. Relationships with relatives are also improving, appearing calmer and more predictable now.

May will bring pleasant surprises to those who are single. New acquaintances with intelligent, promising, and interesting people are very likely this month, especially in the second half of May.

Health. In May, your energy levels are quite high, and illnesses will not be a concern. However, those who are fatigued or suffer from long-standing chronic ailments should consider taking a break. An ideal escape would be a spa hotel near a blue sea or a cabin in the green wilderness—whichever appeals most. The main thing is to get away from the usual routine and hustle.

TAURUS

The main theme of this month may be domestic matters. In one case, this is related to personal matters, and in another, to professional concerns. As the saying goes, "Everybody has its own burden".

Business. Complex situations that arose in the recent past are slowly but surely heading toward a favorable resolution. This primarily applies to the financial sphere, where things are starting to make sense and become more manageable.

Entrepreneurs and managers will need to undertake the reconstruction of production facilities. This could be minor repairs, expansion of spaces, or relocating the business to another place. The course of action depends on individual intentions and opportunities, which vary for everyone. However, this time, your operational plans will proceed smoothly, concretely, and predictably.

For employees, it's a positive period. All career-related matters, including seeking help from management, can be handled well, provided they are well-argued. Preparatory work, like leveraging family connections, is encouraged. However, improvisation and spontaneous decisions should be avoided.

Money. Financially, May is quite stable. In addition to regular income, support may come from parents or close ones. This support can be both moral and financial. Alternatively, a favorable loan is also realistic.

Love and Family. For those focused on personal life, complex issues of home improvement are on the agenda. This could mean the successful completion of a long renovation or the acquisition of items that beautify the home.

Spouses will work in full agreement with each other during this time. Long-time lovers and newlyweds may be setting up their home, feathering their nest. In this, they may receive help from parents or older family members. Long-standing disagreements seem to be resolved, and a good time lies ahead.

Health. For most of the month, your energy levels are quite high, and illnesses are not a concern. However, fluctuations in energy might be noticeable on 14th, 15th, 27th, and 28th.

GEMINI

May is a calm and productive month. It's a good time to look back on the challenging path you've already traveled and your progress.

Business. In all matters this month, it's essential to secure the support of friends, colleagues, and partners. They will be eager to help you in any way they can. Both international connections and partnerships within your own country are developing well. Successful negotiations and trips are likely.

When resolving issues, you might need to leverage not only official and obvious connections but also more discreet ones. This approach will undoubtedly help you succeed both now and in the near future.

Despite clear favorable circumstances, you may face some problems in mid-May. These will be temporary and won't affect your progress. There may be some misunderstandings with colleagues from other cities or countries, which will be resolved later. The most challenging period is from May 12 to 18.

Money. Financially, May is calm and stable. No significant changes are expected in this area, and both expenses and income are predictable.

Love and Family. May is a positive period for your personal life. Spouses and lovers may go on a trip that will be very rewarding. Meetings with relatives living in other cities or countries are possible. Relationships in married couples are smooth and harmonious, with no upheavals or misunderstandings expected this month.

Single individuals might meet someone special, possibly during a trip to a place far from home.

In all matters this month, both personal and professional, relatives may play a significant role. With their support, any tasks will be successfully resolved.

Health. In May, your energy levels are slightly lower. This applies especially to the elderly and those with weakened health, who should take extra care of themselves. Young and healthy individuals will benefit from maintaining a healthy lifestyle and ensuring they get enough sleep.

CANCER

An excellent period lies ahead! After a long stretch of misunderstandings and various problems, you can confidently say that the difficult phase is finally coming to an end.

Business. This month is undoubtedly good for all professional matters. Entrepreneurs and managers can look forward to new projects with promising financial prospects, and employees will have the opportunity to negotiate for a new job or a promotion at their current place. A very important period is ahead, with the path fully open, and you are taking your first steps in this direction in May.

Friends or people with power and influence may play a significant role in all activities this month. After lengthy negotiations, you will be able to resolve important financial issues and plan for the future. After lengthy negotiations, you will be able to resolve important financial issues and plan for the future.

Money. Financially, this month can be considered positive. Money will come in regularly, and the amount will noticeably increase as a result of your professional developments. The key dates for receiving the largest sums are May 4, 5, 14, 15, 23, 24, and 31.

Naturally, there will be expenses; many of you will have to repay old debts, loans, and solve household problems. However, the growing income will more than cover all possible expenses.

Love and Family. Personal life might take a backseat this month as work and social life will occupy most of your time and energy. However, those who recently started construction or major repairs will be able to find time to complete these challenging household tasks.

Relationships with spouses are quite stable, and if there were any problems in the past, they are now resolved. Even divorced couples will be able to find a way to settle long-standing issues.

Health. In May, your energy levels are quite high, and illnesses are not a concern.

LEO

Throughout May, you may feel a significant surge of energy. This boost will help you move mountains or make them move towards your magnificent plans and endeavors.

Business. This month is very fortunate for all professional activities. Your connections with colleagues from other cities or countries are developing well, and a successful trip is possible. All agreements with distant partners will benefit your business, improving your professional and financial positions.

Entrepreneurs and managers can count on the successful completion of ongoing projects, as well as new interesting proposals. Large-scale events related to business expansion and possibly construction are ahead.

Employees will have a good opportunity to climb the career ladder at their current place or move to a more prominent position in a larger organization. In short, May brings many opportunities, and it's up to you to make the most of them. Complex legal and financial issues with friends or high-ranking individuals are almost resolved or are in the process of being positively resolved.

Money. Financially, this month can be considered successful. Money will come in regularly, and you'll notice a steady increase in your income. The key dates for receiving the largest sums are May 6, 7, 16, 17, 25, and 26.

Your expenses will be minimal and will be comfortably covered by your growing income.

Love and Family. Personal life is not as successful as work. Stern Pluto is firmly situated in the part of your chart that governs marriage and long-term relationships. What does this mean? On one hand, it signifies a reassessment of existing relationships, and on the other, their complete transformation. Relationships that do not meet changing conditions must end. This is a long process that may take years, but it begins precisely in 2024-2025.

So, be more attentive to your partners and remember that it takes two to tango. Honesty in relationships comes to the forefront now, and any deviation from this rule will be punished by Pluto. This advice from the stars is relevant for a long time, so remember it and behave accordingly.

Health. In May, your energy levels are very high, and illnesses are not a concern.

Besides the Sun, Mercury, and Venus, Mars supports you as a powerful source of energy. It's up to you how to use this energy, whether for harm or for good. Additionally, May is an excellent time to take up sports, dancing, or any activity you have always wanted to pursue.

VIRGO

Movement and change are the main themes of this month. For some, these changes may be significant, while for others, they might be minimal. It all depends on plans, intentions, and opportunities.

Business. May presents a dual direction for professional matters. On one hand, things are progressing, but on the other, you constantly need to look back and shore up your support. This involves various organizational and operational activities that may have been ongoing since last month.

Connections with colleagues from other cities or countries are developing well, and a successful trip is possible. Many of you will have plans and opportunities to start a business in distant places, and if this has already happened recently, you can think about strengthening or expanding your business.

Both in May and continuing into June, most Virgos will be at the peak of their professional capabilities, and it's important to make the most of this. Employees can solidify their positions at their current jobs or switch to more promising roles. The stagnation that many of your sign have experienced for a long time is completely over, and great things lie ahead.

Money. Financially, this month is quite good. Money will come in regularly, as is a natural continuation of your professional success. The key dates for receiving the largest sums are May 8, 9, 18, 19, 27, and 28.

Love and Family. There are no significant changes in your personal life for now. Grim Saturn, which has been in the sector of the sky responsible for marriage and long-term relationships for the past two years, continues to exert its influence. This planet has a special effect—if a relationship has run its course, Saturn can end it, but if mistakes are recognized, it can restore it.

Many Virgos have likely felt this purifying effect, and if there was a breakup in the recent past, now is the time to take a pause. Patience and waiting are your strengths, and this strategy will prove correct now. Focus on yourself, your work, home improvements, and other necessary tasks.

Those with stable and reliable relationships may also engage in household concerns. You might be arranging a home in another city or country. Many Virgos may go on a trip in May, where they will have a good rest.

Health. This month, your health is strong, and you're full of energy. With this combination, you'll easily ward off any potential illnesses.

LIBRA

Compared to previous months, May can be seen as relatively calm. Nonetheless, you will be able to accomplish a lot, both in your work and personal life.

Business. The main achievement of this month is likely to be successful negotiations with partners, like-minded people, and individuals in high positions. In addition to discussions about cooperation, you will also be able to resolve important financial issues.

Relationships with colleagues from other cities or countries will feel more peaceful and cooperative. There are slow but steady positive trends in this area, which is encouraging.

However, entrepreneurs and managers should pay more attention to their subordinates. This area is not developing as well as it should for the growth of the business, and it seems to have become a chronic issue. Measures will need to be taken, if not now, then a bit later.

Employees can expect positive changes in their work, though these may come a bit later. For now, you can hold negotiations and secure the necessary support.

Money. No financial problems are expected in May. Besides regular earnings, you can count on support from close ones, as well as bonuses and various payments. These might include income from bank deposits, profits from shares, and other unexpected windfalls. Those wishing to obtain a loan can apply this month.

Love and Family. In most cases, the main events of May will center around your personal and family life. Relationships between spouses and lovers are stable and harmonious, with possible travel plans or preparations for a trip.

Additionally, May is a month of domestic concerns. Many Libras will improve their homes, apartments, or country houses, with the help of close ones.

May is an excellent month for new acquaintances. Single and disillusioned individuals should seize this opportunity. Positive influences from the stars might bring people into your life who truly matter. So, make an effort to be more social and always stay in shape. As the saying goes, "God helps those who help themselves."

Health. Throughout the month, elderly people may feel a slight drop in energy, with the most challenging days during the Full Moon from May 11-13. However, no major problems are expected, especially if you lead a healthy lifestyle, do morning exercises, and spend more time in nature or at least in a nearby park.

These simple yet important rules will help maintain mental clarity and physical vigor.

SCORPIO

The upcoming period is favorable, active, and quite stable. Take into account the opinions of those around you and often remember the saying, "No man is an island." By doing so, you will achieve more.

Business. There will be a lot of work this month, including potential negotiations about future professional opportunities. This is likely to involve a transition to a new job or the development of a new venture. Diligent employees might find themselves particularly engaged in these activities.

Entrepreneurs and managers will be concluding projects related to business expansion, construction, or major renovations, with new opportunities on the horizon. May is a good time to recruit new energetic team members and to outline and refine future goals.

Money. The financial situation is improving, with more money coming in. The approximate dates for receiving the largest sums are May 4, 5, 13-15, 23, 24, and 31. Expenses will be minimal and fully covered by increasing income.

Love and Family. Personal life won't be as active as professional matters. Those with families will continue to be occupied with their children's needs, potentially incurring expenses related to the growing generation. At the same time, the support of a partner in all activities this month cannot be overstated. A close one will provide both moral and financial assistance, which will be especially valuable in case of construction, repairs, and other household tasks.

Long-term couples may decide to start living together this month. Those who had conflicts in the recent past might find ways to reconcile. If love is still alive, this is quite possible; if not, there is no point in forcing it.

Singles and adventure-seekers might meet someone new and start a passionate romance. This could happen at work when a colleague unexpectedly reveals another side of themselves. Office romances are still very much a possibility.

Health. In May, you may experience fluctuations in well-being and mood. To balance these swings, ensure you get enough sleep, spend more time in nature, start your day with exercises, and use positive affirmations like, "Today is a good day, and great things await me."

SAGITTARIUS

This lovely spring month will allow you to act boldly, without looking back at circumstances. The stars are on your side and will support you in every way possible.

Business. May is quite positive for professional activities. Although reaching your goals may not be easy, you will put in maximum effort and not deviate from your plans. Entrepreneurs and managers seem focused on expanding their business and embarking on new, large-scale projects. Negotiations with partners who are willing to participate in the joint venture are likely.

For employees, a specific phase in their professional life is concluding. In some cases, changes will affect the organization, while in other scenarios, there will be a desire to pursue something different. Some ideas on this topic may emerge this month, and their implementation is just around the corner.

Connections with colleagues from other cities or countries are developing well, and a successful trip is possible. Creative individuals will experience increased popularity, which will undoubtedly reflect positively on their earnings.

Money. May is excellent in terms of finances. Significant profits from past work are possible, as well as prepayments for future projects. Some Sagittarians can expect bonuses and dividends from bank investments. The approximate dates for receiving the largest sums are May 6, 7, 16, 17, 25, and 26.

Love and Family. This month promises to be quite interesting in your romantic life. A new romance that adds vibrant colors to your life is not ruled out. It might happen during a trip or within a circle of people who have come from afar.

Parents will be pleased with their children's successes, and meetings with children living in other cities or countries are likely. Many Sagittarians will go on a trip, which will turn out very well.

Health. Usually, your well-being in May leaves much to be desired, but this May could be a pleasant exception. However, during the Full Moon from May 11-13, it is advisable to be cautious, as the energy of this period can be challenging, conflict-prone, and accident-prone. Also, be extra careful during trips and while driving.

CAPRICORN

This month, you can indulge yourself a bit and forget that life is only about work. Now is the time to engage in activities you never had time for before.

Business. However, for the incurable workaholics among you, even this beautiful spring month will find you making time for work. Administrative tasks, such as office renovations and organizing financial documents, will go smoothly.

Relationships with colleagues from other cities or countries are improving. Hostile interactions are decreasing or becoming less relevant, but there's still much work ahead to resolve old issues completely. Travel and meetings with former partners or old adversaries are possible.

Creative professionals, such as artists, singers, journalists, and musicians, will thrive this month. They will have more work and increased popularity.

Employees might spend more time on family matters and romantic relationships. Even while at work, their thoughts may revolve around personal issues. Hence, the stars recommend taking a short vacation to focus on what you truly desire. Your work won't collapse if you spend some time away from the office.

Money. In financial terms, May is relatively neutral. Expenses will alternate with income, but by the end of the month, you'll likely maintain a positive balance. It's worth noting that most of May's expenses will be pleasant—rest, spending time with children, and giving gifts to loved ones. This aligns with the astrologer's view that money is earned for these very purposes.

Love and Family. May is an excellent time to fully immerse yourself in family matters. Harmonious couples can tidy up their home, apartment, or cottage and spend more time with their children and grandchildren. Complicated relationships with relatives will improve day by day. At the very least, the problem is no longer as pressing as it was in the recent past.

Your home may see more pleasant visitors than usual, so homemakers should prepare in advance. Many Capricorns will have the opportunity to travel. New places will help you reset and view life from a more optimistic perspective. Travel is also recommended for couples in love—it will strengthen relationships and lead to important, possibly life-changing decisions.

May is also an excellent time for single individuals. The chance of meeting someone who could become a reliable partner is very high, so be sure to socialize and stay in good shape.

Health. In May, the energy levels of most Capricorns are quite high, and even those who were unwell in the past will recover quickly. It's a great period to refresh your wardrobe and visit beauty salons. This month, everyone can find something that truly resonates with them.

AQUARIUS

The pace of this month is not particularly fast. Therefore, don't set grandiose goals—or rather, you can set them, but don't expect rapid progress. After all, great things take time to resolve.

Business. May is more suited for rest and addressing family matters. However, those for whom life is work will still be able to accomplish quite a bit this month.

Entrepreneurs and managers will resolve relationships with distant colleagues, potentially engage in negotiations, and even enjoy a successful trip. Additionally, they will be able to successfully address complex issues related to real estate, land, and construction—initiatives that were started in the recent past for the expansion and development of their business.

Employees may take a temporary break from work to focus on family problems. During work hours, it's worth organizing affairs, sorting through documents, and reflecting on relationships with colleagues and superiors. Overall, this month is calm and quite good.

Money. Financially, May is stable, but no more than that. Major profits are not expected, but neither are losses. Both income and, most importantly, expenses are predictable and reasonable.

Love and Family. As mentioned, the main events of May are likely to occur in the sphere of family or romantic relationships. Many Aquarians will take a short vacation and head to the sea and sunshine. Alternatively, you could tidy up your home, apartment, or cottage, perhaps even do some minor renovations.

May is a great time to take care of loved ones, visit parents, help children, and simply enjoy the company of those you know and love. Lovers might decide to move in together, with the support of parents or older family members.

Singles can look forward to new contacts and a vibrant romance. Even if it turns out to be brief, it will still add some excitement to life.

Relationships with relatives will become warmer and better. Trips and meetings with relatives living in another city or country are possible.

Health. This month, you might experience a certain energy dip. To overcome this trend, start your day with some exercise and a strong cup of coffee.

PISCES

An energetic and highly productive period lies ahead. Bravely flap your fins, and the current will carry you right where you need to be!

Business. May is exceptionally favorable in the professional realm. You will excel at quickly resolving emerging issues without making mistakes, a highly valuable skill.

Connections with colleagues from other cities or countries will flourish, with successful negotiations and potential travel opportunities.

May particularly favors creative projects and unconventional solutions. However, practical matters will also be handled successfully.

Entrepreneurs and managers will complete work related to business expansion, involving construction or large-scale renovations. In all endeavors this month, managers can confidently rely on their subordinates, and employees can depend on their colleagues. There will be plenty of work for all Pisces, but the benefits will be substantial.

Complex relationships with partners concerning real estate are approaching a favorable resolution. Many issues will be resolved through financial means or other material assets.

Money. May is quite good financially. Money will flow in regularly, with noticeable increases.

Many Pisces will earn additional profits from significant work done in previous months and in May.

Additionally, there are potential earnings from successful real estate transactions. The estimated dates for the largest sums are May 4, 5, 14, 15, 23, 24, and 31.

Love and Family. Personal life this month may be just as important as work. Most Pisces will continue improving their homes, and this busy process is nearing completion. Old disputes related to real estate, especially for divorced or divorcing couples, are also coming to an end.

Relationships with relatives will significantly improve, with potential trips and meetings with family living in other cities or countries.

Many Pisces will head to distant lands, warm seas, and sunny places, or, in a more modest version, to their cottages. However, staying home will not be an option for anyone.

Health. This month, you are in excellent shape, and all ailments will steer clear of you. May is a great time for sports, shopping, and a complete makeover, so choose what suits you best.

June

New York Time			London Time		
Calendar Day	Lunar Day	Lunar Day Start Time	Calendar Day	Lunar Day	Lunar Day Start Time
01/06/25	7	11:11:20 AM	01/06/25	7	10:37:07 AM
02/06/25	8	12:14:34 PM	02/06/25	8	11:49:35 AM
03/06/25	9	1:15:23 PM	03/06/25	9	12:59:22 PM
04/06/25	10	2:14:30 PM	04/06/25	10	2:07:05 PM
05/06/25	11	3:12:49 PM	05/06/25	11	3:13:41 PM
06/06/25	12	4:11:06 PM	06/06/25	12	4:20:02 PM
07/06/25	13	5:09:50 PM	07/06/25	13	5:26:41 PM
08/06/25	14	6:09:02 PM	08/06/25	14	6:33:32 PM
09/06/25	15	7:08:03 PM	09/06/25	15	7:39:34 PM
10/06/25	16	8:05:35 PM	10/06/25	16	8:42:39 PM
11/06/25	17	8:59:53 PM	11/06/25	17	9:40:03 PM
12/06/25	18	9:49:24 PM	12/06/25	18	10:29:28 PM
13/06/25	19	10:33:21 PM	13/06/25	19	11:10:10 PM
14/06/25	20	11:11:52 PM	14/06/25	20	11:43:04 PM
15/06/25	21	11:45:53 PM	16/06/25	21	12:09:56 AM
17/06/25	22	12:16:39 AM	17/06/25	22	12:32:42 AM
18/06/25	23	12:45:34 AM	18/06/25	23	12:53:04 AM
19/06/25	24	1:14:04 AM	19/06/25	24	1:12:33 AM
20/06/25	25	1:43:40 AM	20/06/25	25	1:32:38 AM
21/06/25	26	2:16:06 AM	21/06/25	26	1:54:57 AM
22/06/25	27	2:53:14 AM	22/06/25	27	2:21:35 AM
23/06/25	28	3:37:06 AM	23/06/25	28	2:55:14 AM
24/06/25	29	4:29:11 AM	24/06/25	29	3:38:58 AM
25/06/25	30	5:29:32 AM	25/06/25	30	4:35:02 AM
25/06/25	1	6:33:30 AM	25/06/25	1	11:33:30 AM
26/06/25	2	6:35:58 AM	26/06/25	2	5:42:42 AM
27/06/25	3	7:45:00 AM	27/06/25	3	6:57:38 AM
28/06/25	4	8:53:25 AM	28/06/25	4	8:14:36 AM
29/06/25	5	9:59:26 AM	29/06/25	5	9:30:03 AM
30/06/25	6	11:02:39 AM	30/06/25	6	10:42:38 AM

You can find the description of each lunar day in the chapter "A Guide to The Moon Cycle and Lunar Days"

ARIES

June is set to be a mixed bag for Aries, marked by both good days and not-so-good ones. Life, as they say, has its ups and downs.

Business. June is a transitional month, influenced by Jupiter changing signs, which alters both the pace of life and your priorities. Entrepreneurs and managers will embark on new stages in their careers, with upcoming construction, renovations, and various operational activities linked to business expansion. Successes are likely, but challenges may arise, particularly unresolved issues with authorities that are likely related to real estate. However, the good news is that these issues are expected to be resolved, albeit not immediately. The motto "perseverance conquers all" fits well here.

Relationships with colleagues from different cities or countries will evolve, potentially leading to a successful trip and the renewal of old partnerships and friendships. Those planning to start a business in another city or country might consider acquiring property.

Employees may consider changing jobs or venturing into their own business, but such decisions should be carefully considered due to significant risks.

Money. Financially, June might be uneven. While you won't be without money, the month's expenses will be hefty. Travel, children's needs, business expenses, and real estate issues will all require substantial funds. However, no budget gaps are anticipated as decent sums will periodically boost your account. Key dates for major income include June 2-4, 13, 14, 22, 23, and 30.

Love and Family. Personal life is unusually calm. Couples and lovers may enjoy a trip together. However, mid-June could bring disputes over various domestic matters, as everyone has different tastes that need to be respected.

Relationships with relatives are harmonious, and it seems that past issues have been resolved for good or for the foreseeable future, depending on individual horoscopes.

Children still require both moral and financial support, regardless of their age. In fact, older children might demand more attention due to their own challenges.

Health. Your health is robust this month; you're energetic, active, and sharp-witted. However, it's important to note that Saturn, a stringent planet, has recently entered your sign. This signifies a need to reassess your habits and eliminate any that are harmful.

TAURUS

June is a positive month for you, particularly in terms of finances and business activities. However, it is important to stay mindful and remember that even good things have their limits.

Business. A significant phase in your career is concluding, paving the way for another crucial and equally important stage.

Entrepreneurs and managers will look towards distant places and countries, contemplating the establishment of new ventures abroad. While currently just plans, these could come to fruition within the year.

Many Taureans will successfully conclude ongoing projects and reap considerable profits. Nonetheless, life is never without its clouds, and some may face legal issues.

Entrepreneurs and managers who are fond of taking risks should exercise caution, as scrutiny of their actions could intensify. Mid-June is indicative of potential audits, for which preparation in advance is advisable. During this time, problems with superiors or government agencies might arise, so be ready with solid arguments and factual evidence. Disagreements with distant colleagues might also occur, but they can be resolved with some flexibility.

Money. June is one of the best months of the year financially. Money will flow consistently from both official and unofficial sources. Key dates for substantial income include June 5, 6, 15-17, 23-25. Expenses will be few and are all predictable and reasonable.

Love and Family. In personal life, Taureans might decide on significant changes, such as moving. Many will be drawn to distant places by love. Married individuals might also plan relocations, with initial steps possibly being taken soon. However, mid-month it will become apparent that complex issues need addressing, including problems with documentation and foreign laws. Throughout the year, many of these issues will be resolved, hence any efforts in this direction are highly encouraged by the stars.

Relatives will play a significant role in the month's events, though relationships may not always be smooth. You will be able to gauge what might happen in your specific situation, but there will be cause for concern.

Health. In June, your energy levels are not very high, but no serious health issues are expected. The stars strongly advise caution during travel and while driving, especially during the period from 10th to 20th of June.

GEMINI

Times are changing – Jupiter is moving into Cancer, and Saturn is entering Aries. For you, this means new opportunities and new challenges. In short, business as usual!

Work. The forward momentum that many Geminis experienced recently is continuing. Entrepreneurs and managers will see an increase in their income as a natural result of the hard work they've put in. However, this progress may come with some problems. These issues might manifest as financial claims from friends or influential people in your life. Whether these claims are justified depends on past situations, but there is a reason for concern.

At the same time, new opportunities will emerge, which, despite the problems, will surely be realized in the future.

Employees may change jobs or job directions, but it's crucial to discuss the terms of future cooperation thoroughly, especially regarding finances.

Connections with colleagues from other cities or countries are developing with mixed success. Some issues may arise between June 13th and 17th, and the stars advise avoiding trips, both business and personal, during this period.

Money. Financially, this month is quite contradictory. On one hand, your income is increasing and there is hope for progress in this area, but on the other hand, expenses are also high. Some may need to pay off old debts and past obligations, while others might struggle to collect old debts. Additionally, many expenses will be related to children and loved ones. So, money comes and goes, and the stars strongly advise you to keep this process under control.

Love and Family. The movement of Jupiter encourages many Geminis to focus on household matters. Heroic plans for renovations or, in a more serious case, buying new property are emerging. These are just plans for now, but they will become a reality over the year.

Relationships with relatives will improve, and help from elder family members may be available. A trip or a visit from close ones living in another city or country is possible.

Lovers might make an important decision about living together and start "building their nest."

Some issues with a family member may arise in the middle of the month. Nothing critical will happen, but circumstances might force you to change plans or postpone them.

Health. This month, you are healthy, energetic, witty, and attractive, which will be noticed by everyone you encounter. However, the stars strongly recommend being careful in travel and while driving throughout the month. The most challenging period in this regard is from June 13th to 17th.

CANCER

This month, Jupiter changes signs. Moving from the problematic for you sign of Gemini, this powerful planet enters your home sign of Cancer. Since Jupiter is the planet of luck, this means that your life will slowly but surely start to improve.

Business. For professionally active Cancerians, June is a transitional, concluding month. Entrepreneurs and managers will be able to complete various business activities related to expanding their enterprises. Ahead lies active work, forward progress, new ventures, and new opportunities.

Employees might consider changing jobs and take the first steps in this direction. These efforts will definitely pay off later. Ongoing legal issues, if any, are also coming to an end. The theme for this period is saying goodbye to what hindered your development, work, and life, and embarking on a long journey towards a new future.

However, some problems, as remnants of the past, may still arise. For example, in the middle of the month, entrepreneurs might face disagreements with official bodies, while employees could have conflicts with their superiors.

Additionally, conflicts with friends, allies, or high-ranking patrons are possible. The main reason here is money, unresolved financial issues, and it's likely that you will have to settle these.

Money. June's financial situation is quite turbulent. On one hand, you won't be short of money, but on the other, expenses are significant, with the majority falling between June 13th and 17th. However, Jupiter offers you good prospects in both business and finances, so settle your debts if you have any, and move forward.

Love and Family. In your personal life, the agenda involves resolving complex domestic issues and various housing-related problems. Many Cancerians are planning a move, and this summer, you are likely to relocate to a new or fully renovated home.

Relationships for lovers are not very stable, and mid-month disagreements may arise due to differing views on life, or in the worst case, financial issues. It's unfortunate when love and money are intertwined, and this time, excessive materialism could lead to a breakup. If this happens to you, learn from it and avoid repeating past mistakes in the future.

Health. In June, your energy levels are low, but this situation won't last long. By next month, things will start to get back to normal, and gradually you will feel more confident and better.

For now, take care of yourself and if you feel unwell, seek help from a good doctor, avoiding self-treatment methods. This advice is especially relevant for those weakened by chronic illnesses and the elderly.

LEO

Jupiter's move into the sign of Cancer, which is foreign to you, signals a shift in priorities. The key now is to consolidate your achievements and strengthen your base.

Business. Most of June will undoubtedly be favorable for you. Expect intensive negotiations with partners, like-minded individuals, and influential figures. The goal is to expand your business, which is particularly relevant for senior managers and entrepreneurs. This process may require significant effort and resolution of various issues. You might encounter legal challenges, especially if you have business interests in another country. Alternatively, there could be serious disagreements with partners about business development, particularly its financial aspects. In the worst case, your activities might attract the attention of regulatory bodies, leading to complications.

However, no task is insurmountable, so roll up your sleeves and take action without delay. You have many people around you who are willing and able to help.

Employees might face issues with their superiors in mid-June. It's important to note that this will likely be due to your own overconfidence and lack of flexibility and diplomacy. Remember that a boss is still a boss, and maintaining professional decorum is crucial. The bluntness and even aggressiveness that many Leos exhibit in the first and second ten-day periods of June will meet with a strong response. As they say, "When an unstoppable force meets an immovable object."

Money. Financially, June is rather unstable for you. While you won't be short of money, expenses will be significant. On the one hand, this is due to professional obligations, and on the other, family and household needs.

Love and Family. For those focused on personal life, June is a month of movement and change. This primarily concerns housing and relationships with loved ones. Questions like "Where to live?" and "Who to live with?" may arise, especially for those who recently experienced a breakup or a sudden change of partner. Answers to these questions may not be immediate, but in six months or so, things will settle into place.

Harmonious couples might discuss plans related to construction or purchasing a home and are likely to realize these plans within the year.

Those planning to move to another country may face problems, so the stars advise postponing such plans for a year or a year and a half. In the meantime, you can analyze and refine your plans as needed.

Health. In June, your energy levels will be quite high, and you will likely avoid illnesses. A slight decline in well-being is possible during the New Moon from June 25th to 28th, so reduce your activity and take care of yourself during this period.

VIRGO

An active, bright, yet quite intense month lies ahead. The stars promise you decisiveness in actions and insight in thoughts, which can help you move mountains.

Business. In June, many of you will have a substantial workload. Entrepreneurs and managers will complete ongoing projects and plan for the future. Everything will proceed smoothly, without delays or problems. The future, according to the stars, looks bright and appealing.

However, past issues remain relevant and will need to be addressed now and later. For example, complicated relationships with partners will enter a new phase, directly related to finances or other material assets. There may also be disagreements with friends or higher-ups regarding debts or other financial obligations. Resolving this situation will be possible if both sides are willing to compromise; otherwise, it will be a stalemate.

Relationships with partners from other cities or countries will develop with mixed success. Complications are likely in the middle of the month, especially between June 15th and 18th. These issues may be unpredictable, so it's wise to consider all possible options to avoid getting caught off guard.

Employees might be offered a new job or additional tasks to their current ones, naturally resulting in higher pay.

Money. Financially, this month might be uneven. On one hand, you won't be short of money, but on the other, problems will arise. Some of you will need to settle old debts, while others may struggle to receive due payments on time. The estimated dates for receiving the largest sums are June 7th-9th and 23rd-25th.

Love and Family. June will have a strong focus on business, pushing personal life temporarily to the background. However, those whose life revolves around love and family might face difficulties. Divorced or separating couples will begin a new phase involving financial issues. This area will not run smoothly, possibly due to the partner's lack of necessary funds.

June will also be challenging for those in love, who may drift apart or enter into conflicts for various reasons. The stars advise you to be more attentive to each other and, in case of arguments, first reflect on your own mistakes.

Stern Saturn, still in the area governing relationships, urges you to recognize your mistakes and analyze the past. If something isn't right, remember that there is no punishment without fault. This is Saturn's warning.

Health. This month, you are healthy, energetic, and illnesses will bypass you. However, be cautious while traveling and driving between June 14th and 18th. It's best to avoid long trips during these days and reschedule them for a later date.

LIBRA

A bright and unconventional month lies ahead, where you can expect the unexpected and embrace unique solutions that lead to success. Go for it!

Business. The main focus this month will be on resolving relationships with colleagues from other cities or countries. Trips and negotiations are likely, and they will be successful. However, relationships with certain partners may deteriorate, leading to disagreements over unresolved financial issues. This won't stop your progress, but it will create some challenges along the way. Entrepreneurs will begin implementing new, large-scale projects, which is the right move—great times are ahead, and many of your plans will come to fruition.

Employees will find new opportunities, whether through a new job or a promotion at their current one. In some cases, these opportunities might involve relocating to another city or country.

Money. Financially, June is quite contradictory. The largest expenses will arise in mid-June, specifically from June 15th to 18th.These may be related to business expansion, resolving complex issues within your network, or demands from friends or higher-ups. Those not involved in business might spend significant amounts on the needs of children and loved ones. Nevertheless, money will come in regularly, and the prospects are promising.

Love and Family. For many professionally active Libras, personal life might take a back seat this month due to the importance and volume of work.

However, if your life revolves around family, love, and children, the stars warn of a challenging period ahead. Stern and demanding Saturn moves into the sector of the sky that governs marriage and stable partnerships, meaning that flexibility, diplomacy, and delicacy are essential now and in the future.

In June, nothing will prevent you from taking a trip together, spending more time with your children, and supporting your loved ones in all their endeavors. Lovers should be particularly attentive to each other between June 14th and 18th, as unexpected quarrels and grievances may arise during this period. Parents might also face issues with their children around this time.

Health. Your energy levels are high in June, and illnesses will stay away.

SCORPIO

You're in for a challenging yet potentially very productive period. Life is in constant motion, and the stars advise you to go with the flow that time offers you.

Business. For most Scorpios, one phase is ending and another is beginning.

Entrepreneurs are wrapping up significant projects related to business expansion—possibly involving construction, major renovations, important acquisitions, and other substantial business activities. Ahead lies active work related to expanding professional horizons, often involving other cities or countries.

On this path, many of you will face obstacles that may vary greatly in each case. For example, entrepreneurs might encounter issues with partners who have different visions for the business's future or wish to split it. Problems with employees who may not meet current demands are also possible. Those planning to start a business in another country should thoroughly study its laws, as certain difficulties may arise that need to be overcome.

Employees might consider looking for new jobs, with the entire year ahead being favorable for this change. However, the first steps can be taken now, in June and July. You might face problems with colleagues who could obstruct your progress or simply ignore your contributions. Despite these challenges, there are positives. The key is to muster the strength and resources to overcome them, making it worth putting in maximum effort.

Money. The financial situation is stable but not spectacular. There won't be significant achievements, but there won't be any major setbacks either. Besides regular expenses, there might be income from real estate transactions and help from a close person. Those planning to take out a loan can expect a favorable outcome.

Love and Family. Families may enter the final phase of home improvement. Alternatively, selling an old house and planning a move, possibly to another city or country, is possible. Family relationships may not be very stable this month, following the saying, "There's a thin line between love and hate."

Even the slightest disagreement could turn the situation around completely, with the most challenging period being from June 14th to 18th. The motto for this difficult time is: "Calmness, patience, and more calmness."

Health. In June, your energy levels are low, and special care is needed for the elderly and those with weakened health. Young and healthy individuals should maintain a healthy lifestyle and avoid dangerous situations.

Be cautious during travels and when driving from June 14th to 18th. If a long trip is planned, it's better to reschedule it.

SAGITTARIUS

This month is all about people. Achieving your goals will only be possible with a strong team. The proverb "One man in the field is not a warrior" has never been more relevant.

Business. June is characterized by a plethora of contacts, most of which will be quite productive. Entrepreneurs and managers will think about a new stage in their ventures, likely involving expansion and reaching a larger scale. This will require significant organizational work, including supporters, partners, and assistants. Meetings with them are likely in the near future.

Some of you may plan to collaborate with colleagues from afar and ultimately achieve your goals. However, be cautious in mid-June, as unexpected complications may arise. Pay extra attention from June 14th to 18th when you might face various obstacles. Study the laws of foreign countries, be meticulous with documents, and review all potential complications. Only a careful and diligent approach will help you overcome these challenges.

During this same period, managers might face misunderstandings with subordinates, and employees could have issues with colleagues.

Changes in professional activity are also likely for those currently employed. A long professional cycle is ending, and many of you will feel the desire to make significant changes in your work. Some steps in this direction will be taken now, and others later. The entire year ahead will provide opportunities to decide on what to do and how to live.

Money. Financially, this month could be quite challenging. Money might be continuously going out, and the largest expenses will likely occur between June 14th and 18th. Most of these expenses will probably be related to personal matters, such as the needs of children and close ones.

Love and Family. Expect a high level of emotional intensity in your personal life, especially in romantic relationships, where situations may change drastically. This is a time when positivity can swiftly turn to negativity, and vice versa. The most dangerous period is mid-June, from June 14th to 18th. During this same period, parents might face problems with their children, leading to significant expenses.

Many of you will start planning to acquire real estate, possibly in another city or country. While these are just plans for now, they will likely materialize over the year.

Health. This month, you will be needed by everyone around you. The abundance of meetings, impressions, and heavy workloads both at home and work will lead to fatigue and exhaustion. This will be especially noticeable during the New Moon from June 25th to 27th. During this period, reduce your activity and devote time to yourself.

CAPRICORN

Saturn, your ruling planet, is changing signs and immediately clashing with Jupiter. This marks the beginning of a new phase in your life—active, yet tense.

Business. This month promises a lot of work and relentless efforts to overcome various obstacles. One significant challenge may arise from ongoing disagreements with partners, primarily concerning real estate or land. Your partners will exhibit uncommon stubbornness, but you won't lack persistence either. This situation will feel like "an irresistible force meeting an immovable object," and resolving it won't be quick. Much of the summer will be spent in disputes and negotiations. The most challenging period is from June 14th to 20th, when serious disagreements and conflicts are likely. Entrepreneurs and managers of all levels will need to address these issues. Meanwhile, regular work will continue, and most tasks will be successfully completed.

Employees might find themselves juggling family matters and work, managing to keep up with both responsibilities like a "servant of two masters."

Money. The financial situation in June is unstable. A significant portion of what you earn will be spent on various current needs. According to the stars, many expenses will be related to the needs of children and close ones, particularly from June 14th to 17th.

Love and Family. The main events this month will likely unfold at home and within the family. Fragile and disharmonious couples will enter a risky period, with their relationships under celestial pressure again. This time, property issues, especially regarding real estate, will dominate the agenda. Disputes over who owes what and who owns what could last all month, with the most unfavorable period being June 14th to 20th.

In contrast, harmonious couples may use this time to resolve any issues related to their home.

Additionally, many families will face problems with their children, leading to significant expenses. In some cases, you'll need to address issues your children are facing, while in others, you'll invest in their education and upbringing.

June 14th to 20th is also a challenging period for most lovers. Arguments may arise unexpectedly over trivial matters, so it's crucial not to let emotions take over. Take a pause and thoroughly analyze the problem. Over time, you might find that the issue isn't as significant as it initially seemed.

Health. Your energy levels in June are low, so take care of yourself and remember the saying, "God helps those who help themselves."

AQUARIUS

In June, you should control your emotions, as the month will be dynamic but also chaotic. The stars suggest being disciplined and not overly impulsive.

Business. Saturn, your ruling planet, changes signs in June and immediately conflicts with Jupiter. This indicates that you might face several issues in certain areas of your life. Entrepreneurs and managers might experience misunderstandings with colleagues from other cities or countries, possibly regarding the fulfillment of mutual obligations. Conflicts related to real estate or other assets are also likely, where both sides may have different perspectives on the situation. In many cases, these issues could be interconnected. The most intense problems will arise in mid-June, particularly from the 14th to the 18th.

It is unlikely that all these issues will be resolved within the month, and you may need to continue addressing them in the future. Looking ahead, it's safe to say that these problems will eventually be resolved over the year, requiring diligent work on your part.

Despite these challenges, June brings some good news. You'll receive support from your surroundings, and someone close to you may assist as well. Work will proceed as usual, and new opportunities may arise.

Employees might consider changing jobs or seeking a promotion. Such opportunities will likely appear this summer.

Money. The financial situation in June is far from stable. There will be significant expenses, some related to work and others to personal life. However, work continues, and it will bring the expected income.

Love and Family. For many Aquarians, personal life might take center stage this month, but challenges are likely. Couples experiencing discord might enter another conflict, this time over property issues. If it's a matter of divorce and division, this process might drag on. It will take time for both parties to find an acceptable compromise.

Harmonious couples may tackle complex property issues together, relying on wisdom and love. Relationships with relatives might worsen, but this situation could be temporary and may resolve itself later. Children will bring joy and might serve as a crucial link between quarreling spouses.

For lovers, this month could be turbulent, not necessarily due to their relationship but because of various disturbances in their environment. However, if love is strong, everything will be overcome in the end.

Health. Your energy levels in June are quite high, but be cautious during travel and when driving. The entire month is tricky in this regard, especially from the 14th to the 20th.

PISCES

The pace of this month may be quite slow. As the saying goes, "Slow and steady wins the race," and it seems particularly fitting for you now.

Business. For most entrepreneurs and managers, the primary task will be completing projects related to business expansion. This likely involves construction and various administrative activities that may have occupied you for an entire year. Now it's time to finish what you started and evaluate the results. The only downside is the cost. Many of you may need to part with a significant sum in mid-month, indicating that completing your plans might require more funds than initially expected.

Employees might find themselves torn between home and work, and personal matters could take precedence. It might be wise to consider taking a vacation or a few days off – opportunities for this will certainly arise.

Many Pisces may face issues with colleagues from other cities or countries, with the most challenging period being from June 14th to 20th. These misunderstandings will eventually be resolved, but for now, be patient and tackle the most difficult issues. The root of these problems might be the inappropriate behavior of subordinates or colleagues, so keep a close eye on things and remember the saying: "A chain is only as strong as its weakest link."

Money. June's financial situation is characterized by conflicting trends. Money will come in and go out, but by the end of the month, your financial balance may be negative. The largest expenses will occur from June 14th to 19th, due to both business and personal matters.

Love and Family. For many Pisces, the main events in June will happen at home and with family. Loyal couples and committed lovers may invest time and money into creating their cozy nest. Fortunately, these demanding activities are coming to an end. Disagreements over home improvements may arise frequently, but the most challenging time will be mid-month, from June 14th to 20th. During this period, financial issues may come to light, and your partner may have their own perspective on the events. Additionally, many families may face problems with children, leading to significant expenses.

Another potential issue in June could be conflicts with relatives. This is not a new problem, but an old issue resurfacing in a new way.

Health. In June, your energy levels will be low, and the stars strongly recommend that you take care of yourself and practice moderation in all things. Be particularly cautious during travel and while driving throughout the month, especially from June 14th to 20th.

July

New York Time			London Time		
Calendar Day	Lunar Day	Lunar Day Start Time	Calendar Day	Lunar Day	Lunar Day Start Time
01/07/25	7	12:03:31 PM	01/07/25	7	11:52:30 AM
02/07/25	8	1:02:51 PM	02/07/25	8	1:00:25 PM
03/07/25	9	2:01:32 PM	03/07/25	9	2:07:23 PM
04/07/25	10	3:00:14 PM	04/07/25	10	3:14:08 PM
05/07/25	11	3:59:17 PM	05/07/25	11	4:21:00 PM
06/07/25	12	4:58:27 PM	06/07/25	12	5:27:28 PM
07/07/25	13	5:56:47 PM	07/07/25	13	6:31:59 PM
08/07/25	14	6:52:43 PM	08/07/25	14	7:32:01 PM
09/07/25	15	7:44:34 PM	09/07/25	15	8:24:58 PM
10/07/25	16	8:31:07 PM	10/07/25	16	9:09:17 PM
11/07/25	17	9:12:04 PM	11/07/25	17	9:45:15 PM
12/07/25	18	9:48:01 PM	12/07/25	18	10:14:23 PM
13/07/25	19	10:20:06 PM	13/07/25	19	10:38:37 PM
14/07/25	20	10:49:40 PM	14/07/25	20	10:59:46 PM
15/07/25	21	11:18:08 PM	15/07/25	21	11:19:24 PM
16/07/25	22	11:46:57 PM	16/07/25	22	11:38:58 PM
18/07/25	23	12:17:41 AM	18/07/25	23	12:00:00 AM
19/07/25	24	12:52:03 AM	19/07/25	24	12:24:17 AM
20/07/25	25	1:31:59 AM	20/07/25	25	12:54:07 AM
21/07/25	26	2:19:12 AM	21/07/25	26	1:32:20 AM
22/07/25	27	3:14:38 AM	22/07/25	27	2:21:42 AM
23/07/25	28	4:17:24 AM	23/07/25	28	3:23:11 AM
24/07/25	29	5:24:52 AM	24/07/25	29	4:34:26 AM
24/07/25	1	3:12:27 PM	24/07/25	1	8:12:27 PM
25/07/25	2	6:33:41 AM	25/07/25	2	5:50:39 AM
26/07/25	3	7:41:19 AM	26/07/25	3	7:07:24 AM
27/07/25	4	8:46:34 AM	27/07/25	4	8:22:10 AM
28/07/25	5	9:49:20 AM	28/07/25	5	9:34:13 AM
29/07/25	6	10:50:08 AM	29/07/25	6	10:43:56 AM
30/07/25	7	11:49:44 AM	30/07/25	7	11:52:04 AM
31/07/25	8	12:48:49 PM	31/07/25	8	12:59:26 PM

You can find the description of each lunar day in the chapter "A Guide to The Moon Cycle and Lunar Days"

ARIES

July may not be particularly fast-paced, but it will give you the opportunity to pause, reflect, and strengthen your base. As the saying goes, "Slow and steady wins the race."

Business. The first half of the month is the best time for professional endeavors. During this period, entrepreneurs and managers can successfully continue activities related to business expansion. Some of these activities may involve other cities or countries. One phase of your work is wrapping up, and another equally important one is beginning, likely involving real estate and administrative tasks extending into 2025-26. It seems you are laying a strong foundation for future business development, and the stars are on your side.

The second half of July is less favorable – Mercury starts retrograde on the 18th and will continue until August 10th, bringing delays and various problems. One such issue might be a shortage of skilled employees - staff shortage. Misunderstandings with previous colleagues are also possible.

Employees might spend most of this month focusing on family matters, so it might be wise to consider taking some time off to avoid the stress of juggling work and home. July, especially the second half, is an excellent time to step back from work and spend quality time with loved ones. Those who remain at work should be more attentive to their colleagues and handle complex issues with diplomacy. If there are changes within the company, it is important to assess how they align with your needs.

Money. July's financial situation is not particularly stable. Money will come and go, but this process is well-thought-out, and no unpleasant surprises are expected. Everything is proceeding as it should.

Love and Family. For many Aries, the main events of July will take place at home with family. Plans to change your life, buy a new house, apartment, or country house may emerge, and these plans will likely come to fruition within the year. Some of you may take the first steps this month, while others can do so later.

Relationships with relatives could be unstable this month, with a potential for serious conflict in the last third of July. To avoid problems, try to be more tolerant of your loved ones' flaws and offer criticism gently and delicately, keeping in mind that everyone has their own perspective on life.

This advice also applies to those in love, who might be too sharp-tongued and impatient in their speech. Remember, "Silence is golden," and act accordingly.

Health. Throughout July, you may experience some energy decline. The stars advise you to take care of yourself and spend more time outdoors, which is a great way to restore your strength.

Additionally, the stars recommend being cautious while traveling and driving, especially during the last third of July.

TAURUS

This month deserves all good words. Problems are gradually being resolved, and new opportunities are on the horizon. In short, you won't have time for boredom.

Business. In professional and financial matters, it's best to focus on the first half of the month. During this period, you'll be at the peak of your intellectual form and able to find optimal solutions to even the most complex tasks.

Entrepreneurs and managers will rely on partners from other cities or countries. There may be trips, negotiations, and resolving recent issues. Planning new initiatives is possible and even necessary now, with their start happening a little later.

The second half of the month is less dynamic and more suited for steady work, reflection on what's been done, and rest.

Employees can make progress in all areas—both professional and financial—during the first half of the month. There may be offers for new jobs or new responsibilities at their current place. The second half of July, however, is better for personal and family matters.

Money. July looks very promising financially. Venus, your ruling planet, will be in the financial sector of your chart all month, meaning you won't have any money problems. Funds will come in regularly, and their amount will significantly increase. Estimated dates for the largest sums are July 2-3, 12-13, and 20-22.

Love and Family. Your personal life this month could be just as important as work. However, things aren't as positive in this area as one might hope. Many families will face issues with children, leading to significant expenses. Keep an eye on your kids and don't let them take advantage of you. The most challenging time in this regard is the second half of the month, especially from July 20 to 26.

This period may also bring problems for lovers, who are advised to avoid arguments and confrontations. Firstly, the reaction will be intense, and secondly, this isn't a situation where "truth is born in a dispute." Mercury goes retrograde from July 18 to August 10, a period prone to errors in judgments and actions.

Relationships with relatives will improve, with possible trips and meetings with loved ones living in other cities and countries.

Health. Your energy levels will be quite high in July, and illnesses are unlikely to trouble you. You might feel some fatigue in the last days of the month, from July 24 to 30. This period is better suited for rest and for activities that don't require much intellectual or physical effort.

GEMINI

Your ingenuity and wit, which you are well-known for, will shine exceptionally bright this month. With these qualities, you'll feel unstoppable.

Business. Expect a lot of activity in the professional sphere this month. You may receive numerous offers from partners in other cities or countries, with promising financial prospects. Relationships with old friends and former partners may be renewed, and there might be talk of relocation, which applies to both employees and entrepreneurs alike. The best time for all matters is the first half of July, when things will progress quickly, without delays or issues.

In the second half of the month, from July 18 to August 10, your ruling planet Mercury goes retrograde. This period is best spent on negotiations and paperwork, which won't be easy. However, with your characteristic perseverance and inventiveness, you'll overcome any obstacles and tackle the tasks that come your way.

If you have travel plans this month, it's best to schedule them for the first half of the month.

Money. July looks promising financially; incomes may increase, while expenses might decrease. Complex financial issues involving friends or influential individuals are likely to be resolved. Most importantly, there are good prospects for work and financial matters.

Love and Family. In your personal life, both successes and challenges are possible. Uranus and Venus are visiting your sign, creating a perfect union for making new acquaintances. The first half of the month is particularly favorable for this, with luck clearly on your side. If you are single and longing for love, this is the ideal time.

Families can also improve their relationships, especially if there is a need for it. There might be trips and meetings with old acquaintances and relatives living in other cities or countries.

The second half of July is less favorable. During this period, you may experience some nervousness and inconsistency in thoughts and feelings. Problems with parents or senior family members might arise.

In another scenario, there could be domestic difficulties, and you might have to deal with complex issues related to real estate. New acquaintances made between July 18 and August 10 are unlikely to be reliable and may quickly disappear, leaving only unpleasant memories. This applies equally to work and romantic relationships.

Health. Your health is not at risk in July, but be cautious in the second half of the month, especially when traveling or driving. The likelihood of mishaps during this time is quite high.

CANCER

You're stepping into a new chapter of life—one that's brighter and more positive. Jupiter, the planet of luck, is moving through your sign, and it's up to you to make the most of its energy.

Business. Typically, Jupiter brings optimism and a lot of energy, and this will be especially evident in the first half of the month. During this time, business activities should go smoothly, helping you take your endeavors to the next level. Entrepreneurs and managers can breathe new life into stalled projects, with substantial support from friends and influential people.

Your connections with colleagues from afar are progressing well, but this area might need some extra attention. Unexpected problems could pop up in the second half of the month, and they'll need to be addressed.

Employees may receive job offers or move up in their current positions. Another possibility is returning to a previous organization but in a more prestigious role.

Money. Your financial situation is improving as your professional standing strengthens. If you're an employee, this might be a good time to ask for a raise. After some discussions, there's a good chance you'll get it.

Money might take center stage if you're starting a new job. Here, the stars advise you to be realistic—don't overestimate what you can achieve, but don't undersell yourself either. Aim for balance, and by August, you should reach your goals.

Love and Family. This month, your personal life might be just as important as your work. Housing issues are mostly resolved, with only the finishing touches left to take care of.

Jupiter in your sign often brings new people into your life, and this month is no exception. You might meet someone intriguing and start an exciting new romance.

Travel is possible, and it's best to plan trips for the first half of the month. In the second half, whether you're traveling nearby or far away, things could get tricky, especially between July 22 and 26.

Relationships with relatives, which should be fairly stable in the first half of the month, might become strained later on. A serious conflict could arise between July 22 and 25.

Health. In July, you'll feel healthy, energetic, and active, keeping illnesses at bay.

However, during the last third of the month, be careful while traveling or driving.

LEO

The upcoming month is an excellent time for a vacation and focusing on your personal affairs. July's motto: "Eat, Pray, Love."

Business. The first half of July is quite productive. During this time, you may meet new people who can be very beneficial for advancing your projects.

Entrepreneurs and managers will have the chance to settle relations with colleagues from other cities and countries, resolving at least some of the most complex issues. Additionally, plans for restructuring or expanding the business might start to take shape.

Employees might spend part of the month on vacation, with the best time for this being the second half of the month. This period is less promising for work, as Mercury is retrograde from July 18 to August 10, which can lead to delays, the absence of necessary people, and other minor inconveniences.

Money. Financially, July isn't looking very favorable. Money will be spent continuously, partly due to work and business development, and partly due to personal life, children's needs, and close relatives.

Many of you may face financial issues with friends or people in high positions. This could involve old debts, unfulfilled obligations, or other financial matters, with the last third of July being particularly challenging.

Love and Family. Significant, perhaps fateful, events are happening in your personal life. Many Leos might be planning changes at home. This could mean building a new house, doing major renovations, or acquiring new property. You'll likely take the first steps in July, and the rest of the year will give you the chance to turn your dreams into reality.

Relationships between spouses and lovers may feel unstable. Your sign is usually good at enduring and waiting, but now you might be prone to instant emotional reactions. The period from July 22 to 30 looks especially tense. Take your time—with some thought, you'll find the best solution, even in difficult situations.

Health. In July, your energy might not be at its peak, so take care of yourself and remember that summer is the perfect time for rest.

VIRGO

The planetary alignment is exceptionally favorable, promising a productive month ahead. Doors are opening!

Business. For ambitious and professionally active Virgos, it's crucial to be energetic in the first half of the month. This is the best time to start projects, big or small. Entrepreneurs and managers of all levels may receive new proposals, while employees might get job offers. Friends or people in high positions, with whom relationships will noticeably improve, may play a significant role in all endeavors this month.

The second half of the month is less favorable. Mercury, your ruler, goes retrograde from July 18 to August 10, causing any endeavors to progress slowly and requiring more effort. You might need to rework certain tasks and make corrections to ongoing projects. On the bright side, it's a good time for error-checking and contemplating your plans. This period is also perfect for taking a break. You've come a long way, so it's worth taking some time off from work.

Money. Financially, July is quite favorable. Money will come in regularly, and you'll see a slight increase. The best dates for receiving significant sums are July 2, 3, 12, 13, and 20-22 Although there will still be many expenses, they'll be fewer compared to recent months. Complex financial issues related to friends or high-ranking individuals are mostly resolved. If there are any remaining claims, they are minimal.

Love and Family. The second half of the month isn't favorable for family and romantic life. During this time, avoid making hasty decisions as there could be errors in judgment and actions. Even the most positive situation could unexpectedly turn around 180 degrees. Think carefully before saying or doing anything.

The most challenging days for all partnerships are from July 21 to 26.

Health. Your energy levels are high this month, but during the New Moon from July 24 to 26, things might change. You could feel unwell or experience fatigue from the intense period. The stars recommend taking a break and not delaying it.

LIBRA

This month, you can celebrate a victory. Everything is going according to plan and dreams. So, move forward with confidence.

Business. In July, you are full of strength and energy, and even your spontaneous decisions could turn out to be successful. Complex relationships with certain partners or opponents become less relevant. In some cases, they are partially resolved; in others, you simply set the problem aside and move forward confidently. Connections with colleagues from other cities or countries remain important, and this time, you'll see a noticeable improvement in these relationships.

The best time for all professional matters is the first half of July. The second half is less favorable. Your task from July 18 to August 10 is to maintain the gains made in the first half of the month. For example, if you were offered a new job or new venture, you should analyze all the pros and cons and make adjustments if you have any doubts. It's the perfect time for a thorough review of documents and for spotting errors, both your own and others'. During this period, the relationships you had established with colleagues from other cities or countries may become strained, particularly from July 21 to 29. The situation will stabilize later, but it's crucial to keep a close watch on developments in this area.

If your plans are somehow connected with friends or high-profile individuals, you may notice some changes. Promises made may seem uncertain, and you may not be able to clear this fog until the second half of August. However, compared to the overall direction, which indicates clear success, all the problems in the second half of July appear to be minor obstacles that can be easily overcome.

Money. Financially, July is very favorable. Money will come in regularly, and you'll see a slight increase. The best dates for receiving significant sums are July 5-7, 14, 15, 23, and 24.

Love and Family. Family and romantic life this month might feel less exciting than professional activities. However, those whose interests are focused on personal relationships could face some challenges.

Saturn, along with Neptune, will remain in the sector of the sky responsible for marriage and other bonds for a long time. This calls for a gentle approach to each other. Even if not everything in a loved one's behavior satisfies you, it's best not to criticize their actions. A cooling-off period is possible even among close couples, and those whose relationship has been under pressure for a long time may think about separation. It won't be immediate, but now it's necessary to monitor any changes in relationships and, even in case of conflict, try not to cross any red lines.

The most challenging time is the last third of the month when the likelihood of quarrels is quite high. During this period, misunderstandings with relatives, both yours and your partner's, are also possible.

Health. In July, your energy levels are high, and any ailments should pass you by.

SCORPIO

Slowly but surely, a door to the future is opening before you. And it looks bright and promising.

Business. The winds of change will touch all areas of your life, including your professional activities. Many of you will feel the desire to change jobs, and negotiations on this topic may be a background not only in July but also in August. Employees might get promoted at their current workplace, with opportunities available.

Entrepreneurs and managers of all levels will complete one significant project and start another, more interesting and productive one. Some of your plans might involve another city or country, with potential trips, meetings with partners, and discussions about future collaborations.

The best time for professional matters is the first half of the month. In the second half, Mercury goes retrograde, causing delays in all professional activities. You might need to refine your plans and discuss the conditions for future work or partnerships. Don't rush this process—let events unfold at their own pace, and it will turn out better in the end.

Money. Financially, July looks stable. In addition to regular income, you might also benefit from unofficial sources. This could include profits from real estate transactions or support from close ones. A favorable loan might also come your way.

Expect significant expenses in the third decade of the month, particularly from July 22 to 28.

Love and Family. Changes are also happening in your personal life. Many families are finishing long-term renovations and preparing to move. This could be moving to a new apartment or house, and in some cases, to a different city or country.

The last third of July might be challenging for all personal relationships. During this period, both lovers and spouses may have quarrels for various reasons. These disagreements won't be major, but remember—a bad peace is better than a good quarrel.

Health. In July, you are energetic, healthy, and free from any ailments.

SAGITTARIUS

July promises to be a vibrant month, with planets demanding much of your attention. Both your professional and personal lives, as well as household matters, will need your focus. Be ready!

Business. The transition of your main ruler, the powerful Jupiter, into the sign of Cancer signifies a shift in your priorities. It's time to rethink your business strategy and make adjustments to your current work. This applies to all Sagittarius individuals, whether employees or entrepreneurs. Many bosses and businesspeople will embark on large-scale organizational tasks—potentially involving construction, real estate transactions, or defining your role within various structures you work with.

This is a lengthy process, but the initial steps can be taken now, in the summer of 2025. Connections with colleagues from other cities or countries become crucial. Many of you will tie your business development to distant locations, leading to negotiations with distant colleagues that will progress with mixed success.

Employees might be thinking about quitting to start their own business, but this is a long journey requiring both resources and significant responsibility. However, as the saying goes, "The journey of a thousand miles begins with a single step," so make sure you have a clear plan before moving forward. Alternatively, organizational changes might lead you to apply your talents in a different role, such as in another department.

The best time for professional activities is the first half of July. During the second half, from July 18 to August 10, Mercury goes retrograde, which will bring obstacles, delays, and misunderstandings in relationships. Don't rush things; consider delays as blessings that protect you from mistakes. This is a good time to find and correct errors in your projects. Moreover, late July is an excellent time for a break— think about taking a vacation!

Money. Financially, July could be challenging. Money might be constantly going out, either due to work or personal life. However, you won't be completely strapped for cash—successful credit negotiations, support from business partners, or help from loved might come through.

Love and Family. Your personal life may be just as significant as your work this month. Many of you will be focusing on real estate issues, such as planning major renovations or purchasing a new home, apartment, or vacation property. Some of you might even plan these activities in another city or country.

Family connections will take on more importance, with a trend toward reuniting with children living elsewhere. Many parents might be planning to expand their families. Relationships with spouses and lovers will generally be stable, and any misunderstandings that arise in the last third of July will be manageable.

If you have a trip planned for the second half of July, consider visiting familiar places to avoid disappointment. New acquaintances are possible between July 1 and 15, which could brighten the lives of those who are currently single. However, in the second half of the month, be cautious with new people, as they might not be as reliable as they first appear.

Health. Your energy levels will be low in July, but serious complications can be avoided if you focus on rest, a healthy lifestyle, and getting enough sleep.

CAPRICORN

July is an excellent time to express your views and persuade others of their merit. However, it would also be wise to listen to your opponents. Being a true diplomat will be key to your success, both in professional affairs and personal relationships.

Business. July promises to be filled with numerous meetings and interesting, valuable new connections. Entrepreneurs and managers at all levels will be able to find partners to further develop their business, both locally and in distant places. Additionally, there will be opportunities to strengthen your team by bringing in new skilled employees.

Complex issues related to real estate may be resolved successfully or are in the process of being settled. Employees could receive additional tasks on top of their existing ones, and the stars see great benefit in this. The best time for all professional activities is the first half of July, so plan your most important tasks and meetings for this period.

From July 18 to August 10, Mercury goes retrograde, which means that the pace of events will slow down, and various obstacles and delays will appear. Trying to force things through during this time is likely to be frustrating, so work calmly with what the time offers. Progress might be slow, but as long as it's in the right direction, there is no need to worry.

Money. Financially, July is stable; money will come in regularly, and you'll notice a steady increase. The approximate dates for the largest sums to arrive are July 2, 3, 12, 13, 20-22, 30, and 31. Expenses will be minimal and all planned in advance.

Love and Family. For many Capricorns, the main events may unfold in their personal and romantic lives. Long-time lovers may think about strengthening their relationships, perhaps discussing marriage and living together. Even if the main event doesn't happen this month, there's no need to be disappointed—time is on your side, and everything you've dreamed of will eventually come true.

For long-term couples, relationships might feel like they're cooling down, or in the worst case, nearing separation. This is especially true if the marriage has long been unsatisfactory for both parties. The appearance of a new, interesting person could definitely end relationships that lack true attachment and love. Such encounters are likely during this period.

Many Capricorns are still dealing with real estate matters, and the situation varies: some may be dividing property, while others are planning their next purchase. In some cases, this involves another city or country.

Health. You will be active, energetic, and charming this month. However, the last few days of July may bring a significant drop in energy. Diets, detox programs, a temporary break from social media, and trips to nature will all be beneficial, helping to harmonize both thoughts and feelings.

AQUARIUS

Your life is constantly changing, but it doesn't seem to get any easier. Events are coming at you in a powerful, intense flow, and you'll need to stand firm against the current. Go for it!

Business. July's events may revolve around work, which will appeal to the workaholics among you. Entrepreneurs and managers might embark on new projects with good financial potential. This could lead to increased influence within your circle and new professional opportunities.

Complex relationships with colleagues from other cities or countries are gradually being resolved, although some conflicts might just be on hold. Employees could be offered a new job or additional responsibilities. Though challenging, this is a significant step on your professional path and will be beneficial for your future.

The best time for all professional endeavors is the first half of July. In the second half, from July 18 to August 10, Mercury will be in retrograde, slowing the pace of events. You can expect problems with your environment, delays in document processing, and the absence of key people. On the bright side, this slower pace will protect you from mistakes and hasty decisions, allowing you to evaluate the situation more carefully.

Money. Your financial situation is stable. Money will come in regularly, and the amount will noticeably increase. There will also be considerable expenses, mostly related to personal life. However, by the end of the month, your financial balance will be positive.

Love and Family. Your personal life may take different turns this month. Relationships with relatives remain tense, but conflicts are subsiding, even if complete reconciliation isn't yet possible. Household chores, such as major repairs and construction, are now behind you, and a move may be on the horizon. Those dealing with other complex housing issues will also see progress.

In many families, problems with children may arise in the second half of the month, bringing associated expenses. This period is challenging for both spouses and lovers, especially if unresolved issues linger from the past. You might experience cooling off, misunderstandings, and distrust. It's not the time to confront or blame each other during Mercury retrograde; instead, it's wiser to revisit the past and analyze your mistakes. Now is the perfect time to do so.

Health. Your energy levels are somewhat low in July, and overall, it's a period when you need to carefully monitor your health. Identify your weak spots and consult a good doctor if necessary. This advice is especially important for the elderly and those with weakened health.

PISCES

July is looking quite positive for you. You will be able to handle a variety of tasks, showcase your wit, and become the star of any party. So, go ahead with confidence!

Business. July is more suited for rest and attending to personal and family matters, while work can wait. However, for those who can't resist work or have obligations that keep them at the office, you'll still be able to make contributions this month Entrepreneurs will wrap up important activities related to business expansion, possibly involving major construction or other real estate operations. Employees can calmly handle their current tasks, but the stars suggest that your thoughts might be elsewhere. So, consider taking a break, especially since opportunities for rest will arise this month.

July is an excellent time for people in creative professions—your popularity will increase, and so will your earnings. The best time for all professional matters is the first half of the month. In the second half, Mercury goes retrograde, causing significant slowdowns in all affairs. For you, this is a good chance to evaluate what's happening and calmly finish what you've already started.

Money. The financial situation is modest There won't be a lot of money this month, but support from close people, parents, or a spouse might come through. There will also be chances to secure a favorable loan.

Love and Family. Your personal life will be vibrant this month. Home improvement projects are coming to an end, and there are still many plans related to developing existing relationships. This could mean the birth of children or plans related to pregnancy.

Those who are still single may meet someone special and start an exciting romance. Parents will be pleased with their children's achievements, and the atmosphere in most families will be warm and festive.

Additionally, July will be full of parties and various festive events. Some complications in relationships between spouses and lovers could arise in the last ten days of the month, but the situation will quickly resolve.

Health. This month, you are healthy, energetic, successful, and efficient in solving any tasks. July is a great time for shopping, self-improvement, and any cosmetic procedures.

August

New York Time			London Time		
Calendar Day	Lunar Day	Lunar Day Start Time	Calendar Day	Lunar Day	Lunar Day Start Time
01/08/25	9	1:47:52 PM	01/08/25	9	2:06:29 PM
02/08/25	10	2:46:56 PM	02/08/25	10	3:13:09 PM
03/08/25	11	3:45:28 PM	03/08/25	11	4:18:25 PM
04/08/25	12	4:42:18 PM	04/08/25	12	5:20:17 PM
05/08/25	13	5:35:51 PM	05/08/25	13	6:16:13 PM
06/08/25	14	6:24:46 PM	06/08/25	14	7:04:12 PM
07/08/25	15	7:08:18 PM	07/08/25	15	7:43:44 PM
08/08/25	16	7:46:41 PM	08/08/25	16	8:15:49 PM
09/08/25	17	8:20:47 PM	09/08/25	17	8:42:14 PM
10/08/25	18	8:51:51 PM	10/08/25	18	9:04:52 PM
11/08/25	19	9:21:14 PM	11/08/25	19	9:25:23 PM
12/08/25	20	9:50:23 PM	12/08/25	20	9:45:16 PM
13/08/25	21	10:20:46 PM	13/08/25	21	10:06:00 PM
14/08/25	22	10:53:59 PM	14/08/25	22	10:29:15 PM
15/08/25	23	11:31:48 PM	15/08/25	23	10:57:01 PM
17/08/25	24	12:15:55 AM	16/08/25	24	11:31:51 PM
18/08/25	25	1:07:28 AM	18/08/25	25	12:16:25 AM
19/08/25	26	2:06:21 AM	19/08/25	26	1:12:23 AM
20/08/25	27	3:10:47 AM	20/08/25	27	2:18:46 AM
21/08/25	28	4:17:57 AM	21/08/25	28	3:31:58 AM
22/08/25	29	5:25:15 AM	22/08/25	29	4:47:37 AM
23/08/25	1	2:07:07 AM	23/08/25	30	6:02:39 AM
23/08/25	2	6:31:03 AM	23/08/25	1	7:07:07 AM
24/08/25	3	7:34:46 AM	24/08/25	2	7:15:41 AM
25/08/25	4	8:36:36 AM	25/08/25	3	8:26:33 AM
26/08/25	5	9:37:03 AM	26/08/25	4	9:35:44 AM
27/08/25	6	10:36:42 AM	27/08/25	5	10:43:51 AM
28/08/25	7	11:36:02 AM	28/08/25	6	11:51:23 AM
29/08/25	8	12:35:09 PM	29/08/25	7	12:58:21 PM
30/08/25	9	1:33:43 PM	30/08/25	8	2:04:07 PM
31/08/25	10	2:30:52 PM	31/08/25	9	3:07:07 PM

You can find the description of each lunar day in the chapter "A Guide to The Moon Cycle and Lunar Days"

ARIES

August is ahead of you—bright, festive, and a bit lazy. In other words, 'Work done, have your fun.' Well, time for fun has arrived!

Business. The first half of August is not particularly productive for professional matters. Mercury moves retrograde until August 10, which means there won't be any significant achievements during this period. The best thing you can do is to get your affairs in order and analyze your relationships with partners. Conflicts with them are quite likely from August 8 to 11, but with the efforts of your friends and associates, the situation will smooth out.

Relationships with colleagues from other cities or countries will slightly improve, and it's possible that old partners will soon be replaced by new ones, with whom relationships will be more productive. Employees might take a vacation in August and spend time with their loved ones.

The best time for all professional activities is the third part of August. During this period, you can "grab the bull by the horns" and push forward stalled projects. Strengthening connections with both nearby and distant colleagues is also likely in this period.

Money. Financially, August looks uneven, if not outright costly. However, there's good news—the expenses this month are pleasant and beneficial. Rest, entertainment, trips, and advantageous shopping— all of this is likely for this wonderful summer month.

Love and Family. August is the ideal time for relaxation and personal activities. During this period, you can visit familiar places, meet with old friends, and spend time with your children. The younger generation might particularly need your support now, both morally and financially.

For lovers and couples, August could be challenging. In the first half of the month, relationships may experience coldness, some uncertainty, and in some cases, serious conflict. On one hand, you may be cold and unresponsive, while on the other hand, your partner might not be very tactful.

In short, the stars have complaints about both sides, which should be taken into account. Support during this period might come from parents or older family members.

Many Aries will start another phase of home improvement, or at the very least, will have some plans regarding this.

Health. In August, you are healthy and charming but somewhat nervous and inconsistent. Remember that August is a calm month, and there is no need to rush things. Take your time, align yourself with the mood of the stars, and this will be the surest path to harmony and success.

TAURUS

The pace this month isn't very fast, so don't rush. Act according to the circumstances and remember the saying, "Slow and steady wins the race."

Business. This month isn't particularly favorable for professional activities. The best approach is to avoid setting large tasks. You can set them, but don't rush their implementation. Mercury is in retrograde until August 10, which means it's a challenging time with potential delays and minor inconveniences in all professional matters. This period is more suitable for rest and attending to family matters. Consider this and know that nothing will happen if you spend a couple of weeks away from work.

The second half of the month is more dynamic but also more problematic. During this time, entrepreneurs and managers may face issues with subordinates, while employees may encounter problems with colleagues. Unexpected inspections, visits from official agencies, and the emergence of legal issues are also possible. However, you can count on support from your superiors or influential individuals.

Connections with colleagues from other cities or countries are developing quite successfully, and this will be one of the best gifts of August. Trips planned for the period from August 10 to 20 should be very successful.

Money. Financially, this month looks quite prosperous. Money will come in regularly from both official and unofficial sources. The latter might include support from close people, parents, and profits from various real estate operations.

Love and Family. In many cases, personal life this month may take precedence over professional activities. In the first half of the month, various household chores related to housing, rest, and communication with loved ones are likely to take priority. Trips planned for August will go very well, especially if scheduled for the second ten-day period of the month.

Throughout August, intensive contact with relatives and support from them is likely. The first ten days of August are good for reconnecting with old contacts. Old friends, former lovers, and people with whom your relationships were interrupted in the recent past may reappear on your horizon. Lovers may meet a loved one living in another city or country, and joint trips are also possible.

Health. In August, you are healthy and energetic, but the stars advise you to watch your weight and consider a healthy diet, as summer offers such opportunities.

GEMINI

Your ruler, Mercury, is retrograde until August 10, so refrain from making hasty decisions in both professional and personal matters. As they say, "Haste makes waste."

Business. It would be wiser to postpone major and important initiatives until mid-month or at least until August 11. Focus on organizing and completing ongoing projects during the period from August 1 to 10. This is also a good time for reconnecting with old friends and influential individuals. In the future, these connections could prove not only useful but could fundamentally change your career and life.

Significant professional events may occur from August 10th to 20th, when an interesting and profitable proposal from distant colleagues is likely. A trip and productive negotiations may be on the horizon, where courage and decisiveness will be required from you. During this period, your decisions are likely to be successful.

In the last third of August, despite the generally favorable conditions of the month, minor issues may arise, such as confrontations with friends or influential individuals. However, these situations should be resolved by the end of the month.

Money. Financially, August looks very favorable. Money will come in regularly, and the amounts will noticeably increase. Expected dates for the largest sums are August 1, 2, 10, 11, 19, 20, 29, and 30. Expenses will be minimal, with the majority occurring in the last ten-day period of the month.

Love and Family. August can bring many pleasant surprises in your personal life. Many of you will have the opportunity to completely transform your life. This could be related to work, personal life, or education. Projects involving relocation are likely to materialize in the future.

In the last third of August, families may experience issues with children, potentially leading to significant expenses. This period is also challenging for most lovers, with potential conflicts and unexpected disagreements. However, these disputes will be short-lived, so there's no need to worry. The stars advise being delicate and not succumbing to emotional outbursts.

Health. Your energy levels are quite high in August, so any minor ailments will likely bypass you.

CANCER

Your streak of good fortune continues. Jupiter, the planet of great luck, is heading towards your sign, soon to be joined by Venus, the planet of minor luck. This means that Fortune is on your side.

Business. The best time for all professional activities is the last 20 days of August. The first 10 days are also favorable, but more suitable for organizing current affairs and analyzing future projects.

Entrepreneurs and managers should carefully review the financial aspects of future projects, while employees should thoroughly discuss salary matters if considering a new job or a promotion at their current position.

These negotiations and reviews are best carried out in the last 20 days of August. This is the time to revive long-dormant projects, breathe new life into old ventures, and renovate workspaces.

Money. The financial situation is stable with a clear tendency towards improvement. Events occurring now will lay a solid foundation for financial stability and pave the way for achieving a new financial level in the future.

Love and Family. Personal life in August is as important as work. Many of you will complete significant home improvement projects and may even start planning the next phase. Fortunately, opportunities for this will be available.

Relationships with spouses and partners are generally harmonious, although conflicts may arise in the third ten-day period of August.

For singles, the ideal time is also the last 20 days of the month. During this period, a fateful meeting is likely, which could lead to marriage. So, socialize more and always be at your best.

Health. You are healthy, active, and capable of making a strong impression on everyone you meet. However, the stars advise you to pay closer attention to your parents and elderly family members, as there may be issues with them in the last third of August.

LEO

For most of the month, you may not feel particularly confident or energetic. Therefore, don't rush or plan any significant events in August, whether in your work or personal life.

Business. During the first 10 days of August, Mercury is retrograde in your sign, which usually brings unnecessary fuss, mistakes in work, and difficulties in communication. The stars recommend dedicating this period to rest, but if that's not possible, focus on completing ongoing projects and carefully analyzing future plans. The period from the 10th onward is more productive; during this time, entrepreneurs and managers can continue activities related to business expansion, such as major construction or significant renovations.

Old connections are being restored, and there is potential for active development of contacts with colleagues from other cities or countries. However, complications in relationships with distant colleagues are possible in the third ten-day period of the month. Thanks to your efforts and those of your friends, the situation will be quickly resolved. Nonetheless, the stars recommend keeping your documents in order, as they may be needed in the last third of August.

This advice is also relevant for those who might face pressure from regulatory authorities or are dealing with legal issues.

Money. Financially, August is relatively neutral. Income may not be significant, but profit from unofficial sources is likely, such as various real estate transactions, support from business partners or close people, and large loans. The period from August 10 to 20 is particularly indicative in this regard. Expenses are few and are predictable and reasonable.

Love and Family. In your personal life, household activities will continue. These may include changes related to housing, such as selling the old and buying new property. Alternatively, it could be a major renovation that completely changes your living conditions.

Spouses will live peacefully in August; shared responsibilities will only strengthen their bond. Relationships with relatives will be active, with possible visits from family members living in other cities or countries. For most of the month, relations with relatives will be smooth and harmonious, with only the last third of August potentially bringing conflicts involving all family members. Thanks to your efforts, the conflict will quickly subside, but it's worth analyzing its cause, as the problem may arise again in the future.

Health. This month, you are healthy and energetic but also fussy and nervous. The stars recommend dedicating the first ten days of August to rest — there will be opportunities for this. Be careful during travel and while driving in the last third of August.

VIRGO

In the first ten days of August, Mercury, your ruling planet, is retrograde, which will slow down your plans. The stars advise not to rush but to focus on analyzing the current situation.

Business. Most of August, particularly the first ten days, is not very favorable for professional activities. It's not a good time to start new projects, but it's perfect for putting your current affairs in order.

If possible, take a vacation and spend the first half of the month by the warm sea or at your country house. If that's not possible, reconnect with old contacts and seek the support of influential people. Such opportunities are likely to arise in the in the middle of August.

New professional opportunities may arise from August 10th onwards. These may be unexpected but somehow linked to past endeavors.

The most active—and at the same time the most stressful—period is the last third of August. Financial disagreements with partners, friends, or official bodies may arise, but these issues will be quickly resolved, so there is no need to worry.

Money. The financial situation is stable but nothing extraordinary. There won't be any major achievements, but there won't be any financial ruin either. Be prepared for significant expenses on August 12-14 and 26-28.

Love and Family. The situation in your personal life remains unstable. Couples experiencing difficulties may face old grievances resurfacing. Resolving these issues will not be easy, but with some effort and a desire to keep disputes private, you can overcome them. Divorced couples might face similar situations. Harmonious couples can jointly resolve this month's challenges, both moral and financial.

Health. Your energy levels are low in August, so special caution is advised for those who are weakened, elderly, or suffering from chronic illnesses. Young and healthy Virgos are recommended to visit a spa, swim, or go to a bathhouse. All Virgos should watch their diet and consider a light regimen.

LIBRA

A bustling month full of various concerns lies ahead. Overall, things are going well, and the planets are favorably aligned. However, Mercury is moving backward until August 10th, which may cause some delays. Despite this, luck is on your side, so everything is manageable.

Business. The first ten days of the month may bring some unrest among your circle. Some friends or influential people might delay fulfilling their promises or even temporarily disappear from the scene temporarily. This situation is temporary, and everything should fall into place by mid-month.

Relations with colleagues from other cities or countries will significantly improve this month, and successful negotiations or a trip are possible in the second half of August.

The position of employees will significantly improve, with potential promotions, increased influence, and other professional successes. Even opposition from certain individuals won't hinder your progress. Your position is stable and will only strengthen day by day.

Money. Financially, your position is stable, with regular income that will noticeably increase. The expected dates for receiving the largest sums are August 1st, 2nd, 10th, 11th, 19th, 20th, and 28th-30th. While expenses will also be significant, they are all related to personal life.

Love and Family. The situation in your personal life is not as favorable as in your professional life. The process of distancing between spouses continues, with occasional flare-ups of arguments. The most challenging times are the first ten days of August and the last days of the month. In some cases, children might help reconcile quarreling spouses, smoothing over the rough edges in their relationship.

Health. In August, you are healthy, energetic, and ready to "move mountains."

SCORPIO

The complex situations you've dealt with in the past are nearly resolved. What's left will be managed in due course.

Business. Changes in your professional life continue. Throughout the month, negotiations about a new job are likely to be successful. While there may be some uncertainty during the first ten days of August, everything will be resolved positively in the middle of the month.

Connections with colleagues from afar are developing well, and you may receive important and pleasant news from 10th to 20th of August. A trip may also be possible during this time. In some cases, the new job or business will be related to another city or country.

Entrepreneurs and managers are concluding complex projects related to business expansion, possibly finishing major construction or renovations. The first ten-day period of the month, which will be the most challenging part of August, may bring problems with subordinates or colleagues for many Scorpios. There might also be inspections, so it is wise to prepare in advance.

Money. Your financial situation is stable, with regular income and promising prospects. Everything is heading in the right direction, and the future will confirm this.

Love and Family. Your personal life is also progressing. Many Scorpios are preparing for a move, whether it's to a new house, another city, or even another country. It all depends on your plans, intentions, and opportunities. The groundwork is almost ready; only the final step remains. Those who have recently made the decision may find suitable housing this month.

Relationships in families are harmonious, with spouses supporting each other in all endeavors.

Health. Your energy levels are quite high in August, but unexpected complications such as flare-ups of chronic illnesses or sudden accidents are possible in the first ten days. The most challenging days in this regard will be from August 8th to 10th.

SAGITTARIUS

The motto for August: "Movement and Change." Another remarkable aspect of this month is that the more energy you spend, the faster it will replenish.

Business. The primary task for professionally active Sagittarians will be to develop connections with colleagues from other cities or countries.

Entrepreneurs and managers will be able to address several organizational tasks, such as scouting for real estate to expand their business. In some cases, this may occur in distant locations.

Employees can look forward to a vacation, with the first ten days of the month being ideal for this purpose. During this period, Mercury is in retrograde, so achieving significant results in work will be unlikely. The period from August 10th onward is more promising for all professional activities, so it's best to schedule important events during this time. This period is also perfect for new acquaintances. People who enter your life now may prove to be reliable and useful in the future. However, those you meet between July 18th and August 10th are unlikely to bring much benefit—they may disappear, leaving behind unpleasant memories. Naturally, this only applies to new acquaintances; the stars welcome the renewal of old connections.

Money. Financially, August is stable but not exceptional. The month won't bring large incomes, but expenses will also be moderate. From August 10th to 20th, you can expect support from business partners and help from close ones. Obtaining a favorable loan is also possible. Some Sagittarians may gain profits from various real estate transactions.

Love and Family. In your personal life, a period of change is unfolding, primarily driven by a desire to transform your life. Many Sagittarians plan to purchase real estate, often in another city or country. Children may bring many concerns; they might be going through a challenging phase, and you'll need to support them with words, actions, and money. This is particularly evident in the first ten days of the month, which might significantly complicate the situation in this area.

The first ten days of August are also challenging for most lovers. A major quarrel could occur, potentially ending the relationship. Of course, this mainly applies to relationships that have already run their course. If this is your situation, don't worry—the world is vast, and there are plenty of people out there for you. The 20 days of the month are notable for a high likelihood of meeting someone interesting.

Health. Your energy levels are quite high in August, and illnesses won't trouble you. Plan trips related to work and leisure for the last 20 days of the month, as they will be more successful during this time.

CAPRICORN

August is a slow month. The calmer and more modest you are during this period, the better it will be for you.

Business. In terms of professional activities, August can be divided into three distinct periods. The first ten days of the month are frankly unsuccessful and even conflict-prone. It is recommended for employees to communicate less with their superiors and for entrepreneurs to be cautious with inspecting authorities and government bodies. The likelihood of complications in both cases is quite high. Taking a vacation might be a good way out, so step back from work and take care of yourself.

The period from August 10th to 20th is more active and successful. During this period, influential partners may appear on your horizon, and there may be proposals for a new direction in business or its expansion. Disputed real estate issues that have been encountered in the past are generally solvable, although some troubles may still occur in the first half of the month.

The last ten days of August are bright, dynamic, and quite promising. It is during this time that stalled plans will begin to move forward, and this positive process will continue into the future.

It should also be noted that various organizational and household concerns may form the backdrop of the entire month. You are used to this, so everything will work out as planned and dreamed.

Money. The financial situation is unstable. There will be many expenses, but most of them are planned and reasonable. In one case, this is related to business, and in another, to family and children's needs. Financially, the last ten days of August are the most promising, which is directly related to success in business.

Love and Family. August is a traditional vacation period. However, the first ten days are quite challenging. Spouses may often quarrel, with the main reason likely being real estate issues. This situation mostly applies to those who have long been on the brink and are planning a final breakup or divorce. Harmonious couples will also have to deal with real estate issues and take care of parents and elderly family members.

The period from August 10th to 20th is the most interesting for romantic life; during this time, there is a real possibility of an interesting meeting that can develop into a deep, serious romance, possibly even marriage. Long-time lovers may decide to live together or get married. August is also an ideal time for a vacation, so it is worth planning it in advance. If the first ten days are more suitable for trips to familiar places, then the rest of the month can be spent exploring new destinations.

Health. For most of August, your energy levels are low, so lead a healthy lifestyle and do not burden your body with excesses. This is a great time for a trip to a sanatorium, visiting a bathhouse, going to a spa, and massage salons. In short, pamper yourself!

AQUARIUS

The key to this month is to foster good relationships with those around you. This applies equally to work and love.

Business. In all professional matters this August, caution and diplomacy are recommended. Your reaction to even minor difficulties in relationships with partners can be overly harsh.

On the other hand, in the first ten days of August, your partners might behave inconsistently and illogically. Some may not keep their promises, and some might just disappear from the scene. You won't be able to influence this situation, so the best tactic is to wait patiently, understanding that everything happens in its own time. During this period, Mercury is retrograde, leading to various delays, which in your case are related to partners.

Complications in relationships with colleagues from other cities or countries are likely in the first ten days of the month, particularly from August 7th to 10th. During this time, you might also face inspections and the exacerbation of old legal issues or other challenges depending on your personal situation.

The best time for all professional activities is from August 10th to 20th. During this period, new and interesting opportunities may arise, particularly for entrepreneurs and managers at all levels. Employees may strengthen their positions in their current jobs, and new job offers are also possible.

Money. Financial positions in August are stable but not extraordinary. The approximate dates for the most significant income are August 1st, 2nd, 10th, 11th, 19th, 20th, 28th, and 29th. Most expenses will occur at the beginning and end of the month, and these are mainly related to personal matters, according to the astrologer.

Love and Family. The situation in your personal life appears quite turbulent. In the first third of the month, you might be displeased with the insincere behavior of a close person, their coldness, and aloofness. On the other hand, you might also behave in a way that raises questions for your partner. The stars recommend thinking carefully before saying or doing anything to avoid regretting it later. Relations with relatives also seem complicated, with misunderstandings and conflicts likely from August 7th to 10th. The period from August 10th onwards is calmer; during this time, spouses and lovers may realize their mistakes, paving the way for reconciliation.

Children bring joy as positive changes occur in their lives, which will become evident by mid-month.

Health. This month is not particularly favorable for health. Elderly and weakened individuals are advised to pay close attention to their bodies and seek medical help if necessary. At the same time, August is suitable for trips to a sanatorium, spa treatments, and any self-care. Be cautious during travel and while driving from August 7th to 11th.

PISCES

August is a challenging month; it will present a variety of tasks, each requiring your attention and participation. The advice is simple—don't try to chase too many goals at once, or you might end up with nothing.

Business. In the first third of the month, you may encounter delays and problems. Entrepreneurs and managers might face misunderstandings with subordinates who won't show their best side. Remember, your careful management can prevent many issues, so be proactive.

Employees may experience misunderstandings with colleagues and workplace intrigues, which are best ignored. Financial demands from partners or colleagues are also likely in the first ten days of August, which you will need to address.

From August 10th onwards, the periods are calmer and potentially more productive. Those dealing with complex real estate issues will complete one challenging phase and can move on to the next, which looks innovative and interesting, though it will require significant resources. However, most of you are creative individuals, so things will go well in this area.

Money. Your financial situation is modest but stable. Besides regular earnings, you can expect pleasant surprises such as gifts, bonuses, or even a lottery win. You can also rely on strong support from close people. Major expenses are likely from August 7th to 10th and may be related to work or personal life, household, and family needs.

Love and Family. Personal life is generally calm, especially from August 10th onwards. The first 10 days of the month are challenging for both lovers and spouses, with likely misunderstandings, confusion, and household problems. After August 10th, things will stabilize, and everything will run more smoothly.

August will bring many interesting events related to children, and in the second half of the month, it will become clear that the older ones are thriving and the younger ones are behaving well and admirably. Your children might even demonstrate a unique and rare talent. Many families may welcome new children or grandchildren.

For lovers, the period from August 10th to 20th is also a great time. If you already have a close person, the relationship will significantly improve, and if not, the chance of meeting someone special is quite high. Those engaged in various real estate transactions can complete one stage and move on to the next, which might involve home decoration, buying furniture, and other necessary household items.

Health. In August, your energy levels are not high, but no serious problems are expected, especially if you maintain a healthy diet and remember the benefits of good sleep.

September

New York Time			London Time		
Calendar Day	Lunar Day	Lunar Day Start Time	Calendar Day	Lunar Day	Lunar Day Start Time
01/09/25	11	3:25:18 PM	01/09/25	10	4:05:09 PM
02/09/25	12	4:15:42 PM	02/09/25	11	4:56:04 PM
03/09/25	13	5:01:10 PM	03/09/25	12	5:38:50 PM
04/09/25	14	5:41:37 PM	04/09/25	13	6:13:52 PM
05/09/25	15	6:17:37 PM	05/09/25	14	6:42:41 PM
06/09/25	16	6:50:16 PM	06/09/25	15	7:07:04 PM
07/09/25	17	7:20:51 PM	07/09/25	16	7:28:45 PM
08/09/25	18	7:50:45 PM	08/09/25	17	7:49:18 PM
09/09/25	19	8:21:26 PM	09/09/25	18	8:10:12 PM
10/09/25	20	8:54:28 PM	10/09/25	19	8:33:04 PM
11/09/25	21	9:31:31 PM	11/09/25	20	8:59:48 PM
12/09/25	22	10:14:16 PM	12/09/25	21	9:32:46 PM
13/09/25	23	11:03:55 PM	13/09/25	22	10:14:33 PM
15/09/25	24	12:00:35 AM	14/09/25	23	11:07:04 PM
16/09/25	25	1:02:54 AM	16/09/25	24	12:09:59 AM
17/09/25	26	2:08:23 AM	17/09/25	25	1:20:23 AM
18/09/25	27	3:14:35 AM	18/09/25	26	2:34:13 AM
19/09/25	28	4:19:47 AM	19/09/25	27	3:48:17 AM
20/09/25	29	5:23:20 AM	20/09/25	28	5:00:57 AM
21/09/25	30	6:25:13 AM	21/09/25	29	6:11:49 AM
21/09/25	1	3:54:37 PM	21/09/25	1	8:54:37 PM
22/09/25	2	7:25:51 AM	22/09/25	2	7:21:12 AM
23/09/25	3	8:25:44 AM	23/09/25	3	8:29:36 AM
24/09/25	4	9:25:17 AM	24/09/25	4	9:37:27 AM
25/09/25	5	10:24:36 AM	25/09/25	5	10:44:49 AM
26/09/25	6	11:23:24 AM	26/09/25	6	11:51:09 AM
27/09/25	7	12:20:54 PM	27/09/25	7	12:55:09 PM
28/09/25	8	1:15:55 PM	28/09/25	8	1:54:47 PM
29/09/25	9	2:07:12 PM	29/09/25	9	2:47:56 PM
30/09/25	10	2:53:49 PM	30/09/25	10	3:33:14 PM

You can find the description of each lunar day in the chapter "A Guide to The Moon Cycle and Lunar Days"

ARIES

After a laid-back summer, it's time to buckle down and dive into work. You'll have plenty of energy and determination, but you might lack focus and patience.

Business. The main achievements in your professional sphere are likely in the first 20 days of September – this is the most active period of the month. Entrepreneurs and managers might consider several directions in their work. On one hand, there are large-scale projects involving expansion, construction, and renovation; on the other hand, there are agreements to be made and regular tasks to be completed. Relationships with partners might be somewhat turbulent, with occasional disagreements and conflicts. These will be minor and short-lived but could be irritating.

Employees should stick to simple and straightforward tasks in September. This month is more suited for meticulously strengthening your base and dealing with the less visible but essential tasks. From September 20th to 26th, be attentive to your surroundings – issues with colleagues, subordinates, and minor frictions with friends might arise. In other words, it will be a typical work life.

Connections with colleagues from other cities or countries remain relevant, with active contacts possible throughout September, especially in the last week. A trip might be on the cards at the end of the month.

Money. The financial situation is stable but not more than that. There won't be significant income, but expenses will be minimal. In tough times, you can rely on support from a loved one, parents, or close friends.

Love and Family. The main theme in your personal life this September might be home improvement. If you've already started such projects, you can continue them at a steady pace. If they're still in the planning stage, there's nothing stopping you from beginning this month. Relationships with your spouse may lack stability; your partner might be overly assertive, if not aggressive. However, this could be a case of "lovers' tiffs," where moments of irritability are followed by reconciliations. You'll need to be flexible and willing to compromise to keep the peace. Children will bring joy, as things are going well for them.

Health. In September, pay attention to your diet and consider planning a healthy eating regimen, especially if you had an indulgent summer. Elderly people and those with chronic illnesses should maintain a moderate lifestyle and avoid excessive strain.

TAURUS

In September, you'll magically manage to balance work with various recreational activities. In other words, "the scamp has a finger in every pie."

Business. September might not be the most promising month for professional activities, but it's practically ideal for relaxation. However, if taking a break isn't an option or if you're a workaholic, you can still accomplish a lot this month. Strengthen connections with colleagues from other cities or countries, go on trips, establish beneficial contacts for your business, and enjoy yourself. Essentially, you'll be able to combine business with pleasure.

Additionally, opportunities will arise for you to showcase your achievements and positions to a broader audience, such as hosting project presentations or finding other ways to promote yourself. September is an excellent time for creative professionals—actors, artists, musicians, and writers. You might come up with interesting ideas that will be well-received by the public.

The best time for professional activities is from September 4th to 16th. During this period, luck will be on your side, and you can achieve your goals. The first days of the month, from September 1st to 5th, may bring some problems, such as disagreements with distant colleagues or financial issues. From the 20th of September, misunderstandings with old friends or high-ranking individuals are possible. However, all these troubles will be short-lived and won't affect the overall favorable outlook for the month.

Money. The financial situation in September is unstable, but a significant sum might come in around mid-month. This will offset the considerable expenses you'll face, most of which will be related to personal life, leisure, and the needs of loved ones.

Love and Family. Personal life might take precedence over work and career in September. Many Taureans will go on trips, meeting with loved ones residing in other cities or countries. Relationships with relatives will improve, and even minor disagreements likely in the first ten days of the month won't impact the overall positive trend of September. Parents will have more time for their children, possibly even taking a trip together.

September is also a festive month, offering more opportunities to socialize, attend birthdays, and parties, and attract a lot of positive attention.

Health. In September, you'll be healthy, energetic, and able to make a strong impression on everyone you meet. However, be careful while traveling and driving from September 1st to 5th.

GEMINI

September is generally a favorable month, with only a few challenging days at the beginning and end. For the most part, you can expect smooth sailing from the stars.

Business. This month, many Geminis will focus on organizational and administrative tasks. On a smaller scale, this might involve tidying up paperwork and your workspace, while on a larger scale, it could mean renovating your office or other workspaces. Connections with colleagues from other cities or countries remain important, and in some cases, organizational activities may take place far from home. There might also be a return home from distant places. The most promising period for professional activities is from September 6th to 19th.

From September 1st to 5th, minor professional misunderstandings are likely. Employees may experience miscommunication with their superiors, while entrepreneurs might face complications with government authorities. In the last ten days of September, disagreements with friends or high-ranking individuals are possible. However, these issues will likely be part of the usual work routine and won't significantly impact your overall progress.

Money. The financial situation in September looks stable but not exceptional. Income this month will be standard, with no windfalls expected, but expenses will also be reasonable. There may be some profit from real estate transactions and support from parents or a spouse.

Love and Family. In many families, the main events in September will revolve around home and family. The agenda includes various household transformations, such as renovations, purchasing furniture, and other household items. In some cases, this might occur in another city or country. Family relationships are calm, with spouses working together to handle household tasks and overcome financial challenges.

At the end of the month, disagreements with parents or older family members are possible. Alternatively, you may need to take care of relatives and possibly solve their problems. Children will require significant attention, both morally and financially, but as they say, "that's a sacred duty."

Health. In September, you will be healthy, active, and attractive. With this combination of qualities, any illnesses will stay away.

CANCER

The upcoming month promises to be excellent, with almost everything going your way. You'll experience such a surge of energy that staying in one place will be impossible. So, get ready to move forward!

Business. The main focus this month will be on developing connections with colleagues from other cities or countries. From September 7th to 20th, travel and successful negotiations are likely, potentially reviving previous collaborations. Along with this, new opportunities will arise, benefiting both employees and entrepreneurs.

You'll have excellent chances to make significant progress at work, tackling the most challenging tasks and achieving what once seemed nearly impossible. Minor issues that may arise from September 1st to 5th, as well as in the last third of the month, will be easily overcome. Early in the month, you might face some disputes related to real estate, and at the end, there may be minor friction with distant colleagues.

Money. Financial stability in September is expected, with a clear trend toward improvement. Venus will be in the financial sector of your chart for most of the month, ensuring you won't be without money. Significant amounts are expected around September 1st, 9th, 10th, and 17th-19th. Expenses are minimal and well-planned.

Love and Family. Those focused on their personal lives can enjoy September as they wish. Couples and spouses might take a trip together and have a great time. Interaction with friends will be joyful, and you might receive pleasant and useful information from them. New acquaintances will come easily, and their development will be swift.

A positive aspect of this month is that new relationships formed now could be quite long-lasting. The stars will support you in any new endeavors, something that hasn't happened for a while. September is also an excellent time to start studying and gaining new knowledge. Your intellectual abilities are at their peak, so take advantage of this.

Health. Your health will be strong, and you'll have plenty of energy for work, loved ones, and maintaining your fitness. Overall, things are looking very good for you.

LEO

The main task this month is to resolve various situations that have arisen around you. Some things will go your way, and some won't. As they say, "That's life."

Business. The planets are aligning in a way that new acquaintances are constantly entering your circle. They can have a significant impact on your affairs, and it's up to you to determine the future of these relationships. Entrepreneurs are advised to carefully review potential offers, especially their financial aspects. Remember, "All that glitters is not gold," and proceed cautiously.

Connections with colleagues from other cities or countries remain relevant, but much in this area still seems uncertain and unstable. With time, what is now just beginning may come to fruition. Those dealing with legal issues might seek to resolve them with the help of new allies and old friends. Although no clear progress is expected at the moment, work in this direction could pay off within a year. Time flies, so be patient and address issues as life presents them.

Money. A significant amount of time may be devoted to financial matters this month, with both problems and successes likely. Many will receive income from unofficial sources, including support from close friends, sponsorships, or loans. The bulk of expenses will fall in the last third of September and will vary depending on past circumstances. Some may need to repay old debts, while others might struggle with financial issues in their personal lives.

Love and Family. As usual, personal life is complex. Old connections fade away, making room for new ones. This process can be painful but inevitable. Divorcing couples may find it difficult to resolve various financial issues, and problems related to real estate are possible. Harmonious couples will continue with household changes, such as renovations, construction, and other costly activities.

Relationships with relatives are challenging, with potential grievances surfacing at the beginning and end of the month. It's best not to react to these complaints, as the issues will likely resolve themselves with time.

Health. Your energy levels are low in September, so lead a healthy lifestyle and remember the benefits of rest and adequate sleep. From September 1st to 6th, be especially careful during travel and while driving. These days are prone to accidents, emotional instability, and conflicts.

VIRGO

A time is approaching when all the higher planets—Pluto, Neptune, and Uranus—are forming positive aspects to your Sun. This means that life continues to evolve, and all changes are for the better.

Business. The planetary energies are aligning in your favor, capable of doing a lot for you. This chance might not come again soon, so the time to act is now. Employees might unexpectedly receive job offers, likely facilitated by influential friends. If negotiations began last month, they will likely come to fruition now.

Entrepreneurs might secure lucrative orders with good financial prospects. The challenging aspect of this month involves disagreements with certain individuals over unresolved financial matters, especially from September 1st to 6th. In the last third of the month, you might face conflicts with old partners who remain rigid and uncompromising.

Money. Despite clear professional successes, financial matters are complicated. The issue isn't a lack of income but rather high expenses. As they say, "What comes in, goes out immediately." This could be due to family and children, old debts, or previous obligations.

You might also be investing in your business's future, which could be the best option.

Love and Family. Complex personal processes continue. Many Virgos are still haunted by the past, whether it's a dissolved marriage or a failed love story. The stars advise leaving the past behind and moving forward. Nothing can be changed, so focus on the future. New people are entering your life, and friendships may develop into something more. In the last third of the month, Venus moves into your sign, making it a great time for romance and love. However, this same period could bring challenging situations with past partners, involving old grievances and resentments. This applies only to couples with a problematic history.

Harmonious couples will spend September focusing on home, children, and everyday concerns.

Health. This month, you are healthy, energetic, and ready to move mountains.

LIBRA

The stars remain favorable to you, allowing you to manage people, situations, and all the tasks that will demand your attention.

Business. The main focus this month is to establish your position regarding colleagues from other cities or countries. Changes are happening in this area, and most of them are positive. New partners may replace old ones, and these new partners might be more cooperative. However, positive developments still seem unstable, so it's not time to relax yet.

Entrepreneurs and managers should pay closer attention to their subordinates, while employees should be more cautious with their colleagues. The most challenging time in this regard is the last third of September, when complex issues requiring your attention and involvement may arise, potentially leading to conflicts. In the first third of the month, employees should be more attentive to their superiors, and entrepreneurs should be cautious in their interactions with official bodies. Mars in your sign might provoke you to be more abrupt, in cases where a different approach could solve the issues.

Overall, your professional positions are strong, and the problems in September will only be minor obstacles on your path to success.

Money. Your financial situation in September is stable, with regular income. The expected dates for significant sums are September 7, 8, 15, 16, 25, and 26.

Love and Family. In all personal relationships, diplomacy is key. First, Saturn, periodically visiting the sector of your chart related to long-term partners, requires you to be considerate of your loved one. Second, Mars is in your sign this September, and this aggressive planet might push you towards reckless actions. Keep this in mind and be more delicate with your close ones. This is the only way to avoid unpleasant situations, conflicts, and complaints. In short, everything is in your hands, and you bear the full responsibility.

Health. Your energy levels are low in September, but this is not critical. A few days of rest will restore your vitality and clear your mind.

SCORPIO

The beginning and end of the month might not be very fortunate for you, but the middle of it is extremely positive. Plan your activities according to the stars' recommendations to achieve excellent results.

Business. Changes in your affairs continue, and in some cases, this involves work or starting a business in another city or country. Alternatively, it could mean actively developing connections with colleagues from afar. If you are not planning to move or work in another city or country, you can successfully explore new professional areas.

While many things will go well, there could still be some problems. Between September 4th and 8th, unexpected issues may arise, potentially involving secret intrigues. In the last third of the month, disagreements with friends or people who have provided you with important services in the past are likely. It's important to note that these problems are temporary and won't affect the overall positive progression of events. The middle of the month is especially favorable, many of your plans will start to come together. During this period, you might receive help from friends or supportive influential people, which will positively impact all your endeavors.

Money. Your financial situation is unstable, as expenses remain high this month. However, in the most difficult cases, you will likely receive help from close people, your spouse, or parents. There could also be profits from various real estate transactions or a favorable loan.

Love and Family. In your personal life, there aren't many changes overall. However, in the last third of the month, parents might face problems with their children that have occurred recently. This could involve a temporary separation or issues that require your support, both emotionally and financially. The last third of September is particularly indicative in this regard. During this same period, lovers might also experience disagreements, potentially involving friends. Nevertheless, all these issues seem solvable, so try to be more delicate and flexible.

Health. In September, you are healthy and energetic, so illnesses will likely bypass you. However, be cautious during travels and while driving from September 4th to 8th.

SAGITTARIUS

New doors are opening to a bright future. However, embracing it may mean letting go of much of what you've already achieved. Fortunately, you still have time to make your decision, giving you complete freedom of choice. For now.

Business. Your activity levels this month could be at their peak, and professional luck is on your side. As a result, many things will go well for you. Connections with colleagues from other cities or countries are developing nicely. Many of you may slowly but surely start thinking about opening your own business in another city or country. This project might involve significant acquisitions, such as real estate. For some, these are just plans, while for others, there are actual steps being taken in this direction.

If you're employed, you might be considering different future job opportunities, as much of your current situation no longer satisfies you. However, no changes are expected just yet, though negotiations and some movement toward future employment are quite likely. Meanwhile, everything at your current job continues smoothly, with no stress in sight.

Money. September looks stable financially. Money will come in regularly, and the luckiest among you will see a noticeable increase. Expected dates for the most substantial sums are September 2, 3, 11, 12, 20, and 21. The biggest expenses are likely at the beginning of the month, between September 2 and 5.

Love and Family. Your personal life might take a back seat this month, as professional interests are more pressing. Nonetheless, there is a tendency toward change here as well. Many of you will plan a future move and can start thinking about how to make it happen and securing the necessary resources.

Relationships among spouses are stable, though the generally positive atmosphere of the month might be disrupted by unexpected but short-lived arguments. The situation could be more complicated for those who try to juggle two relationships. Here, you might face complex scenarios that force you to choose between an old attachment and a new love. Luckily, the freedom of choice remains.

Health. Your energy levels are high this month, and illnesses will stay away.

CAPRICORN

The month looks incredibly promising. Barring a few minor incidents, significant success can be predicted in all your endeavors. Go for it!

Business. The main focus for professionally active Capricorns will be on developing connections with colleagues from other cities or countries. New partners with innovative and modern ideas may appear, promising considerable profits, which will undoubtedly interest bosses and entrepreneurs. Employees might receive additional tasks and could even get new job offers.

The most productive time in September is between the 5th and the 20th, when the most significant successes are likely. However, there may be problems with some partners, bosses, or government agencies from the 4th to the 6th of September.

In the final third of the month, issues with colleagues from other cities or countries are also possible. Fortunately, all complex matters will be short-lived and can be resolved in the usual work routine.

Money. Financially, September is quite stable, with the largest sum likely arriving in the middle of the month.

Love and Family. Your personal and romantic life may develop rapidly this month. September could see you falling head over heels in love, having a disagreement, and then making up again. Spouses and lovers might take a short trip, which will turn out very well. A challenging aspect of this month is the recurring misunderstandings with relatives. The last 10 days of September are particularly indicative in this regard, making conflicts most likely during this period. The bad news is that if an argument does occur, it could bring up past issues where relationships with family were less than ideal.

Health. In September, you are healthy, energetic, and very charming, which will be noticed by everyone you meet.

AQUARIUS

In September, you may experience an energy slump, so it makes sense not to plan anything extraordinary this month. Sometimes it's okay to just go with the flow and focus on what the time presents.

Business. The main task for many Aquarius individuals will be to reassess relationships with colleagues from other cities or countries. New, sometimes unexpected developments may unfold in this area. New partners might appear on the horizon, allowing you to reset relationships that have caused issues in the recent past.

However, not everything may go as you wish. From September 4th to 9th, you might face problems in various areas of your work, which will be resolved in the usual course of business. Despite this, the overall trend in your affairs is quite positive.

Those with longstanding legal issues may encounter new financial claims in September, which won't be too difficult to fend off, especially given your experience with such matters. Employees are advised to work steadily and be cautious with colleagues in the first third of September, as intrigues, misunderstandings, and conflicts are possible.

Money. The financial situation in September looks quite turbulent. Expect many expenses this month, mostly related to personal life and the needs of children and loved ones. The largest amount of money will be spent in the last 10 days of September.

Love and Family. For many Aquarius individuals, the main events in September will occur in the realm of romantic or family relationships. Parents will be concerned about their children's future, investing time, emotions, and considerable funds into their development and education. Those who recently completed major renovations or construction may add the final touches to their work this month.

Single individuals and those seeking adventure are promised new acquaintances by the stars, likely related to work. Some may be intrigued by new colleagues, while others might see more than just friendship in their relationships with old friends.

Health. This month, your energy levels are low, which will be especially felt by the elderly and those weakened by chronic illnesses. Be cautious and take preventive measures in advance to ensure a calmer September.

PISCES

September promises to be festive and romantic. If you have any energy left for work, you'll have ample opportunities to shine.

Business. Expect a dynamic work period ahead. Partnerships are crucial, and you'll witness an interesting phenomenon: old connections will fade away, making room for new ones. Your task during this period is to part ways with former colleagues gracefully and build strong relationships with new ones. This will require wisdom, tact, and flexibility to navigate the challenges that may arise. The stars are confident that you will succeed!

The last third part of September will be the most challenging for relationships with former partners. Creative professionals—actors, artists, musicians, and writers—can expect particular success. Opportunities to showcase your talents to a broader audience and increase your income will arise. In fact, all Pisces will have the chance to present their achievements and gain recognition among peers. Just make sure you have something valuable to offer.

Money. September will be financially turbulent. Significant income is possible in the first half of the month, while substantial expenses are likely in the last 10 days of the month.

Love and Family. For many Pisces, personal life will take precedence over work and career. New relationships will form easily and develop quickly. This is great for singles but may cause problems for those who already have a partner. Remember, making a choice isn't always easy or pleasant and can be challenging and even painful. Keep this in mind and analyze the situation carefully before crossing any "red lines."

Parents will be delighted by their children, and many Pisces are planning to expand their families. Significant sums may periodically be allocated from the family budget for the needs of the younger generation.

Health. Your energy levels will be high for most of the month. However, you'll likely feel tired in the last days of September from all the social events and gatherings. While these activities enhance life, they can also make you yearn for solitude. Listen to your body, and if you feel fatigued, take the time to rest.

October

New York Time			London Time		
Calendar Day	Lunar Day	Lunar Day Start Time	Calendar Day	Lunar Day	Lunar Day Start Time
01/10/25	11	3:35:29 PM	01/10/25	11	4:10:41 PM
02/10/25	12	4:12:39 PM	02/10/25	12	4:41:28 PM
03/10/25	13	4:46:13 PM	03/10/25	13	5:07:18 PM
04/10/25	14	5:17:26 PM	04/10/25	14	5:29:54 PM
05/10/25	15	5:47:36 PM	05/10/25	15	5:50:52 PM
06/10/25	16	6:18:12 PM	06/10/25	16	6:11:41 PM
07/10/25	17	6:50:46 PM	07/10/25	17	6:33:58 PM
08/10/25	18	7:27:02 PM	08/10/25	18	6:59:32 PM
09/10/25	19	8:08:48 PM	09/10/25	19	7:30:45 PM
10/10/25	20	8:57:29 PM	10/10/25	20	8:10:17 PM
11/10/25	21	9:53:27 PM	11/10/25	21	9:00:28 PM
12/10/25	22	10:55:30 PM	12/10/25	22	10:01:37 PM
14/10/25	23	12:01:01 AM	13/10/25	23	11:11:03 PM
15/10/25	24	1:07:18 AM	15/10/25	24	12:24:30 AM
16/10/25	25	2:12:31 AM	16/10/25	25	1:38:22 AM
17/10/25	26	3:15:53 AM	17/10/25	26	2:50:47 AM
18/10/25	27	4:17:28 AM	18/10/25	27	4:01:20 AM
19/10/25	28	5:17:46 AM	19/10/25	28	5:10:19 AM
20/10/25	29	6:17:21 AM	20/10/25	29	6:18:22 AM
21/10/25	30	7:16:43 AM	21/10/25	30	7:26:00 AM
21/10/25	1	8:25:59 AM	21/10/25	1	1:25:59 PM
22/10/25	2	8:16:03 AM	22/10/25	2	8:33:27 AM
23/10/25	3	9:15:08 AM	23/10/25	3	9:40:18 AM
24/10/25	4	10:13:13 AM	24/10/25	4	10:45:21 AM
25/10/25	5	11:09:06 AM	25/10/25	5	11:46:38 AM
26/10/25	6	11:01:25 AM	26/10/25	6	11:41:55 AM
27/10/25	7	11:49:05 AM	27/10/25	7	12:29:30 PM
28/10/25	8	12:31:40 PM	28/10/25	8	1:09:01 PM
29/10/25	9	1:09:27 PM	29/10/25	9	1:41:23 PM
30/10/25	10	1:43:19 PM	30/10/25	10	2:08:14 PM
31/10/25	11	2:14:24 PM	31/10/25	11	2:31:18 PM

You can find the description of each lunar day in the chapter "A Guide to The Moon Cycle and Lunar Days"

ARIES

October might be a tense month for you, filled with challenges that ultimately lead to success. All tasks will be completed, but they will require considerable effort.

Business. Throughout October, you might feel a strong dependence on your partners, both morally and financially. Entrepreneurs and managers will find it challenging to handle their large-scale ventures alone and will definitely need help. This assistance will depend heavily on your ability to get along with those who can offer real support. Given your proud nature and straightforward character, being dependent on others and circumstances can be difficult. However, it's worth remembering the saying "no man is an island" and acting accordingly. Misunderstandings with partners may arise frequently, but in the end, you will achieve your goals, at least partially. If finances are involved, the necessary funds will be obtained.

Additionally, entrepreneurs should pay close attention to their subordinates, as misunderstandings within the team could hinder progress.

Employees may experience minor friction with colleagues throughout the month. Despite these challenges, keep in mind that the main goal is the result, which will definitely be achieved.

Connections with colleagues from other cities or countries remain relevant. Though progress might be slower than desired, it is moving in the right direction – your direction.

Money. Financially, this month could be varied. Your earnings may be minimal, but the primary funds will come from business partners and close people. Sponsorship or a beneficial loan is also possible.

Love and Family. In your personal life, processes that began recently continue. This involves significant changes at home, such as construction, renovation, and other activities aimed at improving your living space. In all these endeavors, the strong support of a close person will be felt. However, not everything may go smoothly in your relationships. You might have to argue occasionally, as everyone has their own tastes and opinions on how to arrange the future home. In this case, the stars advise listening more to your partner's opinions, as this will lead to a better outcome. This advice applies equally to lovers and married couples.

Health. Your energy levels will be low this month, especially towards the end. October demands a lot of effort and dedication, bringing meetings and significant mental strain. Therefore, do not neglect your body's natural needs – rest and a good night's sleep. Find time to relax periodically and take care of yourself.

TAURUS

October calls for a cautious approach, avoiding haste and revolutionary actions. It's wiser to plan your time in advance, set clear goals, and act strictly according to these plans. With this approach, success is guaranteed.

Business. October is a busy and dynamic month, demanding hard work and dedication. In addition to your regular tasks, you'll need to tackle significant and complex issues related to business partnerships, reestablish old connections, and search for new partners and colleagues.

The process of renewal in business continues, requiring entrepreneurs and employees alike to adapt.

Relationships with colleagues from other cities and countries develop as usual, with both achievements and challenges. There is noticeable progress in relationships with former partners, old friends, or people who have previously supported you. Issues may arise from regular work tasks, but these will be resolved in the usual course of business. Those planning to start a business in another city or country are steadily moving towards their goal.

Money. Financially, October looks very promising. Money will come in regularly, and the amounts will significantly increase. Expected dates for major sums are October 2nd, 3rd, 10th, 11th, 20th, and 21st. Expenses will be minimal, predictable, and reasonable.

Love and Family. October is not only suitable for work; the second half hints at successes in love. During this period, old romantic and friendly relationships might be rekindled. Meetings with old acquaintances living in other cities or countries are possible. Many may travel for this purpose, with trips planned for the latter half of October or November.

Relationships with relatives will noticeably strengthen, and their support is likely. There is good progress in your family's affairs, and close ones are ready to share their successes. Thus, positive changes are happening in your personal life, with no complaints about the stars for now.

Health. Your energy levels in October are low, but this is not critical. Maintain a healthy lifestyle, ensure you get enough sleep – these simple rules will help you stay energetic and clear-headed.

GEMINI

The planetary alignment suggests that this month, you'll be able to juggle many tasks simultaneously and excel in all areas. Keep up the good work!

Business. In October, you'll continue the positive trends in your professional activities that began recently. This is an excellent time for decisive steps toward your goals, showcasing yourself in a bright and unconventional manner.

Connections with colleagues from other cities or countries remain important. Many of you will reconnect with old friends and former employers, receiving intriguing offers from them. These may include additional income opportunities or invitations to return to a previous job. In any case, exciting professional and financial prospects are opening up.

On the other hand, you'll face a choice: should you keep things as they are or embrace change? It's unclear if the future will be better than the present, but as you move toward it, the situation will become clearer. The stars recommend not resisting changes but rather gathering information, making a plan, and acting according to the circumstances.

Money. October is quite favorable financially. Money will come in regularly, and the amounts will significantly increase. Expected dates for major sums are October 4, 5, 12-14, 22, 23, and 31. Significant expenses are anticipated in the middle of the month, likely related to personal and family matters.

Love and Family. Personal relationships may be just as important as work this month. Parents will attend to their children's needs, offering both moral and financial support. There's nothing alarming in this area, just fulfilling your parental duties and enjoying the satisfaction of seeing your children benefit from your support. Relationships with relatives, including your own and your partner's parents, will become very significant. In some cases, a close family member may facilitate professional changes.

Health. Your energy levels are quite high in October, and illnesses are not a concern. The second half of the month is favorable for a makeover, shopping, and any procedures that improve both your well-being and appearance.

CANCER

The key positives this month are a high energy level, decisiveness, and an unwavering belief in yourself and the correctness of your decisions. However, the downside is a tendency to be overly categorical, with a "You're either with us or against us" attitude. Strive for balance, and everything will turn out well.

Business. October is more suitable for personal and family matters, so consider taking a vacation or at least a short break. If that's not possible, you can focus on routine organizational tasks, various administrative projects, or office renovations. There's always something to do at work.

Connections with colleagues from other cities or countries become important, and there's a possibility of rekindling relationships with former colleagues or taking a successful trip. You might even receive offers to start a business in a place far from home. Additionally, in the second half of the month, showcasing your achievements to specialists or the public will undoubtedly benefit your career.

Money. Financially, October is stable but not exceptional. Significant income isn't expected just yet, but everything you accomplish this month will lead to financial success in the near future. Most expenses this month will be related to personal life, such as the needs of children and loved ones.

Love and Family. The main events of October might occur in your personal life. It's a great month for lovers who can strengthen their relationships, perhaps by taking a successful trip together. Recent romances are developing well, with increasing chances of evolving into a serious commitment or marriage.

Separated spouses and lovers can reunite, making an important step toward full unity. Parents will spend plenty of time with their children, who will bring them joy. Moreover, October, especially its second half, is a great time for new acquaintances. You'll likely attend more social events, birthdays, and parties, attracting much attention and potentially meeting someone special.

Health. You're in good health this month, but you might occasionally feel the need to relax and take a break. Make sure to do so! You'll certainly have opportunities to unwind and rejuvenate.

LEO

The main task this month is to align your dreams with reality. In other words, your imagination should not exceed your financial means. In this case, luck will definitely be on your side.

Business. This month offers you a chance to bring some of your ideas to life. Entrepreneurs and managers can take the next step in expanding or reconstructing their business, which may include extensions, construction, repairs, and other organizational and operational activities.

Connections with colleagues from other cities or countries remain relevant, and October might bring travel opportunities or visits from distant colleagues. Generally, everything is moving in the right direction, although disagreements may arise occasionally, which will be resolved through normal business processes. Discussions about financial support from partners are likely to be successfully concluded in the second half of the month.

Employees can seek support from relatives and friends to strengthen their positions. Many Leos will need to address various legal issues lingering from the recent past. These issues may become more prominent in mid-October, and you are advised to prepare for potential inspections in advance.

Money. Financially, October is quite favourable. In addition to your usual earnings, you can expect support from partners and favourable credit terms. Those not involved in business can rely on help from loved ones and potential profits from real estate transactions.

Love and Family. Your personal life may be just as important as your work this month. Projects related to home improvement are progressing well. Whether it involves repairs, construction, or significant changes in household arrangements, October promises substantial progress in these areas. However, the stars strongly recommend taking a close look at what you truly want and what you should let go of. You might be surprised by how many things fall into the latter category.

Relationships with loved ones are evolving daily. Some may consider reassessing their relationships, while others might part ways for various reasons. Pluto, firmly established in the sector of the sky responsible for long-term connections, demands change. These changes are inevitable, and their nature will depend on the past relationship and the intentions of both parties.

Family ties will become more active this month, with possible visits from relatives living in other cities or countries. Be mindful, as misunderstandings and intrigues can occur. These can be mitigated by demonstrating flexibility and wisdom. If your relatives discover your "skeletons in the closet," it's best not to focus on it, respond to criticism, or get into arguments. The current situation suggests that "a bad peace is indeed better than a good quarrel."

Health. Your health is generally stable this month, and any periods of weakness can be managed by alternating work and rest and not getting stressed over minor issues.

VIRGO

October is a practical, active, and generally successful month. Pay attention to the details, avoid being overly self-centered, and you will surely see results.

Business. October will present you with several opportunities to strengthen your position. One of the main themes this month is reinforcing old connections as well as establishing new partnerships. Relationships with former partners, which were interrupted in the recent past, will gradually be renewed.

Connections with colleagues from other cities or countries will become increasingly important, with a chance to restore relationships with old partners and long-time friends. This is especially relevant in the second half of October and throughout November. Expect travel, meetings with key individuals, and successful negotiations to be on the agenda during the latter part of October.

The downside of this month may include disagreements with friends or influential people. The root of these issues will likely be material or financial matters, which can be diplomatically resolved after discussions and airing grievances. Employees will have a substantial workload and may need to travel for work. Be cautious with superiors, financial documents, and avoid potential errors in these areas.

Money. October might bring financial ups and downs. Money will come and go, and you may have to part with a significant sum in the middle of the month. Some will have to settle old debts, while others will deal with current financial issues, both in business and personal life.

Love and Family. Those focused on their personal lives this month will reconnect with loved ones living in other cities or countries. If you recently separated, relationships with former partners might begin to mend. This will be challenging, but the key is the willingness of both parties. Old friends, whose relationships are improving, can provide valuable support in this process.

Family relationships will become more active, with possible visits from or trips to see relatives living far away. Overall, October is the perfect time to strengthen connections, travel, meet people, and restore your social standing if it has diminished recently.

Health. Your energy levels may be inconsistent in October. At times, you may feel great, but then suddenly become exhausted. The most critical dates when you might experience energy drops are October 6, 7, 15, 16, 29, and 30.

LIBRA

You will enter your birth month fully prepared and ready for action. Your boundless energy combined with thoughtful actions will help you succeed in your endeavors and earn the approval of those around you.

Business. In all professional matters, you will be driven by noble and, most importantly, progressive aspirations. Entrepreneurs and managers will be able to finalize ongoing projects and announce new plans. The key is that all achievements this month will have tangible, material results, not just theoretical or moral victories.

Your connections with colleagues from other cities or countries will develop predictably, primarily thanks to your diplomatic skills, persistence, and determination. You will be able to win over even the most stubborn opponents. However, the stars advise you to "trust but verify." This approach will be beneficial in dealing with distant colleagues for a long time. Neptune, now influencing your partnership sector, suggests that achieving true sincerity in relationships may be difficult. Everything in this area may seem deceptive or illusory.

Entrepreneurs and managers can count on the support of long-time associates and subordinates in all endeavors this month.

Employees will earn the respect of their superiors and colleagues. In the second half of the month, you might receive a promotion or additional responsibilities. There will be a lot of work, but the stars see great benefits from it.

Money. October is one of the best months of the year financially. Money will come in regularly, and the amounts will significantly increase. You can expect profits from work already done and advances for new projects. The best dates for receiving large sums are October 4-6, 12, 13, 22, 23, and 31.

Love and Family. Work will take center stage this month, pushing personal life somewhat into the background. However, family members will still be able to help their partners with household tasks, taking on a significant portion of the expenses, which they will be well-equipped to handle. You will be able to care for children and relatives, making you the champion for your loved ones.

Relationships between lovers and spouses will noticeably improve, possibly because both parties will realize that any peace is better than a good fight and will act accordingly. However, this peace may be fragile, so it's essential to reassess your relationships to avoid future problems.

Health. You may experience fluctuations in energy this month, alternating between periods of vigor and significant fatigue. You can mitigate this by maintaining a healthy lifestyle, getting plenty of sleep, and listening to your body's needs. If you feel tired, forget about work and simply rest. You have a lot of work ahead, and maintaining your health will be crucial.

SCORPIO

October is relatively calm for you, as much as peace is possible in these turbulent times. It's time to evaluate what you've accomplished and plan for the future, which, according to the astrologer, looks vast and promising!

Business. The best time for all professional activities is the last third of the month, a period for open and decisive actions. The first 20 days of October will also go well, but during these periods, many Scorpios will have to handle various organizational and logistical tasks and resolve minor work issues. You may experience some friction with partners from other cities or countries that will need immediate resolution. You'll succeed if you take matters into your own hands, as only you can manage them effectively. Those engaged in restructuring or expanding their business can make significant progress calmly. In the last third of October, all troubling issues will be successfully resolved, allowing you to move forward confidently.

Money. Financially, this month is quite contradictory. Business development will require funds, which many managers and entrepreneurs will face. You may receive support from business partners, sponsorships, or favorable loans. For those dealing with personal matters, parents or close relatives can provide assistance in difficult situations.

Love and Family. Processes started in the recent past continue in your personal life. If you plan to move to another city or country, you will resolve logistical and legal issues. Family ties are crucial, and you can expect substantial financial help from parents or close ones in many cases. This will be particularly relevant for significant renovations or purchasing property in another city or country.

Old connections are being revived; you may meet with children and loved ones living far away. The second half of October is especially indicative of this, with potential travel that can reunite those separated by time and distance. Renewing relationships with former flames is also possible.

Health. Your energy levels may be somewhat lower in October, as the Sun is not supporting your vitality. However, other planets like Mars, Mercury, and Jupiter are on your side, so nothing serious will happen. Periods of sluggishness and fatigue will alternate with powerful surges of energy. To maintain your well-being during challenging times, balance periods of intense work with adequate rest.

SAGITTARIUS

In October, you'll face the daunting task of bridging the gap between your desires and reality. However, there's hope that you'll succeed, as you are often considered the luckiest sign in the Zodiac.

Business. October is quite favorable for all professional activities. If you need to gain the support of management or favor from influential individuals, now is the time, especially if you are cautious and diplomatic in both words and actions. Conversations with friends or powerful people may involve support for your projects, both moral and financial. Much can be achieved in this area. Whether you're embarking on new projects, construction, or business expansion, any assistance will be very welcome now.

Relationships with colleagues from other cities or countries are generally developing well, with potential trips, meetings, and negotiations that will significantly advance your plans and projects. If you have ideas about acquiring property or expanding your business in distant lands, much progress can be made in the second half of October.

Money. Financially, October is generally successful. You may receive support from friends, sponsors, or a favorable loan. Alternatively, close relatives such as parents or partners may help. Expenses will certainly be present, but they will all benefit your endeavors.

Love and Family. Expect significant excitement in your personal life. Many Sagittarians will be frequent guests at parties, creative evenings, and other festive events. The main advantage of this period is the considerable goodwill from various people. The stars suggest making the most of this favorable alignment by reciprocating the positive attention. Relationships with spouses and lovers will be balanced and harmonious, and many families might welcome new children or grandchildren. Those planning to furnish their homes can make significant strides in October. A major breakthrough in household matters is likely in the second half of the month, with all activities proceeding smoothly without delays or issues. Those setting up homes in other cities or countries can also count on the stars' favor.

Health. For most of October, you will be healthy, energetic, and attractive. However, during the last ten days of the month, you may feel some fatigue from social interactions, busyness, and household tasks.

CAPRICORN

An exciting and positive month awaits you. Don't hesitate to set high goals—if not now, when? Great things are in store for you, both professionally and personally.

Business. This month is one of the best of the year for you, so don't waste time. Visits to official institutions and discussions with management could be very productive. If you have legal issues, now is the perfect time to address them. October is also an excellent time to present your projects to both specialists and the public.

Complicated relationships with some partners may lead to disagreements throughout the month, but the involvement of mediators will help smooth things over. Old friends and influential individuals could play the role of "peace doves" this time.

Relations with colleagues from other cities or countries, which have caused problems in the past, will improve noticeably this month. The second half of October, in particular, is promising for peaceful negotiations and reaching compromises on important issues. Another achievement this month will be the harmonious work between managers and subordinates, and between employees and their colleagues. In professional terms, October receives no complaints from the stars.

Money. Financially, this month is also favorable, which is not surprising given the positive professional developments. You will have more money coming in, with the largest sums expected on October 2, 3, 10, 11, 19-21, 29, and 30. Expenses will be few and well-planned.

Love and Family. Your personal life this month could be just as interesting as your professional life. You may find yourself torn between work commitments and the desire to spend more time with loved ones. This is the only contradiction in an otherwise successful month, and the stars suggest that you will handle it well.

Relationships between spouses and lovers will be harmonious, with enjoyable interactions with friends and attendance at various social events. Difficult relationships with relatives will improve noticeably, with possible visits from close ones living in another city or country. You can confidently look forward to the second half of October and the first half of November for these visits.

Health. Your energy levels will be high throughout the month, and illnesses will be kept at bay.

AQUARIUS

This month offers you a great opportunity to establish your own rules. The only advice is to act modestly and diplomatically, as the stars believe this approach will benefit both your work and personal life.

Business. Professionally, October is quite promising, although you will need to fight for your ideas.

Relationships with colleagues from other cities or countries may vary, with successes interspersed with challenges, making it essential for you to keep a close eye on developments. Avoid delegating these matters to colleagues or subordinates who may lack the necessary expertise.

If you have longstanding legal issues, be particularly attentive to ongoing processes to ensure resolution.

Interactions with superiors and official institutions will be constructive and beneficial this month. Entrepreneurs will find success in advancing ongoing projects and negotiating new ventures. Employees will gain approval from management and possibly expand their responsibilities, with new job offers not being out of the question. The majority of professional achievements will occur in the second half of October and the first half of November.

Money. Financially, October is stable. You might receive pleasant surprises such as salary increases, bonuses, or profits from completed work. Key dates for receiving significant sums are October 4, 5, 12, 13, 22, 23, and 31. Expenses will be minimal and primarily related to family matters.

Love and Family. October is also favorable for your personal life. Relationships with children will improve significantly, possibly due to notable and positive events in their lives. Many of you will have reasons to be proud of your children. Single individuals can expect an important meeting, possibly during a trip or within a group of people from afar. Alternatively, virtual meetings could also turn out to be quite interesting.

Health. Your energy levels may fluctuate in October, alternating between periods of vitality and weakness. Elderly and weakened individuals are more likely to be affected by these fluctuations and should closely monitor their health, seeking medical assistance if needed.

Young and healthy individuals should maintain a healthy lifestyle and avoid testing their limits with excesses.

Throughout the month, be cautious while traveling and driving!

PISCES

The upcoming month looks wonderful, though it might be financially draining. You are in demand and popular, and now you need to figure out how to use these qualities to your advantage.

Business. For most of you, the main events in October will occur in your personal life. Exceptions include the ever-busy workaholics and all those in creative professions: actors, singers, artists, musicians, and anyone whose work involves words. Even if you don't fall into these categories but have a desire to showcase your talents to a select group of colleagues or the general public, nothing will stop you from doing so.

Connections with colleagues from other cities or countries are significant, with the potential to renew relationships with old colleagues and distant friends. The second half of the month is the best time for professional endeavors. The first half isn't unsuccessful; it just requires more effort to achieve your goals.

Money. Your financial position in October is unstable, which is perhaps the only downside this month. Money will be spent continuously, primarily on personal life, leisure, and the needs of loved ones. And let's not forget shopping.

Love and Family. Personal life may take precedence over professional duties this month. Various but equally interesting developments are in store. Recent romances are progressing well, with relationships becoming more serious, deeper, and more stable. Even any disagreements likely in October can be summed up by the saying, "lovers' tiffs are harmless."

Families will be heavily involved in the affairs of their children, with significant investments in their upbringing, education, and development. Many families might welcome new children or grandchildren, or start planning for this important event. Many of you will continue home improvement projects, investing nerves, money, and time into these efforts.

There will also be time for rest in October. Both spouses and lovers might take a trip, with probable dates being the second half of October and the first half of November.

Health. Your energy levels are low in October, so protect yourself from winter colds and infections. Remember the benefits of maintaining a healthy lifestyle.

November

New York Time		
Calendar Day	Lunar Day	Lunar Day Start Time
01/11/25	12	2:44:02 PM
02/11/25	13	3:13:35 PM
03/11/25	14	3:44:37 PM
04/11/25	15	4:18:51 PM
05/11/25	16	4:58:15 PM
06/11/25	17	5:44:43 PM
07/11/25	18	6:39:20 PM
08/11/25	19	7:41:29 PM
09/11/25	20	8:48:28 PM
10/11/25	21	9:56:52 PM
11/11/25	22	11:04:03 PM
13/11/25	23	12:08:51 AM
14/11/25	24	1:11:12 AM
15/11/25	25	2:11:41 AM
16/11/25	26	3:11:05 AM
17/11/25	27	4:10:05 AM
18/11/25	28	5:09:08 AM
19/11/25	29	6:08:14 AM
20/11/25	1	1:48:17 AM
20/11/25	2	7:06:48 AM
21/11/25	3	8:03:43 AM
22/11/25	4	8:57:28 AM
23/11/25	5	9:46:43 AM
24/11/25	6	10:30:42 AM
25/11/25	7	11:09:30 AM
26/11/25	8	11:43:51 AM
27/11/25	9	12:14:50 PM
28/11/25	10	12:43:46 PM
29/11/25	11	1:11:58 PM
30/11/25	12	1:40:54 PM

London Time		
Calendar Day	Lunar Day	Lunar Day Start Time
01/11/25	12	2:52:11 PM
02/11/25	13	3:12:24 PM
03/11/25	14	3:33:26 PM
04/11/25	15	3:57:02 PM
05/11/25	16	4:25:24 PM
06/11/25	17	5:01:22 PM
07/11/25	18	5:47:56 PM
08/11/25	19	6:46:43 PM
09/11/25	20	7:55:56 PM
10/11/25	21	9:10:50 PM
11/11/25	22	10:26:42 PM
12/11/25	23	11:40:47 PM
14/11/25	24	12:52:18 AM
15/11/25	25	2:01:37 AM
16/11/25	26	3:09:31 AM
17/11/25	27	4:16:48 AM
18/11/25	28	5:23:57 AM
19/11/25	29	6:30:54 AM
20/11/25	1	6:48:17 AM
20/11/25	2	7:36:45 AM
21/11/25	3	8:39:41 AM
22/11/25	4	9:37:19 AM
23/11/25	5	10:27:32 AM
24/11/25	6	11:09:26 AM
25/11/25	7	11:43:36 AM
26/11/25	8	12:11:34 PM
27/11/25	9	12:35:06 PM
28/11/25	10	12:55:52 PM
29/11/25	11	1:15:19 PM
30/11/25	12	1:34:55 PM

You can find the description of each lunar day in the chapter "A Guide to The Moon Cycle and Lunar Days"

ARIES

November is traditionally a challenging month for you. On one hand, you'll be pressured by household and organizational issues, and on the other, you'll need to unravel various complexities in your surroundings, much like Sherlock Holmes.

Business. In November, entrepreneurs and managers will need to work diligently, as all activities will demand attention and participation. Major organizational work, possibly construction, will be on the agenda. Something needs to be changed or finalized in this area, and this situation will persist throughout November.

The stars recommend taking your time and delving into all the details of what's happening. Mercury is retrograde from November 9th to 29th, a time often fraught with delays, misunderstandings, and a return to seemingly resolved issues. Despite the problems, the overall situation is stable. Everything that is required will be accomplished.

Connections with colleagues from other cities or countries remain relevant, although the results of negotiations may be delayed. In this regard, December appears more reliable and predictable.

Employees may be involved in major changes within their organization and should pay close attention to documents, especially those related to finances.

Money. November is quite turbulent financially. Money might be constantly going out, directly related to professional matters where every step forward requires significant funds. Those focused on personal life might spend money on resolving household issues. If you can't handle it alone, you can rely on funds from business partners, sponsorship, or a favorable loan. Those not involved in business will surely receive help from close ones or parents.

Love and Family. Many of you will continue various activities to improve your home, with household problems likely taking center stage, consuming all your time and requiring maximum effort. Be prepared for things not to resolve as quickly as you'd like.

In all complex household matters, you can confidently count on moral and financial support from close ones. Family disputes are likely, but most will pertain to financial matters. However, ultimately, you will reach a consensus.

Health. Your energy levels in November are low, especially during the Full Moon on November 5-7 and the New Moon on November 18-20. Reduce your activity during these periods, protect your body from the whims of autumn weather, and don't worry if things get out of control.

November will provide an opportunity to rest, allowing you to take a break from your duties and dedicate at least a few days to yourself. If you plan to travel, choose familiar places, as new cities or countries may bring disappointment.

TAURUS

This month, approach your affairs and relationships with utmost seriousness. At the same time, be flexible and diplomatic: listen more than you speak!

Business. The main focus this month is on connections and relationships with partners, friends, and influential people. The process of restoring old connections continues, encompassing all areas of life, including partners from other cities or countries. Travel and negotiations are possible, progressing with varying success. Nothing critical or negative will occur, but the pace of activities this month will seem slow. You may need to revisit the same issues multiple times, review documents, and make changes to already established plans. Do not rush; you currently depend on your partners, and any pressure or haste can cause irritation. Mercury is retrograde from November 9th to 29th, leading to inevitable delays in business matters.

Connections with senior relatives may be significant, and if you need support, do not hesitate to ask. This advice applies not only to entrepreneurs but also to employees aiming for advancement within their organization or seeking a position elsewhere.

Money. November is financially stable, but not more than that. There won't be significant profits, but expenses are moderate, planned, and reasonable.

Love and Family. Your personal life this month is hectic but vibrant and interesting. Lovers may reassess their relationships, a process relevant to both parties. If your loved one lives in another city or country, a trip will be on the agenda. Alternatively, your partner might visit you. However, expect fluctuations, doubts about the right choice, and intense discussions.

In difficult situations, the stars advise seeking help from older, wiser individuals. Their advice can help restore clarity of thought, which you might have lost. Those planning to move to another city or country will face minor problems, but these will be manageable in the near future.

Relationships among spouses are stable, and minor disagreements can be ignored as they fall within the scope of typical family life.

Health. In November, you are healthy and active, but anxious and nervous. The stars recommend never rushing and remembering the proverb, "Slow and steady wins the race." The main thing is that you are moving in the right direction, and the pace is secondary.

If a trip is planned, the stars advise choosing places you have visited before.

GEMINI

This month, it's recommended that you keep your head out of the clouds and stay grounded. With your ruler Mercury retrograde from November 9th to 29th, this period demands concentration and attention to details.

Business. November will be an active, industrious, and hardworking month for most Gemini. However, it's probably best not to start new projects this month. Instead, continuing work on already initiated projects promises excellent results.

Entrepreneurs and managers will have the chance to resolve issues with official institutions, while employees will find common ground with their superiors. Contacts with old partners and employers will actively develop, and you might receive proposals from people you haven't seen in a long time. Managers can rely on old, trusted subordinates, and employees on loyal colleagues.

Relationships with colleagues from other cities and countries may temporarily slow down and take a back seat, but they might become significant in the future, potentially determining the direction of your business and life.

Since Mercury will be retrograde for most of the month, all Gemini will have to revisit seemingly resolved issues, correcting errors in projects and ongoing tasks. Pay close attention to details, and November will prove to be very successful.

Money. Financially, November looks very good. Money will come in regularly, and the amount will noticeably increase. There won't be any unexpected windfalls; you'll have to work hard, but the stars see great benefits from this effort. In addition to regular earnings, you might also recover old debts.

Love and Family. In November, personal life may take a back seat to work. There may simply not be enough time or energy for family and loved ones, which could lead to frustration for your partner and increase the likelihood of conflicts.

Some Gemini might need to care for a family member, such as parents or older relatives who require your attention and support. Lovers are advised to be patient if things don't seem to be going smoothly in their relationships. Overall, November requires modesty, restraint, and delicacy in all types of connections.

Health. Your energy levels will be low this month, which will be particularly noticeable to elderly and weakened individuals who may experience flare-ups of old ailments. All Gemini are advised to protect themselves from autumn colds and infections, with the most challenging days being November 5th-7th and 18th-20th.

CANCER

November is a creative and romantic month for you. There will be no reason to have any complaints about the stars!

Business. November is largely suitable for personal life, but if work comes first, you can still do a lot of good for your business this autumn month.

In the first ten days of November, you will be able to rekindle relationships with some long-time colleagues from other cities or countries that were interrupted in the recent past. A trip and successful negotiations are possible, and many will manage to combine business with pleasure—working well and relaxing well. Additionally, in the first ten days of November, you may make new contacts that will be useful in the future.

The last 20 days of November are less dynamic. From November 9th to 29th, Mercury is retrograde, so business matters will noticeably slow down. During this period, many Cancers may experience unexpected disagreements with friends or influential people. Issues you thought were nearly resolved might resurface. Reaching an agreement will be difficult, as both parties will stick to their opinions.

Many Cancers will have the opportunity to take a break from work and relax a bit, with the second and third weeks being the best times for this.

Money. Financially, November is neutral. There will be many expenses, but most of them will be pleasant, such as on leisure, shopping, and spending on loved ones. The good news is that you will have enough money for everything, and in difficult moments, support from loved ones is possible.

Love and Family. November is quite favorable for personal life. Parents will be able to spend a lot of time with their children, who will bring them joy. Meetings with children living in other cities or countries are possible.

November is a month of romantic adventures, which is good news for those who are single and have long been looking for a partner. While the period from November 1st to 8th is good for new acquaintances, the period from the 10th of November onwards is ideal for renewing old connections. However, if new acquaintances happen between November 9th and 29th, the people met during this time might prove to be unreliable, and this will become apparent later.

In the second half of the month, lovers may experience sudden arguments and then sudden reconciliations. Relationships with friends may be to blame, so it's best not to seek their advice on personal issues but to rely on your own judgment. This advice also applies to married couples whose friends have somehow interfered in their relationship.

Health. In November, you are healthy and energetic, able to make a strong impression on everyone you encounter.

LEO

November is a month of significant undertakings that can be described with a military term: "defense and protection of the rear." Such preparations are essential before a major offensive!

Business. One of the main issues in November could be problems with representatives of official institutions, particularly for businesspeople and managers.

Employees might also face troubles with their superiors. The most challenging times are likely to be from November 10th onwards. Prepare in advance and get your affairs in order.

You are heading into a crucial period of organizational and logistical tasks that began recently and are now in full swing. However, since Mercury is retrograde from November 9th to 29th, expect to review and revise many things during this period.

Those involved in business expansion, construction, or real estate transactions will be able to make important and necessary adjustments. Despite delays and annoying obstacles, a positive outcome is assured, which is, of course, the most important thing.

Money. Financially, November is stable. Although logistical tasks will require substantial funds, bankruptcy is not expected. Besides regular earnings, you can count on support from partners, credit, or sponsorship. Profits from various real estate operations are also possible. Alternatively, some financial burdens might be taken on by close ones.

Love and Family. Many Leos will be focused on arranging their homes in November. Don't be disheartened if not everything goes smoothly at first. You can always make adjustments and perfect your plans. If you find yourself torn between professional duties and personal matters, consider taking a leave of absence. This will help you avoid both work troubles and personal issues.

In many families, there may be problems with children who could become rebellious and disobedient.

Relationships between spouses may become complicated, and the reasons can vary. Those who have recently gone through a divorce or separation will start rebuilding their lives. Those who remain together despite celestial pressures must prepare for a transformation in their relationship. What kind of transformation depends on your specific situation, and you might already have an idea of what it entails.

Health. Your energy levels are not very high in November, so try to alternate work with rest and definitely take some vacation days or personal leave. Fortunately, November will provide such opportunities.

VIRGO

November presents a unique opportunity to revisit the past and make the most out of this journey. Be prepared!

Business. For professionally active Virgos, the main focus this month is on strengthening connections. Contacts with colleagues from different cities or countries gain significant importance, and it is possible to resume collaborations that were interrupted for various reasons. Additionally, old friendships and relationships with influential people will be restored. All this will significantly strengthen your position, allowing you to regain some of the standing you may have lost in the past.

Many of you will notice support from your relatives in all your endeavors, though relationships may not always unfold as planned. Keep this in mind when considering involving close ones in your affairs. Relationships with new acquaintances may also be unstable.

With Mercury retrograde from November 9th to 29th, people who enter your life during this time could bring many problems now and in the future. Only time-tested connections, such as former partners, old friends, and those who have helped you in the past, can be relied upon.

Money. Financially, November is stable but no more than that. Both expenses and income are planned for this month, so there will be no surprises in this area.

Love and Family. In your personal life, there will also be a noticeable return to the past. Separated spouses might meet to peacefully discuss past issues and possibly future plans. Even divorced and highly antagonistic couples might experience nostalgic feelings, remembering not only the bad but also the good times. This is especially relevant for couples still connected through their children. Use this opportunity if you want to rekindle an old flame. This advice is also pertinent for estranged lovers.

Many Virgos will reconnect with friends, relatives, and former lovers living in other cities or countries. Trips are quite likely and will be successful if you plan to visit well-known places and familiar people. However, avoid traveling during the New Moon days from November 18th to 20th.

Health. In November, you are active and energetic, and illnesses will steer clear of you. However, be cautious during travel and while driving in the last 20 days of the month.

LIBRA

Radical changes aren't achieved in a single day. But since you clearly understand your intentions and see your goal, nothing will stand in your way. November is an important step on your journey to the top!

Business. In all professional activities, the key is to balance your ambitions with your resources. In other words, carefully assess what you have before you take action. This is especially important for those planning to invest time and money into a significant project. The stars advise you to consider all possibilities, including the less pleasant ones.

Entrepreneurs and managers will find support in trusted employees who, once again, won't let them down. Employees will have the opportunity to earn praise from their superiors and the respect of their colleagues.

Your connections with colleagues from other cities or countries are somewhat uncertain. It's a "neither war nor peace" situation in this area. However, everything is moving in the right direction, albeit slowly and not as obviously as you might wish.

Overall, the pace of this month is slow—Mercury is retrograde from November 9th to 29th, which usually leads to delays. There's no point in resisting this; first, because it's futile, and second, because you are on the right path, and the pace is secondary. This period will give you the opportunity to analyze the past, find flaws, and fix them.

Money. Financially, this month is quite good. Money will come in regularly, and there may even be a slight increase. However, expenses will also rise, and some of them may be unexpected. The dates to expect the largest sums are November 1, 2, 9-10, 18-20, 28, and 29. Correspondingly, money could go out on November 5-7, 11, 12, 18, 19, 25, and 26.

Love and Family. This month, work may take precedence, leaving little time for personal life, so no major changes are expected in this area.

Parents will continue to invest heavily in their children's upbringing, education, and development. If there are changes happening at home, you may need to spend money on various household needs. Differences in opinions on spending could spark arguments between spouses, but ultimately, you'll manage to reach an agreement.

Health. This month, you may occasionally feel unwell, but serious illnesses can be avoided if you maintain a healthy lifestyle and protect yourself from autumn colds and infections.

SCORPIO

This month, it's as if you have a time machine that will take you back to the past. Make the most of this journey and try not to rush. Remember, this month doesn't tolerate carelessness or haste.

Business. The focus remains on relationships with colleagues from other cities or countries. Progress is being made in this area, though not as quickly as you'd like. You may need to revisit the same issues multiple times and solve problems that seemed already resolved. While it's not the best time to start new projects, it's perfect for bringing existing ones to perfection. Old connections will become crucial; in all your affairs this November, they are your main support.

Relationships with some partners may leave much to be desired. Occasionally, this could lead to open conflicts, but it won't harm the overall progress, just bring some adjustments. Those searching for a new job might engage in discussions with old acquaintances, but results might not come immediately. However, this doesn't mean there will be no success—everything will fall into place in due time.

Money. The financial situation is stable, but nothing more. There won't be any significant gains, but there are no expected losses either. So, no major news in this area.

Love and Family. Your personal life this month looks more interesting than work. Many Scorpios will reconnect with old friends or a former flame. This could be a great opportunity to start over; however, this depends not only on you but also on the intentions of the other person. The stars will undoubtedly support you, so no complaints this time. A joint trip is also possible.

Parents may have the chance to visit children living in another city or country.

Relationships between many married couples may be unstable, with possible grievances and frequent quarrels. This is especially relevant for those juggling two relationships. Take note if this applies to you.

Health. In November, you are generally healthy, but a bit anxious and restless. The stars assure you there's no need to worry—everything is fine with you.

SAGITTARIUS

November is a month for slow, discreet actions. The main motto this month is silence!

Business. To make the most out of this autumn month, it's best to forget about meetings, presentations, and the launch of major projects. Now is the time to focus on internal work, carefully refining what has already been started. This is an excellent period for identifying flaws in your work and addressing them.

Those engaged in renovations or construction can make significant progress in these demanding tasks, making November nearly ideal in this regard. However, this month is not favorable for important meetings or interactions with high-ranking individuals or superiors. These recommendations apply to both employees and entrepreneurs.

All professionally active Sagittarius should also note that the pace of events this month will be slow. You may find yourself revisiting the same issues multiple times, encountering misunderstandings from others, and facing a lack of recognition for your achievements. You might even find yourself alone, which, as the stars suggest, is something you need. Many will find time to rest, and it's worth taking full advantage of it. Nothing catastrophic will happen if you step away from work for a while, especially since you also have plenty to do at home.

For those staying at work, be aware that colleagues and subordinates may act hostile and even engage in conflicts with you. The most challenging days in this regard are during the New Moon (November 18th-20th) and the Full Moon (November 5th-7th).

Money. Financially, November is quite favorable. Money will flow in regularly from both official and unofficial sources. The latter could include sponsorship, support from business partners, or a favorable loan. Support from close ones and profits from various real estate transactions are also likely.

Love and Family. Many Sagittarians will devote November to family matters. Once again, household issues are on the agenda. Some are renovating, while others are building a new home, and all of this requires not only money but also attention and direct involvement. So, there are many tasks at hand, and November is a great time to make significant progress in solving household issues. The stars advise not to worry if things don't go smoothly at first; the end result will be positive.

Personal relationships might lose some of their luster; you may not receive as much attention as you usually do. Be mindful of your reputation during the Full Moon (November 5th-7th) and the New Moon (November 18th-20th); unwanted information may come to light, disappointing both lovers and spouses. Overall, November calls for modesty, caution, and attentiveness to those around you. And if new people enter your life, remember the saying: "All that glitters is not gold."

Health. In November, most Sagittarians will experience a noticeable decrease in energy levels. This can lead to the worsening of old ailments and the emergence of new ones. Protect yourself from autumn infections and colds, and maintain a healthy lifestyle.

CAPRICORN

Nostalgia might be the dominant feeling in November. Well, sometimes this feeling is beautiful.

Business. Professionally active Capricorns will have the chance to reconnect with many people this month. These could be partners from other cities or countries, old friends, or individuals who were important and helpful to you in the past. With them, you can work on and discuss not only past but also future projects. A trip or useful meetings may occur, bringing not only professional benefits but also genuine pleasure.

However, the slower pace of this month may not align with your expectations and plans. It's likely that not everything will work out on the first try: you might meet with some people while others may be unavailable for various reasons. If not all matters are resolved in November, don't worry—everything will eventually fall into place as planned and hoped.

Money. Financially, November is unstable. Money will be constantly going out, but the stars suggest that all expenses this month may be of a pleasant nature. Trips, children, and socializing with friends will all require funds. However, there is no sign of financial ruin, as your income has been steadily growing for some time.

Love and Family. For many Capricorns, the main events of November will revolve around their personal lives. Recent romances are developing well, and marriage or cohabitation might be on the horizon.

The situation is more complicated for those who find themselves torn between two relationships. Surprisingly, an old love might rekindle with new intensity, while the new relationship is also hard to let go of. Choosing between the two is always difficult and can cause a lot of emotional pain. How to handle it is up to you, but the stars suggest that nostalgic feelings may be much stronger this month. Conflicts and inner turmoil are likely during the Full Moon on November 5-7 and the New Moon on November 18-20. Family issues, especially with children, may also arise during these periods.

Many Capricorns will spend part of November traveling, visiting old friends or relatives living in another city or country.

Health. This month, you are healthy and energetic, and all illnesses will steer clear of you.

AQUARIUS

An active yet quite contradictory month lies ahead. However, you are moving in the right direction, and everything will work out!

Business. November will be an incredibly busy month.

Employees will have important meetings with management and lengthy discussions on complex and contentious issues. Entrepreneurs will need to present their proposals to various official institutions, patiently awaiting final approvals. Despite possible delays, decisions made at higher levels will smooth out any contentious issues and help advance your ideas.

Throughout the month, managers can rely on their subordinates, and employees can count on their colleagues. Moreover, your talent will be more than sufficient to convince the right people of the validity of your proposals. You may need to revisit and refine projects that were previously shelved. The stars encourage a return to former ideas and long-standing partnerships.

Money. Financially, November looks quite promising. Money will come in regularly, and the amount will noticeably increase. Some Aquarius individuals may even recover old debts or funds that had been lost.

Key dates for significant financial gains are November 1, 2, 18, 19, 22, 23, 28, and 29. Expenses will be minimal, likely related to personal matters.

Love and Family. Family life may take a backseat to work this month. However, not everything will be calm in this area, and conflicts are likely during the Full Moon (November 5th-7th) and the New Moon (November 18th-20th). This situation could become risky only for couples who already have unresolved issues from the past. Stable couples will need to care for their parents or elderly family members, a situation that may not come as a surprise, given that these issues have been brewing for some time.

Health. In November, you are healthy, energetic, and ready to move mountains. With this level of vitality, any ailments will stay far away from you.

PISCES

This month, many of you might feel as though you've grown wings. Staying in one place will be challenging, and the more energy you expend, the more it seems to replenish. The laws of physics don't seem to apply to you!

Business. In November, the main focus for most of you will be developing connections with partners from other cities or countries. A trip might be on the horizon, where you can combine business with pleasure: productive work and a lot of positive emotions. Relationships with former colleagues are being rekindled, leading to extensive discussions on important matters, ultimately resulting in a decision that satisfies both parties.

Despite the positive outlook for November, challenges still exist. While you'll find common ground with some colleagues from other cities or countries, issues may arise with others. Difficult matters may reach resolution during the Full Moon on November 5-7 or the New Moon on November 18-20. These are challenging times, but as the saying goes, "truth springs from arguments." This might just be one of those times.

Money. The financial situation is stable, and in addition to regular earnings, pleasant surprises such as bonuses or gifts from loved ones are possible. November's expenses might also be enjoyable—trips, meeting friends, spending on children, and of course, some shopping.

Love and Family. Your personal life this month looks just as exciting as your work and career. Both couples and lovers may take a trip and have a wonderful time. Meetings with old friends and relatives from other cities or countries are likely.

Parents will be able to spend more time with their children, with possible joint trips or visits to children living far away.

One of November's challenges could be dealing with family relations. An unexpected quarrel might flare up among relatives, and you may find yourself trying to reconcile conflicting interests within your family. Pay special attention during the Full Moon on November 5-7 and the New Moon on November 18-20.

Health. In November, you are healthy, energetic, and able to make a strong impression on everyone you meet. However, throughout the month, the stars recommend being extra cautious during travel and while driving.

December

New York Time			London Time		
Calendar Day	Lunar Day	Lunar Day Start Time	Calendar Day	Lunar Day	Lunar Day Start Time
01/12/25	13	2:12:11 PM	01/12/25	13	1:56:10 PM
02/12/25	14	2:47:45 PM	02/12/25	14	2:21:02 PM
03/12/25	15	3:29:44 PM	03/12/25	15	2:52:03 PM
04/12/25	16	4:20:06 PM	04/12/25	16	3:32:32 PM
05/12/25	17	5:19:33 PM	05/12/25	17	4:25:33 PM
06/12/25	18	6:26:30 PM	06/12/25	18	5:31:38 PM
07/12/25	19	7:37:13 PM	07/12/25	19	6:47:06 PM
08/12/25	20	8:47:52 PM	08/12/25	20	8:06:01 PM
09/12/25	21	9:56:06 PM	09/12/25	21	9:23:50 PM
10/12/25	22	11:01:11 PM	10/12/25	22	10:38:35 PM
12/12/25	23	12:03:30 AM	11/12/25	23	11:50:11 PM
13/12/25	24	1:03:53 AM	13/12/25	24	12:59:23 AM
14/12/25	25	2:03:13 AM	14/12/25	25	2:07:11 AM
15/12/25	26	3:02:12 AM	15/12/25	26	3:14:23 AM
16/12/25	27	4:01:11 AM	16/12/25	27	4:21:19 AM
17/12/25	28	4:59:56 AM	17/12/25	28	5:27:33 AM
18/12/25	29	5:57:36 AM	18/12/25	29	6:31:44 AM
19/12/25	30	6:52:47 AM	19/12/25	30	7:31:36 AM
19/12/25	1	8:44:26 PM	20/12/25	1	1:44:26 AM
20/12/25	2	7:43:58 AM	20/12/25	2	8:24:45 AM
21/12/25	3	8:30:02 AM	21/12/25	3	9:09:40 AM
22/12/25	4	9:10:41 AM	22/12/25	4	9:46:24 AM
23/12/25	5	9:46:23 AM	23/12/25	5	10:16:12 AM
24/12/25	6	10:18:08 AM	24/12/25	6	10:40:50 AM
25/12/25	7	10:47:09 AM	25/12/25	7	11:02:01 AM
26/12/25	8	11:14:44 AM	26/12/25	8	11:21:17 AM
27/12/25	9	11:42:15 AM	27/12/25	9	11:40:00 AM
28/12/25	10	12:11:11 PM	28/12/25	10	11:59:34 AM
29/12/25	11	12:43:13 PM	29/12/25	11	12:21:37 PM
30/12/25	12	1:20:22 PM	30/12/25	12	12:48:15 PM
31/12/25	13	2:04:48 PM	31/12/25	13	1:22:22 PM

You can find the description of each lunar day in the chapter "A Guide to The Moon Cycle and Lunar Days"

ARIES

You will enter the last month of the year in full battle readiness. Your motto: "Through thorns to the stars."

Business. The main task this month will be to resolve connections with colleagues from other cities or countries. This won't be easy, as various obstacles, which might feel like a blow from the shadows, could hinder full cooperation. However, despite these difficulties, most of the problems will likely be overcome by the end of December.

Organizational activities related to business expansion are ongoing, but they will temporarily take a back seat. It is now essential to focus on developing contacts to successfully wrap up 2025.

At the same time, all representatives of your sign are advised by the stars to organize your papers and financial documents, as inspections might occur towards the end of the month.

Money. Financially, December is unstable. Expenses will be high, and at some point, they might exceed income. In some cases, this is due to business expansion, while in others, it relates to personal or family needs. However, by the end of December, the situation will improve, and money will start to flow more frequently. This positive trend will continue into January 2026.

Love and Family. In your personal life, the trends of recent months will continue. Home improvement activities will proceed calmly.

Those planning trips may face several obstacles again. The stars recommend paying closer attention to documents and the countries you plan to visit. It might be wise to postpone travel until next month. The best time for trips is from December 27 to 29.

Relationships within families are stable, with each spouse engaged in their activities, but this won't lead to any issues.

Single people may expand their social circles and are likely to meet someone interesting, possibly linked to a trip. Those staying at home might meet someone who has come from afar.

Health. Throughout December, you will be healthy, energetic, and free from ailments. However, the stars strongly recommend being cautious during travel and while driving.

TAURUS

The final month of the year will be quite challenging for you. When faced with obstacles, exercise restraint and caution. The key is not to force open a closed door, but to stop and consider safer paths.

Business. The primary issue in December will be your relationships with others. Serious disagreements may arise with friends, like-minded individuals, as well as with people who hold influence and power. The root of these conflicts is likely to be unresolved financial matters from the past. You may have to revisit who owes what and who owns what. Entrepreneurs and managers should prepare for audits and unexpected legal issues.

Employees might face changes within their organization. The stars advise you to carry out your duties calmly and, if possible, limit interactions with your superiors. If you do need to interact, be prepared for the possibility that your work may be undervalued. React calmly to criticism, remembering that the pressure won't last long. Come January, the situation will noticeably improve.

Your connections with partners from other cities or countries are developing well; this area of your work looks quite positive.

Money. The financial situation this month is challenging. Money will be going out constantly, and at best, you'll be investing in business or household issues. At worst, you'll be settling old debts and previous commitments. Be cautious and frugal, as the financial downsides this month will likely outweigh the upsides.

Love and Family. Personal life will not be easy. Lovers may face misunderstandings, a cooling in the relationship, and possibly serious conflicts. After the relatively smooth period of the past, this will feel like a cold shower. Trying to rewrite the rules of a relationship while still in it is difficult, and no matter what you do, the reality may be different than expected. If there is something in your relationship that you want to preserve, hold onto that feeling and let go of everything else. This advice applies both to lovers and to spouses, who may also face a crisis of feelings.

In all matters this month, look for support in family ties—here you'll find both moral and financial support.

Health. If you manage to avoid professional and personal difficulties, your health might still let you down. Protect yourself from winter colds, infections, and flare-ups of chronic conditions. Your goal now is to conserve energy—nothing more, nothing less.

GEMINI

The last month of the year will bring you plenty of interactions, and they won't all go smoothly. If problems arise, just remember the saying: "You can't please everyone."

Business. The main issue this month will be recurring disagreements with people in positions of greater power. For entrepreneurs, this could involve various official institutions, while for employees, it could mean conflicts with management. A standoff is on the horizon, where those in charge are unable to move forward, and those below are unwilling to follow.

At the same time, you have plenty of supporters—friends, partners, and like-minded people will back your position, and your opponents will have to take that into account. So, there won't be a dull moment: meetings, negotiations, and conflicts will fill most of December.

On the plus side, you'll have energy, determination, and a strong belief in the rightness of your actions. On the downside, you might be overly categorical, with a "you're either with us or against us" attitude. Be cautious, as this combination can be explosive, making December a month of both significant successes and potential conflicts.

Money. Financially, December is relatively stable. Jupiter, the planet of luck, is in your financial sector, so there's no need to worry about bankruptcy. Money will come in regularly, with the most significant sums likely on December 6-8, 15-17, and 25-26. Most of your expenses will fall toward the end of the year, naturally related to the upcoming New Year, travel, and gifts for loved ones.

Love and Family. Many Geminis will find themselves surrounded by attention from various people in December. There may be interesting new acquaintances, which is great for those who are single but could cause problems for those already in a relationship.

In all matters of personal relationships, you may feel a strong desire to be liked by others. This isn't necessarily a bad thing, but try to maintain a balance—it will ultimately be better for you. In some families, issues may arise with parents or elderly family members. You might need to take care of loved ones, or you could be handling grievances and resolving possible disputes.

Health. In December, your energy levels will be quite high, but you may feel fatigued by the end of the month after a busy period. If this resonates with you, it might be best to spend the New Year holidays as quietly and peacefully as possible.

CANCER

This month, it's crucial to realistically assess your capabilities. Don't promise more than you can deliver, and avoid taking on tasks that are beyond your reach. If you stick to these guidelines, the final month of the year should turn out quite well.

Business. December might bring a lot of work, but it will also come with its fair share of challenges. One of these could be renewed issues with colleagues from other cities or countries. It seems that after a recent truce, distant partners are once again bringing up past grievances and unresolved problems. There could be a resurgence of old legal matters that seemed to have quieted down. Most likely, these issues will revolve around old debts or other financial obligations.

In any case, there's no need to take everything to heart or criticize yourself for minor mistakes. Focus on resolving the issues that arise, and remember that you can handle anything that comes your way. Jupiter, the planet of luck, is currently in your sign and won't leave you unsupported—as long as you are genuinely in the right. If not, you may have to put in a lot of work to correct your mistakes.

Money. Financially, December is relatively stable, with money coming in as expected. There won't be any windfalls—all your earnings this month will be the result of hard work put in recently.

Love and Family. In December, many Cancers might find themselves too busy for love and romance—work takes priority. As a result, relationships may lose some of their luster, both for those in love and for married couples. Remember that a smile and a kind word at the right time can work wonders, so act accordingly.

Health. December is an ideal time for those who are conscious about their health. Older individuals are advised to spend some time in a health resort, as energy levels might be somewhat reduced. Young and healthy individuals are encouraged to give up bad habits and adopt healthier ones.

December is also a good month for shopping, changing your image, and starting a new exercise routine. Throughout the month, be especially careful when traveling and driving.

LEO

December presents you with several excellent opportunities to showcase yourself—now is not the time to be modest! After spending a considerable amount of time in the background, it's your moment to step into the spotlight and let everyone see what you've accomplished.

Business. Entrepreneurs and managers will continue efforts to expand their business. This has been a central theme throughout 2025 and will remain important well into the first half of 2026.

However, December is also an excellent time to present your achievements to a select group of experts or even a broader audience. Creative professionals such as actors, artists, musicians, and politicians are especially likely to find success during this period. While their popularity will rise, bringing great personal satisfaction, it might not translate into significant financial gains.

If you need to sign important documents this month, be sure to read every line carefully, especially when it comes to financial matters. Money and other material assets could be the weak spot in December.

Money. December is a critical month for finances. Money will be going out frequently, and according to the stars, this is mostly related to personal matters. Expenses on children, close family, and gifts for friends and acquaintances will dominate your spending. The consolation is that these are pleasant expenses that will bring joy to your loved ones.

Managers and entrepreneurs might also find themselves spending significantly on advertising and entertainment for their teams.

Love and Family. For many Leos, the main events of December will revolve around family. A large portion of your expenses will be dedicated to your children's needs, including their education and development. Additionally, December is a time for festive gatherings, birthdays, and other celebrations.

New acquaintances, courtships, and light romances are also on the horizon, making the chilly December air feel more like spring for those who are single.

Health. In December, you'll be healthy, sociable, and energetic, with all illnesses likely to pass you by.

VIRGO

The last month of the year is a slow-paced time for you, offering a chance to focus on yourself and your loved ones. Your main goal is to achieve inner balance as you prepare to enter 2026 with strength and serenity.

Business. Professional activity for most Virgos will gradually decline throughout December. While the first ten days of the month might see the development of relationships with colleagues from other cities or countries, the remainder of the month will likely be devoted to organizational and domestic matters.

From December 8th to 30th, many Virgos may face renewed complications in their relationships with partners, potentially due to issues involving property or old financial obligations. Just when you thought a problem was resolved, new issues may arise that you'll need to address before the year ends.

Money. Financially, December appears neutral. Both income and expenses are expected to be predictable, with no unusual surprises.

Love and Family. Your personal life may face some challenges. Relationships with former partners, which seemed to be on the mend, may start to unravel again as old problems, misunderstandings, and resentments resurface. It seems that you haven't entirely let go of the past, and these unresolved issues are still troubling you. You may know the changes you'd like to make, but reality presents a different picture, and you must adapt.

For divorced or divorcing couples, issues related to property may reemerge, and resolving them won't be easy. Children might play a role in smoothing over these difficulties, so take full advantage of their influence. Friends or family members could also provide pathways to resolving past conflicts. Remember, "A bad peace is better than a good quarrel."

Harmonious couples can spend the month preparing their home for the New Year celebrations, drawing on wisdom, patience, and love.

Health. Your energy levels are likely to be low in December, so it's wise to pay attention to your diet and protect yourself from winter infections and colds. This is especially important as you plan to spend New Year's Eve away from home, according to the stars.

LIBRA

We live in times of change, and what seemed stable yesterday may no longer be today. This turbulence will be something many will face in December, including you!

Business. Your professional standing remains strong, but this month will bring its share of challenges. One of these may involve complications with colleagues from other cities or countries. This is likely to be a flare-up of an old problem you thought was nearly resolved, so prepare for another round of struggle, which will once again end in your favor.

The stars continue to advise managers of all levels to be extra vigilant with their subordinates, as another mistake could prove costly this time, affecting both the image of your company and the overall progress of your work. Another issue in December could involve dealings with regulatory authorities. While they won't cause significant harm, these interactions are unlikely to be pleasant.

Employees are advised to be cautious of colleagues who may be more of a hindrance than a help. The good news is that all the problems of December will eventually be resolved, likely because decisions made by higher-ups will smooth out the most contentious issues.

Money. Financially, December is stable. Money will come in regularly, and expenses will be predictable and reasonable. Expect the largest sums around December 6-8, 15-16, and 25-26.

Love and Family. No significant changes are expected in your personal life. Those planning a vacation might face restrictions and obstacles throughout December, making it difficult to move forward with travel plans. In this case, it's best not to force things—consider postponing your trip until a better time.

Many families may experience misunderstandings with relatives who might be dealing with illness or difficult times. Relationships between spouses will remain stable, though professional commitments may prevent them from spending as much time together as they'd like. The same goes for those who are in love.

Health. Your energy levels are fairly high this month, and you're unlikely to face any serious illnesses. However, the stars recommend being especially cautious during travel and while driving throughout December. The risk of accidents and unpleasant incidents on the road is particularly high in the first 20 days of the month.

SCORPIO

In December, you are practical and determined, but your business mindset might face several challenges. Combining frugality with generosity is difficult, but nothing is impossible for you!

Business. December, the last month of the year, is a time to wrap up important ongoing projects.

Your connections with colleagues from other cities or countries are developing well, and those planning to expand their business far from home will continue to make progress. Real estate transactions such as construction, renovation, or purchasing property are also likely.

Many Scorpios can expect profits from earlier endeavors, which they will successfully reinvest into future projects. However, December may bring some challenges, particularly with partners trying to impose their rules on you. Despite these difficulties, your business will move forward, and you will handle the month's troubles quite effectively.

Money. December is a favorable month for all financial activities. Money will come in regularly, with a noticeable increase in your income. However, expenses will also rise. Most of these costs are likely to be personal, such as investments in your children's education, upbringing, and development.

Love and Family. There are some concerning trends in your personal life. Parents may continue to face issues with their children. In some cases, this could be a temporary crisis, while in others, it might indicate more serious relationship problems. You may need to focus on your children's future, investing not only your time but also a significant portion of your family budget.

For those in love, relationships may be far from ideal. Ethical differences could become a stumbling block in some cases, while financial issues might cause problems in others. However, if you approach matters with delicacy and generosity, you can avoid serious conflicts. In another scenario, lovers may suddenly realize they have different life plans, leading to a major argument or even a breakup.

Trying to rewrite the rules of a relationship while you're in it is impossible, but if there is something in the foundation of your connection that you value, hold onto that feeling if you wish to stay together.

Health. Your energy levels are not very high in December, so it's important to avoid excesses and protect yourself from winter infections and colds.

SAGITTARIUS

December is your month! The Sun, Mars, Venus, and Mercury are all in your corner, providing you with plenty of energy. All you need to do is use it for peaceful purposes.

Business. After a dull November spent handling tedious but necessary tasks, your professional life will brighten up in December. Organizational and logistical matters temporarily take a back seat as new projects, meetings, and travel come to the forefront. Your relationships with colleagues from other cities or countries will become more active, with discussions about future projects and, for some, even a new job.

A door to a new future is opening—not immediately, but now is the time to start talking and thinking about it. One challenging aspect of the month may involve real estate issues, which will vary depending on your specific situation. These issues are tied to past complications, so you likely already know what's being referred to.

Money. The best financial period is the last ten days of the month. Significant sums may come in on December 21, 22, 25, 26, 30, and 31.

Love and Family. Your personal life will be filled with various events. Some families may encounter problems with parents or elderly family members, while others might face issues related to housing—especially those involved in construction, renovation, or purchasing property. If these activities are taking place in distant locations, the situation could worsen. However, looking ahead, this problem is solvable, so take the initiative and address it head-on.

December is a month of new acquaintances, which is great news for those who are single. Those already in a relationship should be cautious, especially if things are not going smoothly. A new romance could potentially end your current relationship, so think carefully before starting anything new.

Travel plans for December are likely to go well.

Health. For most of December, you'll be energetic and healthy, but you may feel nervous and restless, leading to a decline in energy toward the end of the month. Try not to overexert yourself in the last days of December, so you can greet the New Year in good health and high spirits.

CAPRICORN

You might feel tired and eager for a break, but the stars have other plans for you.

Business. December will be a challenging month for those who are professionally active. One of the main difficulties may arise from unexpected complications with partners from other cities or countries. Issues that seemed resolved in November might resurface, and new, unpleasant questions could emerge that weren't previously considered important.

Additionally, you might face inspections from regulatory authorities, which are rarely pleasant. The first 20 days of December will be particularly difficult, with the situation only slightly improving towards the end of the month.

Any planned trips for December may either fall through or be unsuccessful, so the stars suggest postponing them to the first month of 2026.

Money. Financially, December isn't looking very favorable, which isn't surprising given the professional challenges. However, you won't be entirely without resources, which is a small consolation.

Love and Family. In your personal life, you may also face a series of challenges that will vary from case to case. Those counting on support from relatives might find it unavailable for various reasons. But this situation is not new to you, and you likely know what this could entail.

If you have planned a long journey or a move, the laws of the foreign country might pose a barrier.

Relationships may become strained for those who are still unsure of their path in life.

Remember that December is also a month of unpleasant discoveries. We all have skeletons in our closets, and one of them might come tumbling out now.

Health. If professional and personal troubles don't get you, your health might. Elderly and vulnerable individuals should aim for a peaceful December, as aside from usual ailments, there's also a risk of accidents.

Be especially careful during travel and while driving. It might be best to avoid long journeys altogether in December.

AQUARIUS

Your career is on the rise, bringing even more tasks your way. This month, keep in mind that staying active and moving forward is key to your success.

Business. In your professional life this month, two opposing trends are emerging. The first is positive: work itself is not particularly challenging, your efforts are being recognized, and your initiatives are supported by your superiors. However, the second trend is less favorable. Relationships with friends, like-minded individuals, and certain influential figures may harbor hidden challenges. The root of the problem is money and financial obligations that you'll need to fulfill. If not, relationships could deteriorate, which is something you want to avoid. Disagreements related to real estate are also possible. The stars advise you to create a clear action plan and tackle tasks step by step. You'll need to rely on yourself, but your talent and ingenuity will be more than enough.

Money. Financially, December is quite challenging. Many of you will feel like you're being pulled in multiple directions: paying off old debts, fulfilling existing commitments, and covering day-to-day expenses that seem to increase by the day. However, you won't be entirely without resources; you'll receive significant sums periodically. In addition to your regular income, there's a chance for a bonus or financial help from loved ones.

Love and Family. Personal life may take a back seat for a while. Work, social interactions, and financial issues are currently more pressing. However, many of you will need to focus on matters related to your children, investing considerable time and money into their upbringing, education, and development.

December is also a month for parties, attending various social events, and showcasing your achievements. New acquaintances are likely, and the people who enter your life this month could be beneficial both professionally and personally.

Health. Your energy levels are strong in December, and you're unlikely to face any serious health issues. Some fatigue from the busy period may set in toward the end of the month, so aim to finish all your tasks by December 25th and take some time for yourself before New Year's Eve.

PISCES

In December, your energy levels may be off the charts. If you can channel it in the right direction, you'll achieve a lot. The stars will be especially favorable to those whose work requires precision and a creative approach. This is your moment to shine!

Business. The major successes in December can be achieved on the professional front. Ongoing projects will wrap up successfully, and new opportunities will emerge.

For entrepreneurs and managers, this means new plans that could receive approval at the highest level. Employees have a good chance of earning their boss's approval, getting a promotion, or securing a position in a more promising organization. There are many opportunities, and it's up to you to seize them.

You might lack some flexibility and understanding of the significance of what's happening right now. So, before making any decisions—whether to reject an offer or accept it—consider all options and possibilities carefully, and the stars will surely support you.

Money. Financially, this month is excellent. Money will flow in steadily, and the amount will significantly increase. In addition to your usual income, bonuses, rewards, and gifts from loved ones are also likely.

Expected dates for large sums are December 1, 8-10, 19, 20, and 27-29. Expenses are few, and all will be offset by growing income.

Love and Family. Your personal life takes a back seat to work in December. Lovers may not get to meet as often as they would like, which could strain relationships.

Supportive spouses will understand and back each other up. The stars remind you that a smile and a kind word can ease tension even in the toughest situations. Also, in matters of personal relationships, trust your intuition—it's likely to guide you well.

Health. Your energy levels are through the roof in December. Surprisingly, the more you expend, the more you'll have. With such an abundance of energy, all illnesses will steer clear of you.

Description of Zodiac Signs

ARIES DESCRIPTION

Sign. Masculine, fire, cardinal.

Rulers. Mars and Pluto in retrograde.

Exaltation. Sun.

Temperament. Choleric, impulsive, aggressive.

Positive traits. Logical, self-confident, decisive, determined, vigorous, persistent, proactive, entrepreneurial, ambitious, optimistic, dynamic.

Negative traits. Irritable, excitable, impulsive, intolerant, stubborn, grumpy, reckless, a tendency to exaggerate and sensationalize, unchecked passion, aggressive, despotic, tyrannical.

Weaknesses in the body. Head, brain, central nervous system, face, eyes, ears, teeth, tongue, nose, mouth, upper jaw, chin.

Metal. Iron.

Minerals. For a talisman, red jasper. Generally: rubies, garnet, diamond, Indian carnelian.

Numbers. 5, 7, 9.

Day. Tuesday.

Color. Red

Aries's Energy

Aries opens the Zodiac and is first in the circle of signs. This is reflected in life, as Aries always tries to be first with everything – and he manages to do it, too! Aries is a fire sign, which symbolizes the material embodiment of the spirit, power, and transformation. In the trigon of fire signs, it is the first manifestation of cosmic fire – a fire of life that erupted, giving way to obsession and the desire to unleash one's natural potential.

Aries is ruled by Mars, which gives its children incredible energy reserves and enviable creativity. This planet is named for the mythological hero associated with victory and incredible powers; in ancient times, he was depicted as an angel with a magic sword cutting through the darkness. The energy of both Mars and Fire makes Aries the most active and powerful sign of the zodiac, with the greatest chances of conquering the highest mountains.

Astrological portrait of Aries

Anyone born under this sign believes in self-affirmation: "I am." He takes initiative, is a confident leader, and moves forward without worrying about the consequences (leaving those concerns to those who follow), guided by ideas that inspire and encourage – this is Aries' highest cosmic task.

Aries is symbolized by a ram, an animal that is direct and courageous as it tackles the challenges thrown at it by Fate. Aries are no different. They conquer the world with strength, assertiveness, and aggression. They are courageous and fearless. They cut straight to the chase, pushing any obstacles out of the way. Aries are never discouraged, they are always moving ahead as they dive into work with a passion, making waves, learn from the school of hard knocks, and in the end, are victorious.

To an Aries, life is a battlefield, and he is ready for anything, has no fear of insults or humiliation, and will not stop in the face of failure or difficulties. Fearlessness often drives an Aries to risk, and for the right cause, an Aries might even risk his or her life. But once in a crisis, Aries has strong intuition, and therefore can rule and cope without any outside assistance.

All of Aries' excess fire makes him or her active, always striving to be the first and the best in everything, with a thirst for fame and recognition. Aries lights up at the sight of a new business and begins to radiate joy and electrify those around him. He is capable of leading large crowds with almost magical influence; this is why he is always in a position of power – either physical or psychological.

Aries is self-absorbed and views the world around him as an extension of himself. The feelings and interests of others are of little interest, and he does not know how to tap into the secrets of the human soul. It is not worth blaming him for that. Aries is able to succeed precisely because of this individualism. However, Aries has something that the other signs do not have – he is honest, noble, and absolutely sincere in every way. Lies and deceit are unknown to an Aries, which softens some of his selfishness. Another valuable quality is Aries' ability to always come to the rescue in times of suffering and need. He is a strong shoulder to lean on during tough times. Once Aries has lent a hand in a difficult time, he will do it again and again, though he may feel hurt if his own worries and concerns go unnoticed.

For all of Aries' bravery, assertiveness, and aggression, he is a very sensitive and defenseless child underneath. It is easy to insult or offend him. However, he quickly gets over any such attacks, as long as you provide him with praise and affection. Despite having a short fuse (Aries can descend into boorishness, scandal, and even fights), Aries will quickly walk away, and he will not waste much sulking before forgiving the offender, especially if he or she has a kind word to say about him.

But don't hold your breath waiting for an Aries to discover tact and the ability to smooth over disagreements and avoid outbursts. These qualities are not on his list of virtues. To an Aries, diplomacy means directness, ingenuity, and honesty. Thanks to their incredible work ethic, Aries tend to be wealthy, though they are never stingy and are willing to share it with others. After all, despite their selfishness, one of Aries' most fundamental needs is to bring joy to others. What's the point of wealth if there's no one to share it with?

How to recognize an Aries by appearances

There are two types of Aries: strong and muscular, or weak and sickly, which is what happens to them if they do not live in harmony with their sign, which requires a healthy diet and constant physical activity. Aries is lively in appearance, speaking quickly and in imperative tones, moving around decisively.

Aries is distinguished by a ruddy complexion. Mars, the red planet, bestows this on its children. Aries' face has a certain roughness, stiffness, and a pronounced nose. Aries women are somewhat masculine in their appearance, with a strong torso, broad shoulders, a narrow waist and hips, and a low, often hoarse voice.

Charting Aries' Fate

Generally speaking, Aries' fate is positive, though his path in life is unlikely to be called "smooth". There will be many changes, crises, and acute situations. Usually, Aries have had a restless youth and later settle down as adults. They always achieve anything they set their mind to, and their dreams and plans come true. But their success is theirs alone – Aries are workaholics, unafraid to take a risk, take great chances in life, and never fixate on past failures. They take Fate by the horns, and will not surrender, no matter what is thrown their way. They simply know no fear and ignore their failures. This, along with their self-confidence are Aries' trump cards.

Aries' impulsivity and scatterbrained nature may become obstacles to success. Aries is inspired by many ideas and perpetually rushing around and has a difficult time focusing on just one thing. They want to do it all, and right now. Therefore, they often do not see things through. The root cause of this is a lack of inner grounding and discipline; Aries is stubborn and often replaces discipline with sheer determination. He simply keeps charging forward, sometimes without even looking where he is going, until he is running into serious obstacles. In order to overcome this problem, he must:

- Find the right way to channel this energy into something inspiring.
- Create a set of behavioral rules for himself. He needs to be educated, have high standards for himself, but not be too strict, as being too

hard one himself will be counterproductive), that is, to show both love and high standards at once, while occasionally indulging himself;

- Learn to think first and have a clear behavioral standard. He can start small – count to 10 before saying or doing anything;
- Do away with black and white thinking – mine-yours, friend-enemy, good-bad) and expand his mind;
- Occasionally look within and reflect on his spiritual impulses and do a "debriefing". Aries is the only sign that does not fall into depression triggered by self-discovery.

TAURUS DESCRIPTION

Sign. Feminine, Earth, fixed.

Ruler. Venus.

Exaltation. Moon.

Temperament. Melancholic, slow.

Positive traits. Persistent, patient, restrained, diligent, thorough, careful, a good judge, consistent, honest, a good temperament.

Negative traits. Stubborn, willful, overly sensitive, pessimistic, lazy, apathetic, sluggish, conservative.

Weaknesses in the body. Neck and internal organs. Thyroid gland, tonsils, frontal sinuses, vocal cords, trachea. The esophagus. Occipital and cerebellum.

Metal. Copper.

Minerals. For talisman – carnelian orange. For general wearing – hyacinth, coral, pink quartz.

Number. 6.

Day. Friday.

Color. Yellow-orange and bright green.

Taurus's energy

It is great fortune to be born under the sign of Taurus and receive the energy of Venus, the ruler of beauty, harmony, love, and prosperity. Taurus is made to flourish and prosper in everything – in love, with money, friends, knowledge, and spiritual values.

The Earth element means that people born under Taurus are practical, incredibly patient, strong, and tenacious. These are their trump cards. Taureans know exactly what they want, and they are determined as they work toward their goals, and these efforts are not in vain! Often, Taureans manage to become wealthy and well-known, with few exceptions.

Astrological portrait of Taurus

Taurus's motto is "acquire, accumulate, possess". They are extremely practical, and their goal is to take ideas in the spiritual phase and make them take shape by creating, building, and strengthening. In everything Taureans do, they are guided by common sense. They are materialists and pragmatists who place great importance on comfort, satisfaction, and prosperity. They are ready to overcome any obstacles on the way to financial stability – but they are not driven by greed or a passion for hoarding wealth, but rather a need to feel comfortable in this world. This is the only way a Taurus can be effective in life, when she feels the ground beneath her feet. The best support you can give a Taurus is material possessions or monetary savings. Taurus is distinguished by her poise and emotional stability – it is hard to get him/her to lose control, and even harder to prove something to her.

Taureans will hold onto certain beliefs until they have been disappointed. They are stubborn, though they would not agree with that description. Taureans are willing to gain strength, experience, and knowledge over a long time in hopes of achieving their goals and then make an overnight breakthrough to see unprecedented results.

Taurus is patient, reliable, responsible, and consistent in everything. As long as this determination lasts, she can withstand just about anything. She is loyal to friends, business partners, and loved ones, so long as they are honest with her.

Taurus still has some shortcomings. First of all, she is conservative. On the other hand, however, conservatism can be necessary and even a virtue in serious matters. That is why if Taurus shows a healthy level of conservatism, that is only an advantage. Taurus's desire to follow the established order also means she is capable of achieving great success.

Taurus also has some unusual qualities. She is hypersensitive. At her highest level of spiritual development, she will literally achieve the state of being a medium, perceiving objects in her world at the most subtle levels of energy. Many Taureans are often soothsayers, psychics, and healers who are capable of accumulating natural energy. J.R.R. Tolkien describes the highest level of Taurus in Lord of the Rings. Hobbits are true Taureans, capable of having fun, living an earthly life, and also guarding eternal values. Other Taureans should strive for the same.

How to recognize Taurus by appearances

A typical Taurus is calm, charming, and friendly, with a harmonious build, though she may tend to gain weight. Men tend to be large and robust. Taureans inspire confidence and authority. One might describe them as "well-cut and well-stitched". Women are extremely attractive, with big, beautiful eyes to lose oneself in, curved eyelashes, a flirtatious, upturned nose, and irresistible dimples. They have a dense build and a rounded shape and are always surrounded by admirers.

Charting Taurus's Fate

A young Taurus is restless, and usually needy, deprived, and her own worst enemy. But during the second half of life, she will see a period of prosperity. Taureans are business-minded, practical people who plan life several years in advance. They are methodical as they move toward their goals, and in the end, their persistence pays off, as they get everything they have been striving for. Everything that Taurus dreamt of is sure to come true. It might not be right away, but gradually, with enormous effort, they will soar to new heights!

Generally speaking, Taurus is healthy, with enviable strength.

GEMINI DESCRIPTION

Sign. Masculine, air, mutable.

Ruler. Mercury.

Exaltation. Mercury, Ascendant Lunar Node.

Temperament. Sanguine, nervous, easygoing, volatile.

Positive traits. Intelligent and intuitive, very perceptive, quick to react, agile, observant, highly imaginative, curious, honest, and full of goodwill.

Negative traits. Superficial, unreliable, immodest, talkative, disorganized, emotionally detached, reckless.

Weaknesses in the body. Hands, respiratory organs, tongue, nervous system, grey matter of the brain, psyche.

Metal. Mercury.

Minerals. For a talisman – gold topaz, yellow beryl. Generally: topaz, tiger's eye, chrysoprase, carnelian.

Numbers. 5, 12.

Days. Wednesday.

Color. Orange-yellow and yellow green.

Gemini's energy

Gemini's personality is formed by the energy of Mercury, the closest planet to the Sun. It rotates far more quickly than the other planets. One side of Mercury is constantly facing the Sun, while the other side faces away from it with temperatures far below zero. This speed and duality are also a good description of Gemini. Geminis rush through life at the speed of light, constantly afraid of not having time to do something, and are reminiscent of Julius Caesar, who was known for being a master multitasker. Gemini is an air sign, signifying strong communication skills, but also a tendency toward inconsistency and superficiality. It is very difficult for a Gemini to focus on one thing at a time and see things through to the end. However, that is not too much of an obstacle in their lives.

Astrological portrait of Gemini

Geminis are cute, attractive, and a pleasure to spend time with. Their best qualities are their energy, mental alertness, intuition, and insight.

They are observant, capable of easily and quickly grasping information, and process it just as quickly. Mercury rules the mental processes, among other things, meaning that Gemini is the sign of intellectuals. People born under this sign achieve great success and have incredible public speaking skills. Coming from them, just about anything can seem true, and they are able to convince anyone of anything. Gemini's duty to himself is to not waste these qualities, and channel them in the right direction instead.

Gemini is restless, temperamental, and inconsistent. He rushes around from one extreme to the other, is in constant motion, and always looking to meet new friends and make new connections at every level. He eats breakfast, lunch, and dinner at the same time, has office romances at work, talks about work issues with their spouse, especially at night, when it is time to go to bed. A Gemini's mood changes from one second to the next. He might be prone to acting irrationally when he is in a bad mood, only to later regret it.

Geminis have a double nature. They can be both happy and sad at the same time. Everything in their lives exists in a duplicate – apartments, families, friends, girlfriends or boyfriends, lovers, and work. Things change with astonishing speed. You might say that to a Gemini, the purpose of life is trying it all.

One of Gemini's more troublesome qualities is inconsistency. If astrologers could rename Gemini, they might refer to this sign as a chameleon, which changes colors in order to camouflage and protect itself. We might add sensitivity to that inconsistency, as Geminis have a tendency to exaggerate the most minute details. They are known for emotional restraint, but this is not out of callousness, but rather a defense mechanism against other peoples' criticisms.

All Gemini tend to hide their true intentions. You will never know what a Gemini is really thinking deep down, even after living with him for decades. They are prone to fantasizing, have rich imaginations, and are inclined to embellish everything. But even in a lie, Gemini is harmless. He is not seeking revenge or to humiliate anyone in order to raise himself up in his own eyes. He is simply protecting his personal space and secrets. He is always interested in those he communicates with, reaching out and easily making a connection. With Gemini, you can always reach an understanding.

How to recognize Gemini by appearance

A typical Gemini is of average height, slim, agile, sociable, and charming. They have thin, pointed facial features.

Charting Gemini's Fate

Gemini's Fate reflects his nature. His life is an endless series of ups and downs. It is very difficult for Geminis to focus on just one thing, even if it is very important. Failing to address this can feed into Gemini's fatalism-they often let things float away from them.

Gemini tends to have an unstable family life, due to his overwhelming desire for new experiences. This sign is not exactly adapted to marriage, at least in the traditional sense.

Nature has gifted Gemini with many talents. If they manage to harness even a modicum of perseverance, they will achieve incredible success. He should avoid throwing himself into things or making hasty decisions.

CANCER DESCRIPTION

Sign. Feminine, water, cardinal.

Ruler. Moon.

Exaltation. Jupiter and Neptune in retrograde.

Temperament. Melancholic, with a tendency toward phlegmatic.

Positive traits. Adaptable, sensitive, romantic, intuitive, emotional, purposeful, patient, persistent, responsible, thrifty, caring, soft, restrained, imaginative, has a good memory.

Negative traits. Irritable, violently reactive, a tendency toward exaggeration, fearful, hysterical, cowardly, resentful, capricious, volatile, lazy, moody, passive, arrogant.

Weaknesses in the body. Stomach, digestive organs, pleura, mucous membranes, breasts, mammary glands, lymph.

Metal. Silver

Minerals. For a talisman – chrysoprase and emerald. In general: pearls, moonstone (selenite), opal.

Number. 5.

Day. Monday

Color. Bright green and purple.

Cancer energy

The volatile Moon changes phases four times in a month, making those born under Cancer sensitive, easily influenced by their emotions, and mood swings. When Cancers are in a good mood, they are friendly and benevolent, but when their mood shifts to bad, it is best to avoid them. Cancers are forgiven for any mistake. What else would they do? After all, they are surprisingly cute and charming.

Despite the fact that Cancers are confident in themselves, they reach out to others. They have an undeniable talent for attracting others, because they need support and emotional energy from others. This is no surprise, given the fact that they are ruled by the Moon, which reflects the light of the Sun. Cancer is a water sign, giving her an astuteness and intuition bordering on clairvoyance, as well as real skills at making money. Few others on the Zodiac are as adept at handling people and leveraging the energy of money. Cancers have turned this into an art form.

Astrological portrait of Cancer

Those born under Cancer are the most sensitive and emotional signs of the entire Zodiac. They have a rich spiritual life, which is always changing, just like the Moon, which is born, grows, climaxes, diminishes, and dies in order to do it all over again. Frequent mood swings are one of Cancer's traits. When Cancer is in a good mood, she is sweet, charming, and friendly. When she is in a bad mood, she has a tendency to slip into a long depression.

Cancer's motto is "I feel, therefore, I am". However, this does not mean we should assume that Cancer's heart is inherently warm or that she tends to feel sympathy for others. Cancers take much more than they give, and mainly have empathy for themselves. They will come to the rescue only when they can be convinced that there is no other option. Cancer seeks to be loved and cared for. However, she remains a bit of a mystery and will never fully reveal herself.

Cancers are vulnerable and sensitive to criticism and will react sharply to ridicule and sarcasm. Cancer is easily offended by a "wrong" look or tone. However, she is capable of defending herself. Cancer's self-defense mechanisms are very strong. A typical response is to lurk silently. Do not think for a second that she will forget or ignore what has happened, however. Cancer rarely forgives insults but believes that revenge is a dish best served cold. She might take a long time to come up with a plan for retaliation, and then leverage a convenient situation. It is best to stay neutral with a person like this.

Cancers tend to be successful people. They are not given to impulsivity or haste, but rather are cautious and risk-averse. Before doing anything, Cancer weighs the pros and cons. Only rarely will she listen to anyone else's advice. She prefers to resolve everything on her own and is not afraid of responsibility. Cancers do what they say and succeed at it. Mistakes are a rarity, thanks in large part to their outstanding intellectual abilities. Cancers perceive all nuances of what is happening around them. All of this is the influence of the Moon, which perceives and reflects the light of the Sun. Much like the Moon, Cancer perceives the outside world and immediately reflects it back.

Cancer's intuition is more developed than most other signs, meaning that she is excellent at understanding how other people are feeling and anticipating how situations will play out. Cancer is able to build a strong cause and effect relationship and find the root causes of certain problems, facts, and phenomena.

It is almost impossible to deceive a Cancer, and they should be treated with kindness. Pressuring them is useless – Cancer has developed a multi-stage defense mechanism, and the only way you can influence a Cancer is to pique her interest.

Cancers are persistent and assertive. If they have decided to do something, nothing will stop them. But in setting a goal, Cancer will never get straight to the point. Rather, she will bide her time, circle around the target, and keep an eye on it until she manages to reach it.

Despite Cancer's love of changes, novelty, and travel, they are strongly drawn to the home and their loved ones, especially their mother and children. To a Cancer, children are the world's greatest gift. Cancer is a home-bound and family sign, the keeper of family traditions. She adores her home and does not feel as relaxed and comfortable anywhere else.

If a Cancer is unable to achieve normal intellectual development, she might develop negative traits such as stinginess, childishness, or become conniving.

Cancers are often spilling over with emotions: it is normal for them to speak in loud tones, argue, or experience bouts of melancholy and even depression. This heightened sensitivity and vulnerability can eventually develop into complexes or neuroses. Cancer tries very hard to fulfill the ideal and be a strong person but continues to feel vulnerable.

Cancer is capable of seeing the true nature of the world around her and its essence, and carries higher ideas, and is a great zealot and creator. She passes all of the dirtiness in the world through her soul but holds onto her own pure soul. This is why it is wise to pay attention not only to a Cancer's outward appearance, but also her essence when dealing with her. If you manage to lure her out of her shell, you will be repaid in the highest form. After all, Cancer is not always on her best behavior, and not because she harbors any ill will. At her core, she is kind and selfless, due to her heightened sensitivity. Her soul cannot withstand the cruelty of the outside world. This might break Cancer, so she is forced to defend herself. If you cannot get her to open up, you will have to deal with her as though she were a child.

How to recognize Cancer by appearances

Cancer does not like to draw attention to herself, though she is very sociable by nature. She behaves modestly and exercises restraint. Cancers are rarely tall, and tend to be obese, though they often look more overweight than they really are, due to the roundness of their figure. They tend to have a round face, like the Moon, which may look childlike due to its puffiness. Their eyes are framed by long, thick eyelashes. They tend to gaze around themselves, often with a slightly sad look. Their thick eyebrows often meet over their nose, and their nose tends to be slightly upturned. Their lips are not distinctive, though often a bit smudged, puffy, and "sensual". Their hair is usually dark and curly, with pale skin and small hands.

Charting Cancer's Fate

Up until about 30-35 years of age, Cancer is fickle, full of worries, disappointments, and conflicts. They do not always succeed in marriage – divorce and separation are possible. Cancers are sensitive, vulnerable people, who depend on the opinions of others. They are characterized by volatile emotional outbursts. All of this may be a red flag to potential partners. This is why Cancers should be taught to reign in their temper from early childhood.

In adulthood, Fate rewards Cancers for all of the challenges they have faced. They will reach a decent position in society and earn a sizeable fortune.

It is important for Cancers to remember that in order to move forward, they need to always be looking backward, that is, to come back to their roots and build on the past. Roots are our first home and family. Build your own nest, and the rest will fall into place. Without a strong home, Cancers lack the support they need to succeed in society.

Excessive caution and suspiciousness can throw a wrench in Cancer's ability to succeed. Cancers are often prone to building safety nets where there is no threat.

LEO DESCRIPTION

Sign. Masculine, fire, fixed.

Ruler. Sun.

Exaltation. Pluto

Temperament. Slightly choleric, with a strong sense of self-esteem.

Positive traits. Proud, self-confident, noble, indulgent, ambitious, determined, passionate, bold, loyal, honest, efficient, eloquent.

Negative traits. Arrogant, insolent, vain, conceited, nervous, cruel, treacherous, demands attention, in love with luxury.

Weaknesses in the body. Left eye in women, right eye in men, upper back, heart, aorta, cardiovascular system, back, spine, spinal cord, ribs, spleen, diaphragm, arterial circulation.

Metal. Gold.

Minerals. For a talisman- rock crystal. Generally- diamond, ruby, chrysoberyl, gold quartz, beryl, jasper, hyacinth, chrysolite.

Numbers. 1, 4, 9.

Day. Sunday.

Color. Purple-red and yellow green.

Leo energy

The Sun is Leo's celestial ruler. It bestows Leo with qualities such as endurance, powerful creative potential, and an incredible range of both soul and generosity. Leo can also be rather vain, however. His ambition means he will not simply stop and rest on his laurels. Leo has a truly regal gaze and is always looking ahead. He has enough innate qualities to satisfy himself. Leo is the sign of winners and rulers. Figuratively speaking, Leos have a special mission, specifically to light the spark of God in themselves to ignite a divine cosmic fire and lead others to the height of spiritual evolution and develop their best qualities. They must understand that the power given to them carries great responsibility.

Astrological portrait of Leo

Leos are born leaders. They aspire to exert control over everything and everyone. Leos like to wear the purple mantle and laurel wreath of a victorious leader in society, and to share this generosity with their neighbors. There are some Leos who do not wish to rule over anyone. These people are individualists who rule themselves and their own destiny. They do not impose their will on anyone, but will not allow anyone to command them, either. No Leo will tolerate orders from someone else. Even if he may occasionally make a concession, he will gradually gain the upper hand by any means necessary.

Usually, Leos do not actively try to take power. Rather, they have been given this job from the very beginning. They are never climbers, and do not push others around. They are totally convinced of their own uniqueness, and subconsciously try to stand out and show others what makes them special. They radiate sunshine and tend to act through intermediaries or assistance. People are drawn to Leo, as they are drawn to the sunlight.

Leos stand out for their great physical and spiritual strength. They are capable of great achievements, and constantly seek to do more. However, they do not openly reveal this, and almost seem embarrassed of their own drive. As far as a Leo is concerned, for the right cause, he is capable of putting it all on the line and going for broke. Fortune is always smiling on him. When it seems that there is no way out, Leo will suddenly find that his supporters and allies open the door to new horizons, seemingly out of thin air.

The most important thing in a Leo's life is his career. He is ready to give it his very all. Family is also very important. Often, Leo views his home as another office. Most Leos have extraordinary talent, and great creative potential. These qualities are on display when Leo manages to fully realize himself. Leo is sincere, trusting, and honest, but also easily influenced by others and prone to ending up in a sticky situation. Leo does not tolerate betrayal in others and is intensely loyal himself.

They are intensely self-sufficient and will never ask anyone else for help, though they are happy to lend a hand to others. They reject anyone's advice, and might make a mistake, but will never regret the experience. Leo simply continues his climb to the top and will eventually conquer his goals. Leo loves the good life, expensive, high-quality things, pleasures, and sports. Physical activity helps him get rid of negative emotions and tension while increasing his energy.

Those born under Leo tend to be friendly and polite, with deep, sincere feelings. They are capable of being very chivalrous, and will never finish off a defeated enemy, just because they can.

Leo's greatest shortcoming is his vanity and pride, which make it difficult to capitalize on all of his virtues. Leo is constant in everything, even his delusions; pressuring him only makes him grow more stubborn, and he has zero humility. As far as Leo is concerned, there are only two opinions – mine and the wrong one. If Leo were to start acting more democratic toward others and treat them with just a little more patience, they would automatically do his bidding. Developing that humility is Leo's great challenge, though he is equipped with the intelligence and drive to win this battle with himself.

Leo feeds off of attention from others. He suffers when no one noticed him. He is easily swayed by flattery, meaning that it may not be difficult to deceive him. If for some reason, Leo is unable to realize his rich potential, he might fall into a real depression and become locked in a vicious cycle.

For this reason, from an early age, Leo needs to be taught to manage his emotions and get used to the idea of rolling up his sleeves and getting to work. Do not encourage him if he is trying to humiliate his peers or tries to prove his point through tantrums and physical violence.

How to recognize Leo by appearances

A typical Leo has prominent, bright features, and a large figure. Their incredible energy is palpable. They are always being noticed, even if discreetly dressed. Generally, they are medium height or tall, with beautiful, almond-shaped eyes, a straight, aristocratic nose, and long, graceful arms. They often have light hair, and men might tend to experience male pattern baldness from a young age. Their body is well-developed, muscular, and usually top-heavy. They have a direct gaze, and a habit of looking right into the eyes of anyone talking to them.

Charting Leo's Fate

Overall, Leo has a good chance of achieving success. When Leo was born, there was a feast in heaven, and God, feeling generous, showered Leo with many blessings. Leos may be known as the favorites of Fortune, but that does not always mean they go through life laughing. They pay a high price for their success, and only gain the strength and opportunities they need after making it through several taxing trials. Even if a Leo does not have any particular talent, he will eventually reach the summit thanks to incredible perseverance. Leo is the sign of victory! He should remember that nature has been very kind to him, and he needs to use his gifts.

VIRGO DESCRIPTION

Sign. Feminine, earth, mutable.

Ruler. Mercury.

Exaltation. Mercury.

Temperament. Melancholic, restrained, cold yet anxious.

Positive traits. Hard-working, business-minded, intelligent and with a great memory, teachable, methodical, punctual, pragmatic, neat, dignified.

Negative traits. Formal, petty, thoughtless, anxious, indecisive, self-centered, self-interested, cunning, prone to flattery, resentful, capricious, greedy, vain.

Weaknesses in the body. Gastro-intestinal tract, solar plexus, pylorus, duodenum, cecum, pancreas, spleen, liver, gallbladder, autonomic nervous system, abdominal cavity.

Metal. Brass.

Minerals. For a talisman: yellow agate and jasper. Generally: yellow sapphire, amber, citrine, chrysolite.

Numbers. 5, 10.

Day. Wednesday.

Colors. Bright green and yellow brown.

Virgo energy

Virgo's personality is colored by the energy of two planets – Mercury and Proserpina. Mercury impacts Virgos differently than it does Geminis, creating a calmer, less independent character. One might say that Proserpina's unhurried effect "slows down" Mercury's influence in Virgo. Virgo and Gemini share a brilliant intellect, but Proserpina is a powerful planet that unleashes the swirl of time. She endows her children with a sense of duty, punctuality, clarity, analytical abilities, a tendency to study the root cause of any problem, grow, and transition to a higher state. In order to that to happen, though, the conscious must work, which is what Virgo has been doing her entire life. Virgo is an Earth sign, making her a practical materialist guided by logic and common sense.

Astrological portrait of Virgo

Virgo is a sign associated with work, service, and duty. It is a sign that is capable of overcoming difficulties. This is why Virgo is always concerned with her health and does not hesitate to seek medical attention. Virgos are willing to work tirelessly for a good cause. Their goals are clear and real rather than simply theoretical ideals. Virgos do not build pies in the sky, and their work is what gives life meaning. Virgos cannot tolerate laziness in others and will not aid those who refuse to work.

Virgos analyze. They are rational, with perfectly developed logic. They have a clear mind, with few illusions about life or other people. Even in love, they are capable of seeing their partner's shortcomings and turn to various methods to correct them. This does not mean that Virgos are devoid of emotions or purely driven by logic, however. Virgo's feelings are there, but she will only rarely reveal them. Even love is first and foremost a duty to Virgo. If someone is truly in need, she will happily step up and do whatever is necessary. Virgo is an intellectual sign, and people born under it constantly strive for new knowledge. They are skilled at absorbing information and memorizing facts. This is why many Virgos are known to their friends as a walking encyclopedia. They seem to know everything and give intelligent, practical advice on any topic. When asked about anything, it is as if they had a file in their head storing complete information on whatever topic is at hand, and they will not be satisfied until they have informed you of all of it. Virgo seeks knowledge to subdue matters with their mind – this is their great, cosmic task.

Virgos are thorough critics. But they are also extremely ambitious and painfully sensitive to any comments. If you start criticizing a Virgo, she will refute all of your arguments, and you will come to regret ever starting the discussion. Virgos are pedantic, judgmental, and calculated, and their ability to impose their opinion on others mean they are impervious to criticism.

Virgos may lack intuition and creativity. They have a need to touch and see everything with their own eyes, and it is difficult for them to grasp the abstract. They subject the entire world to excellent analysis but are less gifted at synthesizing what they perceive. This means that Virgos might have a tendency to miss the forest for the trees. Virgo's home is usually in perfect order. Less pleasant traits may be her coldness and emotional rigidity.

At her highest level, a Virgo is an erudite person full of information, but her greatest battle will be her own pedantry.

How to recognize a Virgo by appearance

A typical Virgo is a slender person with a somewhat disproportional figure. In adulthood, Virgo women may tend to lose more weight than they gain, and will stay in good physical shape, even in old age. Virgos have wide bones, and their facial expressions are serious and stern. They tend to be tall but are rarely excessively so. Their faces tend to be long, as is their nose, which thickens into the shape of a water droplet. Their features are thin and well-defined. They have small eyes. Virgos are modest and often shy, and do not seek to draw attention to themselves, even if they are famous.

Charting Virgo's Fate

In childhood and adolescence, Virgos will face great difficulties. Later, they will manage to reach stability and security. Virgo builds her own happiness through decades of hard work and trial and error. Virgos tend to suffer a crisis in their personal life between the ages of about 18 to 29. They may experience marriage followed by divorce. Perhaps it finding a suitable partner seems impossible. Virgos reach personal harmony rather late in life, after the age of 36, and in some cases, as late as 42.

LIBRA DESCRIPTION

Sign. Masculine, air, cardinal.

Ruler. Venus.

Exaltation. Saturn, Uranus.

Temperament. Sanguine.

Positive traits. Diplomatic, intuitive, loves harmony, idealist, romantic, friendly, tender, fair, noble, light, refined, drawn to beauty, needs a partner.

Negative traits. Lacks self-confidence, volatile, unbalanced, sensitive, weak-willed, detached from reality.

Weaknesses in the body. Groin, uterus, bladder, kidneys, thighs, skin, veins.

Metal. Copper.

Minerals. For a talisman- orange topaz. Generally- hyacinth, orange corundum, diamond, rock crystal, coral.

Numbers. 6, 8, 12.

Day. Friday.

Color. Red-orange and green blue.

Libra energy

Libra is ruled by two planets – Venus (the planet of love, beauty, and prosperity) and Chiron (the symbol of balance and justice). Venus is known to astrologists as "small happiness" (Jupiter is known as "big happiness"). Venus's energy brings Libras good luck, but behind the scenes, Libras need to work hard. They achieve much thanks to their talents, charm, persuasiveness, and ability to smooth over any contradictions. Chiron gives them the key to all kinds of information. Libras can combine that which seems incompatible – they manage to work two jobs, bring enemies and friends together, and maintain a balance, all the while.

The element of air starts off active, before getting carried away. It brings Libra the ability to keep a cool head, remain calm, and seek compromises while getting along with others and avoiding causing a conflict.

Astrological portrait of Libra

Libras are connoisseurs of beauty, aesthetics, and they strive to find the golden mean in everything. Their contradictory natures make it difficult to achieve complete harmony. Libras love people but hate crowds. They are kind and sociable while also experiencing long bouts of depression. They can be intelligent but naïve. Restless and mobile, but never in a hurry. They do not tolerate rudeness but are capable of saying a harsh word in their hearts. It is worth noting that this kind of behavior is just a mask to hide their insecurities. In fact, Libras are good-natured, and any rudeness is contrived rather than their nature. Libra's character is constantly changing, balancing, and rushing from one extreme to the next. From the outside, they may seem to be connected to two totally different people, and they might even appear confused with their own beliefs.

Libras seek stability, comfort, companionship, and partnership. However, they are selective in their contacts, and always keep a relationship with the powers that be. People lacking in intelligence are not attractive to a Libra.

Libras can only flourish in an environment of benevolence and approval. Disharmonious and stressful situations drive them to depression and illness. They try to avoid conflicts and remove any negative energy from themselves. During a heated debate, they will usually side with the winner. At his highest level, Libra is a talented diplomat. Many politicians who manage to straddle two positions at once or provoke two sides in order to benefit from their hostility are also Libras. Despite their conflict avoidance, Libras love to argue for any reason. They take to debates like a fish to water, and always have the last word.

Libras often face contradictory situations. They have a hard time making a choice life puts in front of them. Libra's indecisiveness can be felt everywhere. They hesitate for a long time before making the right decision, and prefer to wait until things have resolved themselves, if they can.

Libras' coldness and detachment can cause them great harm. A lack of positive emotions and rigidity can have a negative impact on their Fate. A Libra's cosmic task is to learn to be sensitive and strike a balance.

Disharmony and imbalance have a very negative impact on Libra. They need to learn the essence of the phenomena around them and understand the cause-and-effect relationship. Chaos takes this ability away from Libra, and they cannot find harmony.

Most Libras have a perfectly developed ability to concentrate in order to make the right choices. They tend to be very wise people, especially in terms of life experience.

Libra's most serious shortcoming is a tendency toward stereotypical thinking and a rigid commitment to principles.

How to recognize Libra from appearances

The only thing that would distinguish a Libra from the other signs by appearance is a charming smile – it is soft, gentle, and mysterious. Libra's figure is balanced, and as a rule he does not tend to put on weight. His appearance is elusive. Wherever he goes, he changes to fit his environment, like a chameleon. Libra is careful with his appearance and is always dressed tastefully. Female Libras need to remember not to get carried away with makeup.

Charting Libra's Fate

Libra is constantly shifting from one direction to another, and so periods of happiness and prosperity are replaced with moments of sadness or disappointment. Libras tend to find prosperity in the second half of their lives. By and large, Fortune is on Libra's side, but Libra's task is to realize this and accept what he has been given.

SCORPIO DESCRIPTION

Sign. Feminine, water, fixed.

Ruler. Pluto, Mars.

Exaltation. Pluto.

Temperament. Phlegmatic, easily choleric, sarcastic.

Positive traits. Passionate, self-confident, restrained, deliberate, determined, persistent, resilient, has high self-esteem, fair, seeks recognition, is able to see an opponent's weaknesses. Richly imaginative, sensitive, a sound judge, prophetically gifted, talented.

Negative traits. Irritable, excitable, willful, critical, deceptive, rude, vindictive, insidious, passion is unbridled, excessively sexual.

Weaknesses in the body. Lower abdomen, groin, reproductive system. Organs of secretion. Bladder and renal pelvis. Gallbladder, veins.

Metal. Iron and bronze.

Minerals. For a talisman – sarder. Generally – ruby, red carnelian.

Numbers. 4, 9, 14.

Day. Tuesday.

Color. Bright red and black.

Scorpio Energy

Scorpio is a water sign ruled by Mars and Pluto. The energy of these two planets is related, and both give off sexuality, fearlessness, determination, and the ability to make decisions in extreme situations. Scorpio is capable of withstanding any battle, making the necessary changes within and rising from the ashes to a new life. Scorpio's main driving force is her incredible sexual appetite, which she gets from both Mars and Pluto. This is reflected in self-expression, love, and creativity. One's sexual energy tends to be expressed outwardly, but the water element holds it back in Scorpio, meaning that their passions live within and rarely splash out.

Astrological portrait of Scorpio

Scorpio is the most complex, mysterious, and sexiest of the Zodiac signs. It is also the strongest sign psychologically – Scorpios are considered to be innate magicians. They possess incredible intuition, and have a real talent for guessing others' thoughts, along with an ability to get those around them to speak frankly and openly. Scorpio is a sign of transformation, perfection, and rebirth. Scorpio's entire life consists of ups and downs, and the lower she falls, the higher she will climb.

Scorpio is mocking and snide, and to her, there are no secrets in human nature. Scorpio's loved ones are open books that she can easily read. Generally speaking, they strive for self-improvement, with a strong will and emotions. Few notice these emotions, however, as they burn inside, given that Scorpios are actually secretive and reserved by nature.

Scorpios are fearless and can tolerate the toughest conditions and recover from any crisis. They despise any weakness in themselves or others, and this is a constant struggle for them. By nature, Scorpios are loners and sometimes, they find it difficult to connect with others. Their personalities are very attractive and charismatic – social, active, and diplomatic, capable of controlling the powerful energy that nature has given them since birth and unwinding the collective energy to subordinate their will onto others. Scorpios are capable of achieving great things in life.

Scorpios are always consistent – in their views, in love, affection, and what they dislike. They can tend toward being overbearing or even authoritarian, but occasionally allow themselves to be manipulated. Scorpio's hardest task is coping with her passions and inner contradictions.

On one hand, Scorpios are strict (both with themselves and others), suspicious, and secretive. On the other, however, they are seeking spiritual transformation and knowledge, and are persistent, determined, fearless, and soft-hearted. This is probably why Scorpios are so attractive, too. They are capable of making a real impression and drawing everyone's attention. They are witty, but that wit can be sharp and even wound. Keep that in mind when communicating with a Scorpio.

Despite Scorpio's secrecy and distrustfulness, she can often be sincere and frank with those close to her. That trust is not easy to earn, however. This is why Scorpios tend to have a very small circle of friends they have known since childhood.

Scorpios must learn how to restrain their passions and angry outbursts. It is very difficult for them to control themselves and their temper. They need to channel that energy into something constructive, preferably creative.

How to recognize Scorpio by appearances

Outwardly, Scorpio does not appear to be particularly strong. Her strength is, after all, spiritual, rather than physical. She may appear to be rather ordinary, but there is something fascinating about her, and it not related to her external beauty.

Scorpios always look right into their partners' eyes. This is a serious, burning, and penetrating gaze. They tend to be ironic and mocking, and over time, develop characteristic crows' eyes.

Female Scorpios are easy to spot by their clothes. They love red and black (they also dye their hair these colors). Often, they prefer tight, revealing clothing, however you will rarely find a Scorpio woman who looks vulgar or tacky.

Charting Scorpio's Fate

A Scorpio's youth is a time of excitement and fateful changes. They reach success slightly later in life – after 30. Marriage is beneficial to them. This is a very sensual sign. When alone, Scorpio becomes an ascetic, channeling her sexual energy into professional endeavors. The quality of a Scorpio's life depends on how she uses her energy. She can channel it into one of three ways.

The first path is the "Scorpian path". Scorpios here have a hard time finding their place in society. In time, they become aggressive and even dangerous. Their worst qualities take over – insidious, treacherous, a lack of empathy, unclear moral principles. They become vulnerable to many vices and dangerous addictions and get into self-destruct mode.

The second path is that of the "eagle". A Scorpio who takes this journey is aware of her power and authority. "I am so strong that I don't need to attack anyone!" is her attitude to life. Such a Scorpio becomes wise, powerful, and fair, and her energy drives her creativity. She is sociable and gifted, great company, an advocate and a fighter against injustice.

The third way is the path of the "grey lizard", or the path of least resistance. Here, Scorpio's energy does not find a worthy channel. She is dissatisfied with herself and others but does nothing to change things, becomes pessimistic, and loses her vitality.

SAGITTARIUS DESCRIPTION

Sign. Masculine, Fire, Mutable.

Ruler. Jupiter, Neptune.

Exaltation. Descending lunar node.

Temperament. Choleric, impulsive.

Positive traits. Strives for freedom and independence. Honest, fair. Persistent, and has good will. Intuitive, a good judge, and has ambitious goals. Optimist, reasonable, compassionate, generous. Skilled at managing tasks, brave, energetic, enthusiastic, ambitious, and free of prejudice.

Negative traits. Craves power, fame, and respect in society. Always wants more. Impatient with any restrictions, oppressive, violent, coercive. Tends to exaggerate, charm, seduce, and build a good opinion and impression of themselves. Loves pleasures, entertainment, and joyful feasts. Tends to be a risk taker, seeking romance and adventure. Excessively polite, sociable, makes rash decisions, direct, abrupt, adventurist.

Weaknesses in the body. Hips, pelvis, back muscles, tendons, and ligaments. Autonomic nervous system.

Metal. Tin.

Minerals. For a talisman – chalcedony. Other good minerals are turquoise, topaz, heliotrope, lapis lazuli, emerald, hyacinth, chrysolite.

Numbers. 3,4, 15.

Day. Thursday.

Color. Indigo.

Sagittarius energy

Jupiter is the planet of luck. Astrologists refer to it as "big happiness". It bestows its children with a special charisma and good luck. Success comes easily to Sagittarians, and they are admired people of honor. But before Sagittarius receives these gifts, Jupiter will put him to the test, and he will have to cross the seven seas in order to find his ideal, which, in the end, will turn out to be within himself. And yet, Sagittarius is incredibly lucky. Jupiter is generous, and Sagittarius always manages to be in the right place at the right time. The fire element gives Sagittarius his organizational skills, energy, and zest for life. Naturally, life reciprocates.

Astrological portrait of Sagittarius

Sagittarians are reckless, life-loving, and open-minded people. They are always positive no matter what the circumstances are, and manage to keep their chin up, so Fate is on their side. Many people envy Sagittarius's success – often people cannot understand how life can be so kind to him. What they do not know is that Sagittarius carefully plans his future success, and always knows his next move in advance. He may give off the impression of flying by the seat of his pants, but in fact, he has a rigid structure and clear life plan. What's more, Sagittarius is highly principled and slightly conservative. He is used to acting intelligently. Yet, he can at times be impulsive and rash. Sagittarius would be wise to learn to wait and analyze his own behavior.

Most Sagittarians are sociable and open. They are characterized by independence and seek to throw off any restrictions they may face – whether internal or external. Sagittarius is incapable of engaging in deception. Intrigue and trickery are not for him, and he is straightforward and open, which those dealing with him need to understand. Sagittarius is not known for being tactful or delicate, though in his mind, he is a model of politeness and diplomacy. He is well-meaning and generous, though he is also capable of standing up for himself. He does not allow anyone to infringe on his rights or property.

Sagittarius is always charming, and that is usually not due to his appearance. Sagittarius's smile lights up a room. His natural charm is an aid as he gains authority and climbs to high positions, which are his main aspirations in life.

Sagittarius is in need of recognition, and it is important for him to be admired by those around him and that they listen to what he has to say. Sagittarians are very good at this, as being in charge and running things is their calling.

Sagittarians travel a lot. They crave new experiences, have a thirst for learning, and want to try everything before their earthly journey is over. It is difficult for them to sit still. They tend to accumulate large libraries, learn on their own, and are excellent teachers, lecturers, and religious leaders. Spiritually, they are open and want to share their ideas with everyone and teach others. At their best, Sagittarians become highly spiritual and might devote themselves to religious activities, missionary work, or simply preach spiritual knowledge.

If Sagittarius does not receive a normal spiritual and intellectual development, he may tend to become authoritarian and arrogant, with a weakness for awards and accolades. He will not tolerate defeat or the slightest criticism.

Sagittarius's most difficult task is to fight his own weaknesses and shortcomings. The most important thing is that his human nature wins, rather than animal nature. After all, Sagittarius is a centaur – half animal (horse) and half human.

How to recognize Sagittarius by appearances

Sagittarians are medium height to tall, with a dense figure and broad bones. They tend to be obese, and so they need to keep an eye on their physical shape from a young age. They have a certain robustness to them.

If you see someone who seems like he would be a great boss, he is probably a Sagittarius. Jupiter places great importance on one's figure. Sagittarius's face is round, but proportional and harmonious. They tend to have a big head, round face, bushy eyebrows, and a good-natured smile. They prefer expensive, brand name clothes. Sagittarius is always surrounded by many fans, and knows how to communicate, tell a story, cheer someone up, and he is not afraid to be funny.

Charting Sagittarius's Fate

In his youth, Sagittarius is full of excitement and anxiety. Sometimes, he experiences personal troubles, but he quickly finds financial prosperity, either by marrying well, receiving an inheritance, or influential patrons who give them a leg up on a strong position. Living off of their own labor is not for Sagittarius. Overall, they are successful people both professionally and in their family life. There is a danger of incurring large financial losses due to their naivete, but they always land on their feet. Sagittarius always manages to make the money back. There is a high chance things will end up in court, but Sagittarius will come out on top.

CAPRICORN DESCRIPTION

Sign. Feminine, earth, cardinal.

Ruler. Saturn

Exaltation. Mars, Pluto.

Temperament. Phlegmatic, with a strong tendency toward pessimism.

Positive traits. Goal-oriented, perseverance, has a strong endurance, restrained, has self-control, ambitious, proud, independent, industrious, efficient.

Negative traits. Selfish, capricious, ambitious, insidiousness, incredulous, cruel, greedy, dissatisfied with herself, moody.

Weaknesses in the body. Knees, bones, skeleton, ligaments, tendons, digestive tract, liver, gallbladder, spleen, pancreas, skin, teeth.

Metal. Iron.

Minerals. For a talisman – black onyx. Generally – opal, blue sapphire, spinel, chalcedony, cat's eye.

Color. Black, blue-black, dark red.

Day. Saturday.

Capricorn energy

In ancient times, Saturn, the ruling planet of Capricorn, was associated with time. The ancient Aryans referred to it as Keyvan, the "lord of time". A calendar was built around Saturn's revolutions around the Sun (32 years), and it still survives today. The Saturnian calendar is not only for counting time, but also for spiritual protection from the heavens and gaining spiritual power. Saturn was revered as the god of the golden age. This means that every Capricorn is capable of rearranging the world, but it would be a mistake to assume that Capricorns are only focused on social revolutions. They start with their own world – their home, family, and themselves. Saturn's children tend to be withdrawn and isolated, as this is a planet of loners and ascetics. Capricorn's life is a journey of trials and self-improvement, but there is also a reward. Saturn allows individuals to slowly but surely achieve their goals through determination and patience. Capricorns always find their place in life and manage to settle down successfully. Capricorn is an Earth sign, and as a result is patient, practical, stable, and clear-headed. She will never miss out on any money-making opportunities, has her feet firmly on the ground, and a clear appreciation of reality.

Astrological portrait of Capricorn

Capricorn is fiercely independent. She is contemplative and analyzes and evaluates all of the events around her. She will not accept anything that she has not seen and heard with her own eyes and ears. She relies on her own strength and will not tolerate any meddling in her life. She is purposeful, and this may be Capricorn's most essential trait. She is very goal-oriented, and incredibly adaptable and tactical as she works to reach her target. She is never satisfied with what she has and continues to strive to reach the very top. She is brimming with ambition, and lives with a sense of higher purpose to achieve something special and change the world. Capricorn is steady as she moves ahead. She is very patient and not afraid of hard work. Sooner or later, almost all Capricorns end up in some sort of leadership position. They respect reliability, and to them, that means money. They are very good with money, never waste it, and always have savings. They aim for financial security and usually achieve it.

Many Capricorns are pessimistic or secretive, with high walls around them. Many are also ascetic and limit themselves in everything. But this is rooted in Capricorn's deep vulnerability. Despite her stiff upper lip and desire to be alone, Capricorn also needs affection. She suffers from her own isolation and is tormented by constant fears and pessimism. If that were not in her way, she might reach her goals twice as fast as she does.

Capricorn is high-minded and knows how to apply this to life. She is willing to sacrifice everything, including her own comforts, and to carefully plan her next step. She is able to worm her way out of anything, has a calm demeanor, and never loses control, no matter how tough things get. Many preachers, pastors, prophets, and missionaries are Capricorns. Her worst qualities are bitterness and irritability, as well as nagging doubt and indecision, along with a general distrust of others. From early childhood, Capricorn needs solid intellectual and spiritual development. Her life's path will be difficult, and for that, she needs personal strength as well as knowledge and money.

How to recognize Capricorn from appearances

Capricorns tend to be slender, but they are rarely very tall. They don't smile much and laugh even less. Their face seems rigid, even when they speak. They have pointed chins, and their eyes are either small and deep set or large. They usually have dark, sometimes curly hair. They are quiet and discreet, do not argue, and prefer to watch things play out from a distance as they draw their own conclusions. They don't talk about themselves much and are usually not the life of the party, though they are excellent at organizing and leading.

Charting Capricorn's Fate

It is unlikely that Capricorn will have a smooth journey through life. There are obstacles, ups and downs, worries, and fears. However, every cloud has a silver lining. Thanks to Capricorn's persistence, skill, and work ethic, she is able to achieve everything she plans, and even manage to enjoy her success, thanks to her longevity. As children and teens, they tend to be sickly, but this improves with age, as they become stronger and more resilient. Once they have overcome all of the hurdles in their way, Capricorns enjoy a period of prosperity that usually begins in middle age (40-50 years).

AQUARIUS DESCRIPTION

Sign. Masculine, air, fixed.

Ruler. Uranus, Saturn.

Exaltation. Neptune.

Temperament. Sanguine, agile.

Positive traits. Progressive, humanist, self-confident, intuitive, social, independent, optimistic, loyal to ideas, original, receptive, impressive, professional.

Weaknesses in the body. Tibia, calves, ankles, joints of the toes, periosteum, tendons, cerebellum, nervous system, blood, heart.

Metal. Uranium.

Minerals. For a talisman, turquoise and sapphire. Generally, aquamarine, falcon eye, obsidian, amethyst, zircon.

Color. Green-blue, grey.

Number. 2.

Aquarius energy

Aquarius is ruled by Uranus, which does not behave like other planets in the solar system. Its axis is deflected from the plane of orbit by 98 degrees, as though the planet were laying on its side. When the Sun is opposite to the North Pole, the southern half of Uranus sinks into the shadows for 20 years. These features of Uranus are a perfect metaphor for those born under its energy. Aquarians are known for their unconventional views and rebelliousness. They see a world thirsty for radical changes, but when push comes to shove, they tread carefully and tend not to get their own hands dirty, preferring instead to inspire others to act.

Astrological portrait of Aquarius

Uranus was revered in ancient times as the god of heaven, thunder, and lightning. Aquarius is not afraid of making changes to his life and is quick to make a decision and act. Uranus is the planet of freedom, spontaneity, and providence, after all. Aquarius is known for his originality, friendship, camaraderie with everyone, eccentricity, and stubbornness. He feels misunderstood, can be defiant, and is often offended. He is not entirely wrong on this count. Aquarius is the Zodiac's most obscure sign, and his behavior often raises eyebrows. He is always unpredictable, marches to the beat of his own drum, and lives based on his own lived experience. He does not always feel it necessary to share his motivations with others.

Aquarius's driving force is absolute justice, which he will defend, no matter whose rights have been trampled. He loves to express his opinions but never imposes them on others. He has respect for individual thought. He has no patience for flattery, hypocrisy, and lies, though he engages in all three. He will not follow the crowd or adjust his ways.

Despite all of this, Aquarius is not a loner or recluse. He loves his circle of friends and needs communication and human contact. These ties are shallow, though, and Aquarius does not let anyone into his soul, no matter how close they are. He is somewhat aloof, with a stiff upper lip and focused on practicality. Inside, however, Aquarius feels isolated and prefers to watch from a distance. He is not a fighter or aggressive in any way, though he will not give up his positions in the face of pressure.

Aquarius sometimes has spontaneous moments of revelation, bordering on prophecy. He can guess others' thoughts and is ahead of his time in his ideas. Aquarius is the sign with the most geniuses. But Aquarius can easily shift his own views and adopt those of his foes. He may not have a lack of clear principles, and a relatively lax attitude toward morality and public opinion, but thanks to his charm, he can be forgiven for many sins.

How to recognize Aquarius by appearances

Aquarius is original and unpredictable in everything, even outward appearances. There is always something extraordinary about him, and he manages to catch everyone's eye. He may be tall with long limbs, and be the picture of contrasts – for example, dark hair with light skin and light-colored eyes. His movements are impulsive and jerky. He is verbose, speaks quickly, and talks with his hands.

Charting Aquarius's Fate

Aquarius's life is full of changes. In his youth, he might spend a lot of time trying to find his path. In adulthood, however, this change becomes internal and therefore more manageable. Aquarians love to travel, especially overseas for long trips, and they bring good luck with them.

PISCES DESCRIPTION

Sign. Feminine, water, mutable.

Ruler. Neptune, Pluto.

Exaltation. Venus.

Positive traits. Highly imaginative, kind, adaptable, tranquil, peaceful, receptive, impressive, modest, compassionate, caring, delicate, gentle, idealistic, religious, deep.

Negative traits. Passive, shy, fanatical, impractical, fantastical, slovenly, volatile, unreliable, self-indulgent, overly sensual, malleable, submissive, dependent, moody, lazy, apathetic.

Weaknesses in the body. Legs – ankles, toe joints, toes. Tendons and ligaments. Digestive, lymphatic, and endocrine systems, heart and circulatory system.

Metal. Platinum and tin.

Minerals. For a talisman – amethyst and chrysolite. Opal, jasper, and coral are compatible.

Numbers. 3, 11, 19.

Day. Thursday.

Color. Purple and indigo.

Pisces energy

Pisces is influenced by the energies of both Neptune and Jupiter. In ancient cultures, Neptune was revered as the ruler of the seas. He represents the primal ocean and chaos where all opportunities lie, but nothing ever comes to life on its own. Neptune is the highest faith, psychic phenomena, hypersensitivity, deep and intuitive understanding of things and capacity for unearthly love. All of these traits are inherent to Pisces, and generous Jupiter bestows them with confidence in their own importance, a happy life, and great vitality.

Astrological portrait of Pisces

Pisces closes the Zodiac. This sign is a mirror of all the others, with a focus on their strengths and weaknesses. Pisces is a self-redeemer who is able to purify others by taking on the negativity. That is Pisces's greatest mission. Empathy, compassion, and the ability to reflect the qualities of any other sign with detachment are her main traits. "I feel, therefore I am" is Pisces's motto. However, in their negative manifestations, Pisces are ambivalent, unreliable, and prone to betrayal at any time. They make big promises and hardly ever follow through. They seek their own benefits and are very dishonest. Pisces always reflect their environment, which will determine their behavior. They are easily influenced by others, though this is usually unconscious. Without even realizing it, they take on the feelings and thoughts of whomever they are talking to. They can get carried away and simply go with the flow like water, not trying to change their own destiny. Pisces lack willpower and the ability to stand on their own two feet or have the inner core they need to resist the influence of others. Pisces is symbolized by two fish swimming in opposite directions. One fish is living, while the other is depicted as dead. This is Pisces – the living fish is in harmony with God and one with the cosmos. The dead Pisces is illusions, speculation of one's own weakness, opportunism, and chaos. At their worst, Pisces are capable of showing the vile human traits, only to be tormented by remorse afterward.

Pisces is a wise sign, with an understanding of others' suffering. They are capable of sacrificing themselves to help others. They are humane, merciful, and optimistic. But they are also overly sensitive and feel others' pain as their own. Pisces make good psychologists, and they are drawn to that which is hidden. They like to wrap their lives in mystery and express themselves symbolically. They tend to fantasize a lot. Others may not always understand Pisces, which causes her to suffer. She hates arguments and scandal but would rather tolerate evil and injustice than actually fight them. She has a good sense of humor, is friendly, humble, and calm. This draws many people in and opens doors. Pisces wants financial well-being but is rarely able to gain it on her own. As Pisces ages, she is eventually able to achieve peace and prosperity.

Pisces's great task is to carry divine love into the world, have compassion for her neighbors, and help them in their spiritual development. Nearly all Pisces are creative – many are musicians, artists, writers, performers, psychologist, or mystics.

How to recognize Pisces by appearances

Pisces is a sign that is constantly changing. Their appearance is a reflection of their inner state. Pisces tend to have large, deep, and alluring eyes, with an inward or wandering gaze that makes them look mysterious and almost absent. Pisces hardly ever look others in the eye. Their eyelids often appear red and irritated. Their skin is soft, pale, and almost transparent. Their hair is thin rather than thick, and their hands are small and soft, even in men. Pisces tend to gain weight, but they keep an eye on their figure.

Charting Pisces's Fate

Pisces's life path is often difficult and full of ups and downs. If she is not guided by someone else's strong hand, she may not achieve success. Pisces needs something or someone to stimulate and inspire her, especially among men. Female Pisces are often strong-minded, strong-willed individuals who forge their own path in life and are very successful in all of their endeavors.

A guide to the Moon cycle and Lunar days

Since Ancient times, people have noticed that the moon has a strong influence on nature. Our Earth and everything living on it is a single living being, which is why the phases of the moon have such an effect on our health and mental state, and therefore, our lives. Remember Shakespeare and his description of Othello's jealousy in his famous tragedy:

"It is the very error of the moon, She comes more nearer Earth than she was wont And makes men mad."

If our inner rhythm is in harmony with that of the cosmos, we are able to achieve much more. People were aware of this a thousand years ago. The lunar calendar is ancient. We can find it among the ancient Sumerians (4000-3000 BC), the inhabitants of Mesopotamia, Native Americans, Hindus, and ancient Slavs. There is evidence that the Siberian Yakuts had a lunar calendar, as did the Malaysians.

Primitive tribes saw the moon as a source of fertility. Long before Christianity, the waxing moon was seen as favorable for planting new crops and starting a new business, for success and making money, while the waning moon was a sign that business would end.

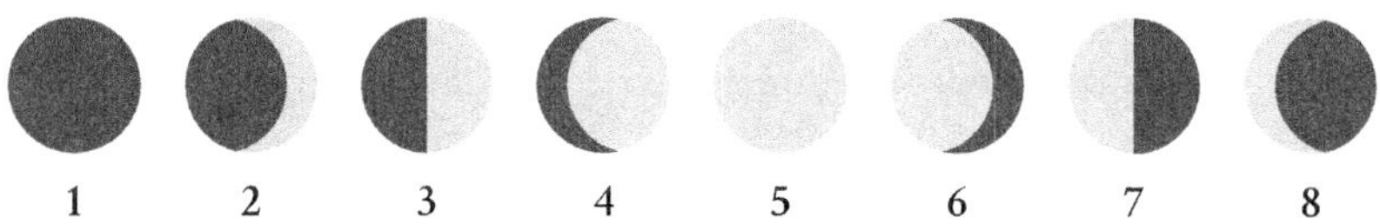

What are the phases of the moon?

- Phase 1 – new moon
- Phase 2 – waxing crescent moon
- Phase 3 – first quarter moon
- Phase 4 – waxing gibbous moon
- Phase 5 – full moon
- Phase 6 – waning gibbous moon
- Phase 7 – third quarter moon
- Phase 8 – waning crescent moon

To simplify things, we can divide the month into two phases:

- Waxing crescent moon - before the full moon
- Waning crescent moon - after the full moon

New moon

We cannot see the new moon, as it is hidden. People might complain about feeling weak, mental imbalance, and fatigue. During this time, we want to avoid taking on too much or overdoing things. Generally, people are not very responsive and react poorly to requests, which is why it is best to look out for yourself, while not keeping your plate too full.

The new moon is a bad time for advertising – it will go unnoticed. It is not worth preparing any presentations, parties, or loud gatherings. People are feeling constrained, not very social, and sluggish.

This is also a less than ideal time for surgery, as your recovery will be slow, and the likelihood of medical error is high.

It is also difficult to get an accurate diagnosis during the new moon – diseases might seem to be hidden, and doctors might not see the real underlying cause of what ails you.

The new moon is also a bad time for dates, and sexual encounters may be dissatisfying and leave you feeling disappointed. Ancient astrologers did not advise planning a wedding night during the new moon.

Waxing crescent moon

It is easy to identify a waxing crescent moon. If you draw an imaginary line between the two "horns", you should see the letter P. The waxing moon is then divided into one and two quarters.

During the first quarter moon, we need to focus on planning – setting goals and thinking of how we will set about achieving them. However, it is still a good idea to hold back a bit and not overdo things. Energy levels are still low, though they are growing along with the moon. It is still a good idea to avoid any medical procedures during this time.

The second quarter is a time for bold, decisive action. Things will come easy, and there is a greater chance of a lucky break. This is a good time for weddings, especially if the moon will be in Libra, Cancer, or Taurus. Nevertheless, it is a good idea to put off any advertising activities and public speaking until closer to the full moon, if you can.

Full moon

During the full moon, the Earth is located between the sun and the moon. During this time, the moon is round and fully illuminated. This takes place during days 14-16 of the lunar cycle.

During the full moon, many people feel more vigorous than usual. They are emotional, sociable, and actively seeking more contact, so this may be a good time for any celebrations.

However, be careful not to drink too much – you can relax to the point that you lose control, and the consequences of that can be very unpleasant. If you are able to stick to moderation, there is no better time for a party!

The full moon is also the best time for advertising, as not only will your campaign be widely seen, people will be apt to remember it.

The full moon is also a favorable time for dates, and during this time, people are at their most open, romantic, and willing to tell each other something important that might take their relationship to the next level of trust and understanding.

Moreover, during the full moon, people feel a surge of energy, which may lead to hyperactivity, restlessness, and insomnia.

It will be harder to keep your emotions in check. You might face conflicts with friends, disasters, and accidents. During the full moon, any surgeries are **not a good idea**, as the risk of complications and bleeding is on the rise. Plastic surgery is also a bad idea, as swelling and bruises might be much worse than in another lunar phase. At the same time, the full moon is a good time to get an accurate diagnosis.

During this time, **try to limit your calories and liquid intake** (especially if you deal with bloating and excess weight), as your body is absorbing both calories and liquids faster during the full moon, and it can be very difficult to get rid of the weight later on.

Waning crescent moon

The full moon is over, and a new phase is beginning – the waning moon. This is a quieter time, when all of the jobs you started earlier are being partly or entirely completed (it all depends on the speed and scale).

Surgery will turn out much better if it is performed during the waning moon. Your recovery will be faster, and the likelihood of complications is much lower. If you have any plans to lose weight, the waning moon is the best time to do that. This is also a good time for quitting bad habits, such as smoking or cursing.

The waning moon can also be divided into the third and fourth quarters.

Third quarter - this is a favorable period, and you are able to resolve a lot of problems without conflict. People are calming down and ready to listen and take in information, while still being active. However, this is not the best time to begin any major projects, especially if you are unsure if you will be able to complete them by the start of the new lunar month.

The third quarter is a good time to get married, especially if the moon is in Cancer, Taurus, or Libra.

Fourth quarter – This is the most passive period of the lunar cycle. You are not as strong as usual. Your energy is lagging. You will be tired until reaching a new beginning. The best thing you can do as the lunar cycle comes to an end is to get things in order, and avoid anything that might get in your way at work or in personal relationships. Examine your successes and failures.

Now, let's discuss the lunar days in greater detail. For centuries, people around the world have described the influence of lunar days, and modern astrologers only add to this work, as they compare old texts to modern life.

The 1st lunar day

The first lunar day is extremely important for the rest of the lunar month. This is a much-needed day to carefully plan your activities and lay the groundwork for the rest of the lunar month. Remember that the first lunar day is not a good day for major activities, but rather for sitting down and planning things.

Avoid conflicts on this day, unless you want them to overshadow the rest of the month. Try to see the positive side of things and imagine that the lunar month will bring you good things both at work and in love. The more vividly you can imagine this, the sooner your desires will come to fruition. Perhaps it would be a good idea to jot down plans that will bring you closer to achieving your dreams. This is the best time for both manifesting and making wishes!

This is also a favorable day when it comes to seeking a new job or starting an academic program.

It is fine to go out on a date on the first lunar day, but limit any sexual contact, as your energy levels are low, and you are likely to end up disappointed.

Getting married on the first lunar day is not recommended.

Avoid getting a haircut – there are many indications that cutting your hair on the first lunar day will have a negative effect on your health and life expectancy.

Under no circumstances should you undergo any major cosmetic procedures, including plastic surgery. Energy levels are low, your skin is dull and almost stagnant. The results will not live up to your expectations, and in the worst-case scenario, you will end up looking worse than before. It is common for cosmetic procedures performed on this day to be disappointing or even useless. Even the best surgeons are less capable.

Your good dreams on the first lunar day foretell happiness and joy. Bad ones usually do not come true.

The 2nd lunar day.

This is considered a lucky day, and is symbolized by a cornucopia. It is not an exaggeration to say that the second lunar day is a favorable time for both work and love. It is a time for action, and a great period to work on yourself, look for a new job, start something new, or complete any financial transaction, whether a sale or purchase. This is also a great time for creative and scientific insights, and a good time for any meeting – whether political or romantic.

Any romantic dates or sexual encounters during the second lunar day are unlikely to disappoint. This is also a good day for weddings or taking a trip with someone special.

During the second lunar day, the moon is beginning its waxing phase, which is a good time for anything you might to do nourish and restore your skin. This is a great time for any cosmetic procedures aimed at preservation, though it is best to put off any plastic surgery until the waning moon. If that is not possible, then the second lunar day is acceptable, if not ideal, and you will not run into any complications.

Folklore tells us that this is not a good day for a haircut, as that may lead to arguments with a loved one.

This is the best time for exercise – your body is in good shape, and you are able to handle new exercise regimens. If the moon happens to be in Scorpio, though, be careful.

This is a good day for anything positive, but avoid any conflicts, discussions about the status of your relationship, or litigation.

Dreams of the second lunar day are usually not prophetic.

The 3rd lunar day.

On this day, we are usually able to make out a thin sliver of the lunar crescent. It is a longstanding tradition to show money during the new month – it is believed that as the moon grows, so will your savings.

However, astrological systems around the world consider this an unlucky, unfavorable day. It is not a good idea to travel, begin any new business, or give into your bad mood.

You might run into many a lot of problems at work on this day, which will cause you a lot of anxiety. However, it is a good day to take a step back and identify and set about fixing any flaws and shortcomings. Remember that everything tends to look worse on this day than it actually is.

It is not the time to ask management for anything – you are likely to walk away disappointed, and end up unfairly reprimanded rather than receiving a promotion or raise. Instead, focus on areas of work that need to be smoothed over or studied further. It will be clear what problems you are facing, and you will easily be able to find a remedy.

Do not rush to criticize your loved ones – things may not be as they appear. "Measure twice and cut once" is your motto on this day.

This is not a good day to get married, as the couple is likely to have a turbulent, short-lived marriage.

You can schedule a cosmetic procedure for this day, but only if it is relatively minor. Plastic surgery should wait.

Do exercises as usual, without overdoing it or adding any new routines.

Dreams on this day do not mean anything.

The 4th lunar day.

These are relatively neutral days, in that they are unlikely to bring anything bad, but they also will not bring you any windfalls. The fourth lunar day is symbolized by a tree of paradise, the tree of knowledge, and the choice between good and evil. Things ultimately depend on us and our final decisions.

This is a great day for anything money-related – signing contracts, agreements, or even taking on credit. There are also a lot of contradictions on this day – on one hand, we are likely to receive money, which is a good thing, but on the other, we will have to give some of it away, which is never particularly fun or pleasant. There is good reason to consider all of your opportunities and possibilities before acting.

It is not a good day to get married, as the wedding will not be as fun as you had hoped. However, the fourth lunar day is, in fact, a good day for sex and conceiving a healthy child.

Be careful on this day if you happen to engage in any physical exercise, as it is not a good idea to overeat or abuse alcohol. Take care of yourself. Any illnesses which began on this day may be extremely dangerous, if they are not dealt with immediately.

Cosmetic procedures are not contraindicated, as long as they are to preserve your appearance. Plastic surgery can be performed if you truly feel it is necessary.

However, avoid getting a haircut, as it is unlikely to grow back healthily, and will become brittle and dull. However, if the moon is in Leo, you can disregard this advice.

Dreams may turn out to be real.

The 5th lunar day.

Traditionally, the fifth lunar day is one of the worst of the lunar month. It is symbolized by a unicorn. Unicorns need to be tamed, but only a virgin is capable of doing so. Many people will feel drained on this day, or frustrated with themselves, those around them, and life in general.

Try to avoid arguments- any conflicts are likely to drag out for a long time, and then you may be overcome with guilt. This advice is relevant for both work and love.

Sexual encounters may be pleasant, but this is not a good day to plan a wedding, as it is likely to lead to a marriage full of unpleasant incidents.

Do not start any new businesses, or ask those around you for favors- you may be misunderstood and rejected.

It is fine to engage in physical exercise, but if you overdo it on this day, you may injure yourself.

Your energy levels are low. Cosmetic procedures may not be effective, and avoid any plastic surgeries.

It is good if you dream something connected with the road, trips or with movement in general. A bad dream might be a sign of a health problem which should be addressed.

The 6th lunar day.

The symbol of the sixth lunar day is a cloud and a crane. This is a philosophical combination that suggests that it is not worth rushing things on these days. This is a very positive, lucky day for both work and love. Creative work will be especially successful, as will any attempts at opening a new business in your field.

The sixth lunar day is a good time for resolving any financial matters. There is one limitation, however – do not give anyone a loan, as they may not pay it back. But you can certainly sponsor and support those who are more vulnerable than you.

This day is a good time to go on a trip, whether close to home or far away.

This is also a good day for dates, weddings, and marriage proposals. Remember that energy is more romantic than sexual, so it is better to give the gift of roses and a bottle of champagne than hot, passionate sex.

It is a good idea to get some exercise, but do not overdo things, though you will probably not want to, either.

Cosmetic procedures will be successful, and you can even have plastic surgery performed, so long as the moon is not in Scorpio.

It is still a good idea to avoid getting your hair cut, as you might "cut off" something good in addition to your hair.

It is better to not discuss dreams as they are usually true. Your dreams of this day can remind you of something that needs to be completed as soon as possible.

The 7th lunar day.

This is also a favorable lunar day, and it is symbolized by a fighting cock, which is an Avestan deity. Avoid any aggression on this day, and instead work on yourself, spend time at home or in nature. Avoid discussing the status of your relationship with anyone, arguing, or wishing bad things on anyone. Everything will come back to haunt you, remember, silence is golden.

Business negotiations and contracts will be successful. You can find support, sponsors, and people ready to help you in both words and deeds.

Lighten up with your colleagues and subordinates. Pay attention not only to their shortcomings, but also to their skills. This is a good day for reconciliation and creating both political and romantic unions.

The seventh lunar day is good for traveling, no matter how near or far from home.

It is also a favorable time for love and marriage.

Exercise moderately, and any plastic surgeries will go very smoothly, as long as the moon is not in Scorpio.

Dreams of this day may become a reality.

The 8th lunar day.

The symbol for this day is a Phoenix, which symbolizes eternal rebirth and renewal, because this day is a great time for changes in all areas of your life. Your energy is likely to be high, and you want to do something new and unusual. This is a good time to look for a new job or begin studying something. Any out-of-the-box thinking is welcome, along with shaking things up a bit in order to improve your life.

However, avoid any financial transactions, as you may incur losses.

Avoid aggression. You can share your opinion by presenting well-founded arguments and facts, instead.

The phoenix rises from the ashes, so this is a good time to be careful with electrical appliances and fire in general. The risk of housefires is high.

Avoid any major financial transactions on the eighth day, as you may end up facing a series of complications. You can pay people their salaries, as this is unlikely to be a large sum.

This is a good day for weddings, but only if you and your future spouse are restless, creative souls and hope to achieve personal development through your marriage.

Any cosmetic procedures and plastic surgeries will go well today, as they are related to rebirth and renewal. Surgeons may find that they are true artists on this day!

You can try to change your hairstyle and get a fashionable haircut on this day.

You can trust your dreams seen on this day.

The 9th lunar day.

The ninth lunar day is not particularly auspicious, and is even referred to as "Satan's" day. You may be overcome with doubt, suspicions, even depression and conflicts.

Your self-esteem will suffer, so don't overdo things physically, and avoid overeating or abusing alcohol.

This is a negative day for any business deals, travel, or financial transactions.

This is a particularly bad day for any events, so keep your head down at work and avoid any new initiatives.

It is better to avoid getting married on "Satan's" day, as the marriage will not last very long. Avoid sex, as well, but you can take care of your partner, listen them, and support them however they need.

Any cosmetic procedures will not have a lasting effect, and avoid any plastic surgery. A haircut will not turn out as you hoped.

Dreams of this day are usually prophetic.

The 10th lunar day.

This is one of the luckiest days of the lunar month. It is symbolized by a spring, mushroom, or phallus. This is a time for starting a new business, learning new things, and creating.

The 10th lunar day is particularly lucky for business. Networking and financial transactions will be a success and bring hope. This is an ideal time for changing jobs, shifting your business tactics, and other renewals.

This is a perfect time for people in creative fields and those working in science, who may come up with incredible ideas that will bring many successful returns.

This is a very successful day for building a family and proposing marriage. This is a good time for celebrations and communication, so plan parties, meet with friends, and plan a romantic date.

One of the symbols for this day is a phallus, so sexual encounters are likely to be particularly satisfying.

The 10th lunar day is the best time to begin repairs, buying furniture, and items for home improvement.

You can exercise vigorously, and cosmetic procedures and plastic surgery will be very effective.

Dreams of this day will not come true.

The 11th lunar day.

This is one of the best lunar days, and seen as the pinnacle of the lunar cycle. People are likely to be energetic, enthusiastic, and ready to move forward toward their goals.

The 11th lunar day is very successful for any financial transactions or business deals and meetings.

You might actively make yourself known, approach management to discuss a promotion, or look for a new job. This is an auspicious time for advertising campaigns, performances, and holding meetings.

Any trips planned will be a great success, whether near or far from home.

Romantic relationships are improving, sex is harmonious, and very desired.

Weddings held on this day will be fun, and the marriage will be a source of joy and happiness.

Exercise is a great idea, and you might even beat your own personal record.

This is an ideal time for any cosmetic procedures, but any more serious plastic surgeries might lead to a lot of bruising and swelling.

A haircut will turn out as you had hoped, and you can experiment a bit with your appearance.

You can ignore dreams of this day – usually they do not mean anything.

The 12th lunar day.

This day is symbolized by the Grail and a heart. As we move closer to the full moon, our emotions are at their most open. During this time, if you ask someone for something, your request will be heeded. This is a day of faith, goodness, and divine revelations.

For business and financial transactions, this is not the most promising day. However, if you help others on this day, your good deeds are sure to come back to you.

This is a day for reconciliation, so do not try to explain your relationships, as no one is at fault, and it is better to focus on yourself, anyway.

Avoid weddings and sex on this day, but if you want to do what your partner asks, there is no better time.

Many may feel less than confident and cheerful during this day, so take it easy when working out. Avoid overeating, stay hydrated, and avoid alcohol.

The 12th lunar day is not the best for getting married or having sex, but the stars would welcome affection and a kind word.

Avoid getting a haircut, or any plastic surgeries. This is a neutral day for minor cosmetic procedures.

Nearly all dreams will come true.

The 13th lunar day.

This day is symbolized by Samsara, the wheel of fate, which is very erratic and capable of moving in any direction. This is why the 13th lunar day is full of contradictions. In Indian traditions, this day is compared to a snake eating its own tail. This is a day for paying off old debts and returning to unfinished business.

Avoid beginning any new business on this day. It is preferable to finish old tasks and proofread your work. Information you receive on this day may not be reliable and must be verified.

It is worth resolving financial problems very carefully, and avoid arguments and conflict.

Do not change jobs on this day or go to a new place for the first time. Do not sit at home alone, though, go see old friends, parents, or older family members.

Minor cosmetic procedures are welcome on this day, but avoid any plastic surgery, as you may experience major swelling and bruising. Avoid any haircuts, too.

As a rule, all dreams will come true.

The 14th lunar day.

It's a full moon! The 14th lunar day is one of the happiest, and it is symbolized by the trumpet. Pay attention – you may run into new, much-needed information. Networking will be successful, and you can confidently sign agreements, meet with people, and attend fun gatherings or other leisure activities. This is one of the best days for advertising, performances, and concerts, and those working in creative professions should keep this in mind, as should those who work in politics. Do not sit in place on this day – you need to get out and see others, make new connections, and try to be visible.

This is one of the best days for communication with and making requests from management, as your initiatives will be noticed and welcome. You might talk about a promotion, raise, or something similarly related to professional growth.

Couples will see their relationship is moving along well on this day, and it is also a good day for getting married.

Any sex on this day will be vigorous and memorable for a long time. The full moon is the best time for conceiving a child.

Any cosmetic procedures will be effective, but avoid any major changes to your appearance, as there is a high likelihood of bleeding and bruising. A haircut will turn out well.

Your dreams of this day will be more or less doubtful.

The 15th lunar day.

It's a full moon! This day is symbolized by a serpent of fire. This is the energy peak of the entire lunar cycle, and a lot will depend on where you are focusing your energy.

You might face a lot of temptations on this day, for example, you might tell someone else's secret or your own to others, and come to regret it for a long time. The stars suggest exercising restraint in both your words and actions, as the 15th day of the lunar cycle is a day of deception and weaknesses.

This is a very active time, and many people might take unnecessary risks. This is not the best day for signing any agreements or contracts. For any performances, concerts, or advertising, however, this is one of the best days of the month.

You can get married on the 15th day, but only if you know each other well and have carefully considered your partnership, without any hasty decisions. This is also a favorable day for a second marriage.

Your romantic relationship is looking wonderful – you are on cloud 9, writing poetry, and deeply convinced of how right your partner is for you – and they feel the same way. It is important that this does not suddenly lead to an abrupt disappointment.

Avoid getting any haircuts on the 15th day of the month, as you may end up with a headache.

Conservative cosmetic procedures and creams will be very effective, but avoid any injections or plastic surgery today. Bleeding, swelling, and bruising are all but guaranteed.

Dreams on the 15th day nearly always come true.

The 16th lunar day.

This day is symbolized by a dove. The full moon is over, and the moon is now in its waning phase. Usually, after the turbulent days of the full moon, people feel a bit under the weather. They are not cheerful, and want to avoid excess worry and give themselves a chance to breathe.

Don't ignore your body's wishes, take it easy with physical activities, and take some time for yourself. You might spend time in nature, in the forest, or at a country home.

The 16th day of the lunar month is a time for moderation in all areas – your behavior, eating, and even in your clothes. If you overate during the full moon period, now is the time to diet a bit or at least avoid fatty foods and meat.

This is not a promising day for resolving any financial matters. Keep your documents in order and get ready for any future meetings, instead. If you help a loved one, your good deed will come back 100 times over.

Avoid getting married today, as well as sex.

Cosmetic procedures are likely to be a success, especially if they are related to cleansing your skin, but it is best to avoid any plastic surgery or injections. Your body is not ready to accept them. A haircut will turn out as you hoped.

Any dreams are likely to come true, but that also depends on a correct interpretation.

The 17th lunar day.

This day is represented by a vine and bell. It is a happy day and both successful and fun-filled. It is also a good time for negotiations, concluding small business deals, shaking up staffing, and creativity. However, you should keep in mind that the 17th day is only favorable for minor business, and you should avoid starting any major events.

Avoid any major financial transactions on this day. Do not give anyone money as a loan or borrow anything yourself, either.

Any travel, whether for business or pleasure, is likely to be a success.

The 17th day is a great time to get married, and an ideal day for dates. Any sexual encounters will bring you happiness and joy.

Avoid getting your hair cut on this day, but cosmetic procedures and plastic surgery will be a success. Women will look better than usual.

Your dreams are likely to come true in three days.

The 18th lunar day.

This day is represented by a mirror. It is a difficult, and generally unpromising day, too. Just as the mirror reflects our imperfections back to us, we need to remember that moderation and modesty are key.

The 18th day is not a favorable time for any business meetings or financial transactions. You can, however work on jobs you already began. It is, however, a positive day for those who work in research or the creative fields.

Your motto of the day is to keep a cool head when it comes to your opportunities and the opportunities of those around you. This is relevant for both work and romantic relationships. It is not a good time to criticize others – any conflicts or arguments may lead to lasting consequences, which you do not need.

Avoid getting married on this day, as well as sexual encounters, which are likely to be disappointing. It is a good time to take a trip together, which will only be good for your relationship.

Avoid getting your hair cut, though this is a relatively neutral day for a haircut, which might turn out well, and though it will not exceed your expectations, it will also not leave you upset. Avoid any plastic surgeries.

Dreams on this day will come true.

The 19th lunar day.

This is a very difficult day and it is represented by a spider. The energy is complicated, if not outright dangerous. Don't panic or get depressed, though – this is a test of your strength, and if you are able to hold onto all you have achieved. This is relevant for both work and love. On the 19th day, you should avoid taking any trips.

The energy of the 19th lunar day is very unfavorable for beginning any major projects, and business in general. Work on what you started earlier, get your affairs in order, think over your ideas and emotions, and check to make sure that everything you have done hitherto is living up to your expectations. Do not carry out any financial transactions or take out any loans – do not loan anyone else money, either. Do not ask your managers for anything as they are unlikely to listen to what you have to say, and make judgments instead.

This is a day when you might face outright deception, so do not take any risks and ignore rumors. Do not work on anything related to real estate or legal matters.

This is a very hard time for people with an unbalanced psyche, as they may experience sudden exacerbations or even suicidal ideations.

This is a very unlucky day to get married. Sexual encounters might be disappointing and significantly worsen your relationship.

Avoid any haircuts or cosmetic procedures or surgeries.

Your dreams of this day will come true.

The 20th lunar day.

This is also a difficult day, though less so than the 19th. It is represented by an eagle. This is a good time to work on your own development and spiritual growth, by speaking to a psychologist or astrologer.

Avoid pride, anger, arrogance, and envy.

The 20th lunar day is a good time for people who are active and decisive. They will be able to easily overcome any obstacles, flying over them just like an eagle. If you have to overcome your own fears, you will be able to do so – don't limit yourself, and you will see that there is nothing to be afraid of. It is a good day for any financial transactions, signing contracts, and reaching agreements, as well as networking.

The 20th lunar day is a favorable time for those who work in the creative fields, as they will be able to dream up the idea that will open up a whole host of new possibilities. Avoid conflicts – they may ruin your relationship with a lot of people, and it will not be easy to come back from that.

This is a lucky day for getting married, but only if you have been with your partner for several years, now. Sexual encounters will not be particularly joyful, but they also will not cause you any problems.

Avoid getting your hair cut, but you can certainly get it styled. The 20th lunar day is a good day for those who are looking to lose weight. You will be able to do so quickly, and it will be easy for you to follow a diet.

Cosmetic procedures will be a success, as will any plastic surgeries.

Pay attention to dreams of this day as they are likely to come true.

The 21st lunar day.

This is one of the most successful days of the lunar month, and it is symbolized by a herd of horses – imagine energy, strength, speed, and bravery. Everything you think up will happen quickly, and you will be able to easily overcome obstacles. A mare is not only brave but also an honest animal, so you will only experience this luck if you remember that honesty is always the best policy.

This is also a favorable day for business. Reaching new agreements and signing contracts, or dealing with foreign partners – it is all likely to be a success. Any financial issues will be resolved successfully.

Those in the creative world will be able to show off their talent and be recognized for their work. Anyone involved in the performing arts can expect success, luck, and recognition. A galloping herd of horses moves quickly, so you might transition to a new job, move to a new apartment, or go on a business trip or travel with your better half.

The 21st lunar day is one of the best to get married or have a sexual encounter.

This is a great time for athletes, hunters, and anyone who likes adventurous activities.

But for criminals and thieves, this is not a lucky or happy day – they will quickly be brought to justice.

Any haircuts or cosmetic procedures are likely to be a huge success and bring both beauty and happiness. You will recover quickly after any surgeries, perhaps without any swelling or bruising at all.

Dreams tend to not be reliable.

The 22nd lunar day.

This day will be strange and contradictory. It is symbolized by the elephant Ganesha. According to Indian mythology, Ganesha is the patron saint of hidden knowledge. so this is a favorable day for anyone who is trying to learn more about the world and ready to find the truth, though this is often seen as a hopeless endeavor. This is a day for philosophers and wisemen and women. However, it is an inauspicious day for business, and unlikely to lead to resolving financial issues, signing contracts, agreements, or beginning new projects. You can expect trouble at work.

For creative people, and new employees, this is a successful day.

This is a good day for apologies and reconciliation.

Avoid getting married, though you can feel free to engage in sexual encounters.

For haircuts and cosmetic procedures, this is a fantastic day. Surgeries will also turn out, as long as the moon is not in Scorpio.

Dreams will come true.

The 23rd lunar day.

This is a challenging day represented by a crocodile, which is a very aggressive animal. This is a day of strong energy, but it is also adventurous and tough. Your main task is to focus your energy in the right direction. There may be accidents, arguments, conflicts, fights, and violence, which is why it is important to strive for balance and calm.

Keep a close eye on your surroundings – there may be traitors or people who do not wish you well, so be careful.

However, this is still a favorable day for business – many problems will be resolved successfully. You are able to sign contracts and receive credit successfully, as long as you remain active and decisive in what you do.

This is not a day for changing jobs or working on real estate transactions or legal proceedings. This is not a favorable day for traveling, no matter how near or far you plan on going.

This is not a promising day to get married – things may end in conflict, if not an all-out brawl.

Sexual relations are not off the table, as long as the couple trusts one another.

Haircuts or cosmetic procedures will not turn out as you had hoped, so avoid them.

Dreams during this lunar day usually mean something opposite of what awaits you, so you can disregard them.

The 24th lunar day.

This is a neutral, calm day that is symbolized by a bear. It is favorable for forgiveness and reconciliation.

This is also a good day for learning new things, reading, self-development, and taking time to relax in nature.

This is a great day for any type of financial activity, conferences, academic meetings, and faraway travel.

The 24th lunar day is a good time for love and getting married, as any marriage will be strong and lasting.

Cosmetic procedures and plastic surgery will be a success, and you can expect a speedy recovery.

Avoid getting a haircut on this day, however, as your hair will likely thin and grow back slowly.

Dreams of this lunar day are usually connected with your personal life.

The 25th lunar day.

This is still another quiet day, symbolized by a turtle.

Just like a turtle, this is not a day to rush, and it is best to sit down and take stock of your life. This is a good time for resolving any personal problems, as the moon's energy makes it possible for you to calm down and find the right path.

This is also not a bad day for business. It is believed that any business you begin on this day is sure to be a success. This is especially the case for trade and any monetary activities.

The 25th lunar day is not a good day to get married, especially if the couple is very young.

This is a neutral day for sexual encounters, as the moon is waning, energy is low, so the decision is yours.

Avoid any cosmetic procedures, except those for cleansing your skin. This is not a favorable day for haircuts or plastic surgery – unless the moon is in Libra or Leo.

You can have a prophetic dream on this day.

The 26th lunar day.

The 26th lunar day is full of contradictions and complicated. It is represented by a toad.

It is not time to start or take on something new, as nothing good will come of it. Avoid any major purchases, as you will later come to see that your money was wasted. The best thing you can do on this day is stay at home and watch a good movie or read a good book.

Avoid traveling on this day, as it may not turn out well.

The 26th lunar day is a negative day for any business negotiations and starting new businesses. Do not complete any business deals or financial transactions. Your colleagues may be arguing, and your managers may be dissatisfied. But if you have decided to leave your job, there is no better time to do so.

This is not a good day to get married, as both partners' expectations may fall flat, and they will soon be disappointed.

The waning moon carries a negative charge, so avoid any haircuts and surgeries, though you can get cosmetic procedures if they are relatively minor.

Your dreams will come true.

The 27th lunar day.

The 27th lunar day is one of the best days of the month, and it is represented by a ship. You can boldly start any new business, which is sure to be promising. This is a great day for students, teachers, and learning new things. Any information that comes to you on this day may be extremely valuable and useful to you.

The 27th day is good for communication and travel, whether near or far from home, and no matter whether it is for work or pleasure.

This is also a good day for any professional activities or financial transactions. If there are people around you who need help, you must support them, as your good deeds will come back 100-fold.

Romantic dates will go well, though any weddings should be quiet and subdued. This is a particularly good day for older couples or second marriages.

The waning moon means that hair will grow back very slowly, but in general, you can expect a haircut to turn out well. This is a great day for plastic surgery or cosmetic procedures, as the results will be pleasing, and you will have a speedy recovery, without any bruising or swelling, most of the time.

However, beware if the moon is in Scorpio on this day – that is not a good omen for any plastic surgery.

Do not pay any attention to dreams on this day.

The 28th lunar day.

This is another favorable day in the waning moon cycle, and it is represented by a lotus. This is a day of wisdom and spiritual awakening. If possible, spend part of the day in nature. It is important to take stock of the last month and decide what you need to do during its two remaining days.

This is a good time for any career development, changing jobs, conducting business, decision-making, and signing agreements, as well as going on a trip. You might conclude any business deal, hold negotiations, work with money and securities.

This is also a good day for any repairs or improvements around your home or apartment.

Any weddings today should be subdued and modest, and restricted to family members only. A loud, raucous wedding might not turn out very well.

Your hair will grow slowly, but any haircuts will turn out very elegant and stylish. Cosmetic procedures and surgeries are not contraindicated. You will recover quickly with little bruising and swelling.

Do not take any dreams too seriously.

The 29th lunar day.

This is one of the most difficult days of the lunar month, and it is considered a Satanic day, unlucky for everyone and everything. It is symbolized by an octopus.

This is a dark day, and many will feel melancholy, depression, and a desire to simply be left alone. This is a day full of conflict and injuries, so be careful everywhere and with everyone. If you can, avoid any travel, and be particularly careful when handling any sharp objects. Do not engage in any business negotiations, sign any contracts, or take part in any networking.

Astrologers believe that anything you start on this day will completely fall apart. For once and for all, get rid of things that are impeding you from living your life. This is a good time to avoid people who you do find unpleasant.

This is also a time for fasting and limitations for everyone. Do not hold any celebrations, weddings, or have sexual relations – these events may not turn out as you hoped, and instead bring you nothing but suffering and strife.

Avoid getting a haircut, as well, as it will not make you look more beautiful and your hair will come back lifeless and dull. Cosmetic procedures can go ahead, but avoid any surgeries.

Dreams are likely to be true.

The 30th lunar day.

There is not always a 30th lunar day, as some lunar months have only 29 days. This day is represented by a swan. The 30th lunar day is usually very short, and sometimes, it lasts less than an hour. This is a time for forgiveness and calm.

You might take stock of the last month, while also avoiding anything you do not need around you. Pay back loans, make donations, reconcile with those who recently offended you, and stop speaking to people who cause you suffering.

This is a good time for tying up loose ends, and many astrologers believe that it is also a good day to start new business.

However, avoid celebrations or weddings on this day. Spouses will either not live long, or they will quickly grow apart.

Do not get a haircut on this day, though cosmetic procedures are possible, as long as you avoid any surgeries.

Dreams promise happiness and should come true.

A guide to Zodiac compatibility

Often, when we meet a person, we get a feeling that they are good and we take an instant liking to them. Another person, however, gives us immediate feelings of distrust, fear and hostility. Is there an astrological reason why people say that 'the first impression is the most accurate'? How can we detect those who will bring us nothing but trouble and unhappiness?

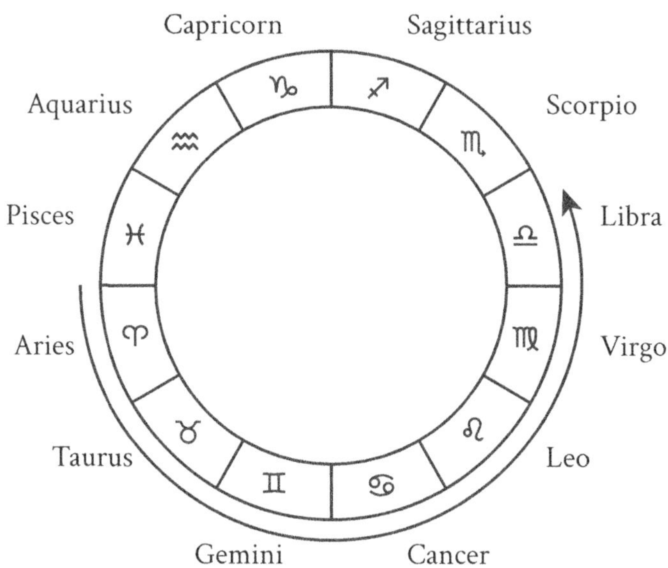

Without going too deeply into astrological subtleties unfamiliar to some readers, it is possible to determine the traits according to which friendship, love or business relationships will develop.

Let's begin with problematic relationships - our most difficult are with our **8th sign**. For example, for Aries the 8th sign is Scorpio, for Taurus it is Sagittarius and so on. Finding your 8th sign is easy; assume your own sign to be first (see above Figure) and then move eight signs counter clockwise around the Zodiac circle. This is also how the other signs (fourth, ninth and so on) that we mention are to be found.

Ancient astrologers variously referred to the 8th sign as the symbol of death, of destruction, of fated love or unfathomable attraction. In astrological terms, this pair is called 'master and slave' or 'boa constrictor and rabbit', with the role of 'master' or 'boa constrictor' being played by our 8th sign.

This relationship is especially difficult for politicians and business people.

We can take the example of a recent political confrontation in the USA. Hilary Clinton is a Scorpio while Donald Trump is a Gemini - her 8th sign. Even though many were certain that Clinton would be elected President, she lost.

To take another example, Hitler was a Taurus and his opponents – Stalin and Churchill - were both of his 8th sign, Sagittarius. The result of their confrontation is well known. Interestingly, the Russian Marshals who dealt crushing military blows to Hitler and so helped end the Third Reich - Konstantin Rokossovsky and Georgy Zhukov - were also Sagittarian, Hitler's 8th sign.

In another historical illustration, Lenin was also a Taurus. Stalin was of Lenin's 8th sign and was ultimately responsible for the downfall and possibly death of his one-time comrade-in-arms.

Business ties with those of our 8th sign are hazardous as they ultimately lead to stress and loss; both financial and moral. So, do not tangle with your 8th sign and never fight with it - your chances of winning are remote!

Such relationships are very interesting in terms of love and romance, however. We are magnetically attracted to our 8th sign and even though it may be very intense physically, it is very difficult for family life; 'Feeling bad when together, feeling worse when apart'.

As an example, let us take the famous lovers - George Sand who was Cancer and Alfred de Musset who was Sagittarius. Cancer is the 8th sign for Sagittarius, and the story of their crazy two-year love affair was the subject of much attention throughout France. Critics and writers were divided into 'Mussulist' and 'Sandist' camps; they debated fiercely about who was to blame for the sad ending to their love story - him or her. It's hard to imagine the energy needed to captivate the public for so long, but that energy was destructive for the couple. Passion raged in their hearts, but neither of them was able to comprehend their situation.

Georges Sand wrote to Musset, *"I don't love you anymore, and I will always adore you. I don't want you anymore, and I can't do without you. It seems that nothing but a heavenly lightning strike can heal me by destroying me. Good-bye! Stay or go, but don't say that I am not suffering. This is the only thing that can make me suffer even more, my love, my life, my blood! Go away, but kill me, leaving."* Musset replied only in brief, but its power surpassed Sand's tirade, *"When you embraced me, I felt something that is still bothering me, making it impossible for me to approach another woman."* These two people loved each other passionately and for two years lived together in a powder keg of passion, hatred and treachery.

When someone enters into a romantic liaison with their 8th sign, there will be no peace; indeed, these relationships are very attractive to those who enjoy the edgy, the borderline and, in the Dostoevsky style, the melodramatic. The first to lose interest in the relationship is, as a rule, the 8th sign.

If, by turn of fate, our child is born under our 8th sign, they will be very different from us and, in some ways, not live up to our expectations. It may be best to let them choose their own path.

In business and political relationships, the combination with our **12th sign** is also a complicated one.

We can take two political examples. Angela Merkel is a Cancer while Donald Trump is a Gemini - her 12th sign. This is why their relations are strained and complicated and we can even perhaps assume that the American president will achieve his political goals at her expense. Boris Yeltsin (Aquarius) was the 12th sign to Mikhail Gorbachev (Pisces) and it was Yeltsin who managed to dethrone the champion of Perestroika.

Even ancient astrologers noticed that our relationships with our 12th signs can never develop evenly; it is one of the most curious and problematic combinations. They are our hidden enemies and they seem to be digging a hole for us; they ingratiate themselves with us, discover our innermost secrets. As a result, we become bewildered and make mistakes when we deal with them. Among the Roman emperors murdered by members of their entourage, there was an interesting pattern - all the murderers were the 12th sign of the murdered.

We can also see this pernicious effect in Russian history: the German princess Alexandra (Gemini) married the last Russian Tsar Nicholas II (Taurus) - he was her 12th sign and brought her a tragic death. The wicked genius Grigory Rasputin (Cancer) made friends with Tsarina Alexandra, who was his 12th sign, and was murdered as a result of their odd friendship. The weakness of Nicholas II was exposed, and his authority reduced after the death of the economic and social reformer Pyotr Stolypin, who was his 12th sign. Thus, we see a chain of people whose downfall was brought about by their 12th sign.

So, it makes sense to be cautious of your 12th sign, especially if you have business ties. Usually, these people know much more about us than we want them to and they will often reveal our secrets for personal gain if it suits them. However, the outset of these relationships is, as a rule, quite normal - sometimes the two people will be friends, but sooner or later one will betray the other one or divulge a secret; inadvertently or not.

In terms of romantic relationships, our 12th sign is gentle, they take care of us and are tender towards us. They know our weaknesses well but accept them with understanding. It is they who guide us, although sometimes almost imperceptibly. Sexual attraction is usually strong.

For example, Meghan Markle is a Leo, the 12th sign for Prince Harry, who is a Virgo. Despite Queen Elizabeth II being lukewarm about the match, Harry's love was so strong that they did marry.

If a child is our 12th sign, it later becomes clear that they know all our secrets, even those that they are not supposed to know. It is very difficult to control them as they do everything in their own way.

Relations with our **7th sign** are also interesting. They are like our opposite; they have something to learn from us while we, in turn, have something to learn from them. This combination, in business and personal relationships, can be very positive and stimulating provided that both partners are quite intelligent and have high moral standards but if not, constant misunderstandings and challenges follow. Marriage or co-operation with the 7th sign can only exist as the union of two fully-fledged individuals and in this case love, significant business achievements and social success are possible.

However, the combination can be not only interesting, but also quite complicated.

An example is Angelina Jolie, a Gemini, and Brad Pitt, a Sagittarius. This is a typical bond with a 7th sign - it's lively and interesting, but rather stressful. Although such a couple may quarrel and even part from time to time, never do they lose interest in each other.

This may be why this combination is more stable in middle-age when there is an understanding of the true nature of marriage and partnership. In global, political terms, this suggests a state of eternal tension - a cold war - for example between Yeltsin (Aquarius) and Bill Clinton (Leo).

Relations with our **9th sign** are very good; they are our teacher and advisor - one who reveals things we are unaware of and our relationships with them very often involve travel or re-location. The combination can lead to spiritual growth and can be beneficial in terms of business.

Although, for example, Trump and Putin are political opponents, they can come to an understanding and even feel a certain sympathy for each other because Putin is a Libra while Trump is a Gemini, his 9th sign.

This union is also quite harmonious for conjugal and romantic relationships.

We treat our **3rd sign** somewhat condescendingly. They are like our younger siblings; we teach them and expect them to listen attentively. Our younger brothers and sisters are more often than not born under this sign. In terms of personal and sexual relationships, the union is not very inspiring and can end quickly, although this is not always the case. In terms of business, it is fairly average as it often connects partners from different cities or countries.

We treat our **5th sign** as a child and we must take care of them accordingly. The combination is not very good for business, however, since our 5th sign triumphs over us in terms of connections and finances, and thereby gives us very little in return save for love or sympathy. However, they are very good for family and romantic relationships, especially if the 5th sign is female. If a child is born as a 5th sign to their parents, their relationship will be a mutually smooth, loving and understanding one that lasts a lifetime.

Our **10th sign** is a born leader. Depending on the spiritual level of those involved, both pleasant and tense relations are possible; the relationship is often mutually beneficial in the good times but mutually disruptive in the bad times. In family relations, our 10th sign always tries to lead and will do so according to their intelligence and upbringing.

Our **4th sign** protects our home and can act as a sponsor to strengthen our financial or moral positions. Their advice should be heeded in all cases as it can be very effective, albeit very unobtrusive. If a woman takes this role, the relationship can be long and romantic, since all the spouse's wishes are usually met one way or another. Sometimes, such couples achieve great social success; for instance, Hilary Clinton, a Scorpio is the 4th sign to Bill Clinton, a Leo. On the other hand, if the husband is the 4th sign for his wife, he tends to be henpecked. There is often a strong sexual attraction. Our 4th sign can improve our living conditions and care for us in a parental way. If a child is our 4th sign, they are close to us and support us affectionately.

Relations with our **11th sign** are often either friendly or patronizing; we treat them reverently, while they treat us with friendly condescension. Sometimes, these relationships develop in an 'older brother' or 'high-ranking friend' sense; indeed, older brothers and sisters are often our 11th sign. In terms of personal and sexual relationships, our 11th sign is always inclined to enslave us. This tendency is most clearly manifested in such alliances as Capricorn and Pisces or Leo and Libra. A child who is the 11th sign to their parents will achieve greater success than their parents, but this will only make the parents proud.

Our **2nd sign** should bring us financial or other benefits; we receive a lot from them in both our business and our family life. In married couples, the 2nd sign usually looks after the financial situation for the benefit of the family. Sexual attraction is strong.

Our **6th sign** is our 'slave'; we always benefit from working with them and it's very difficult for them to escape our influence. In the event of hostility, especially if they have provoked the conflict, they receive a powerful retaliatory strike. In personal relations, we can almost destroy them by making them dance to our tune. For example, if a husband doesn't allow his wife to work or there are other adverse family circumstances, she gradually becomes lost as an individual despite being surrounded by care. This is the best-case scenario; worse outcomes are possible. Our 6th sign has a strong sexual attraction to us because we are the fatal 8th sign for them; we cool down quickly, however, and often make all kinds of demands. If the relationship with our 6th sign is a long one, there is a danger that routine, boredom and stagnation will ultimately destroy the relationship. A child born under our 6th sign needs particularly careful handling as they can feel fear or embarrassment when communicating with us. Their health often needs increased attention and we should also remember that they are very different from us emotionally.

Finally, we turn to relations with **our own sign**. Scorpio with Scorpio and Cancer with Cancer get along well, but in most other cases, however, our own sign is of little interest to us as it has a similar energy. Sometimes, this relationship can develop as a rivalry, either in business or in love.

There is another interesting detail - we are often attracted to one particular sign. For example, a man's wife and mistress often have the same sign. If there is confrontation between the two, the stronger character displaces the weaker one. As an example, Prince Charles is a Scorpio, while both Princess Diana and Camilla Parker Bowles were born under the sign of Cancer. Camilla was the more assertive and became dominant.

Of course, in order to draw any definitive conclusions, we need an individually prepared horoscope, but the above always, one way or another, manifests itself.

Love description of Zodiac Signs

We know that human sexual behavior has been studied at length. Entire libraries have been written about it, with the aim of helping us understand ourselves and our partners. But is that even possible? It may not be; no matter how smart we are, when it comes to love and sex, there is always an infinite amount to learn. But we have to strive for perfection, and astrology, with its millennia of research, twelve astrological types, and twelve zodiac signs, may hold the key. Below, you will find a brief and accurate description of each zodiac sign's characteristics in love, for both men and women.

Men

ARIES

Aries men are not particularly deep or wise, but they make up for it in sincerity and loyalty. They are active, even aggressive lovers, but a hopeless romantic may be lurking just below the surface. Aries are often monogamous and chivalrous men, for whom there is only one woman (of course, in her absence, they can sleep around with no remorse). If the object of your affection is an Aries, be sure to give him a lot of sex, and remember that for an Aries, when it comes to sex, anything goes. Aries cannot stand women who are negative or disheveled. They need someone energetic, lively, and to feel exciting feelings of romance.

The best partner for an Aries is Cancer, Sagittarius, or Leo. Aquarius can also be a good match, but the relationship will be rather friendly in nature. Partnering with a Scorpio or Taurus will be difficult, but they can be stimulating lovers for an Aries. Virgos are good business contacts, but a poor match as lovers or spouses.

TAURUS

A typical Taurean man is warm, friendly, gentle, and passionate, even if he doesn't always show it. He is utterly captivated by the beauty of the female body, and can find inspiration in any woman. A Taurus has such excess physical and sexual prowess, that to him, sex is a way to relax and calm down. He is the most passionate and emotional lover of the Zodiac, but he expects his partner to take the initiative, and if she doesn't, he will easily find someone else. Taureans rarely divorce, and are true to the end – if not sexually, at least spiritually. They are secretive, keep their cards close, and may have secret lovers. If a Taurus does not feel a deep emotional connection with someone, he won't be shy to ask her friends for their number. He prefers a voluptuous figure over an athletic or skinny woman.

The best partners for a Taurus are Cancer, Virgo, Pisces, or Scorpio. Sagittarius can show a Taurus real delights in both body and spirit, but they are unlikely to make it down the aisle. They can have an interesting relationship with an Aquarius – these signs are very different, but sometimes can spend their lives together. They might initially feel attracted to an Aries, before rejecting her.

GEMINI

The typical Gemini man is easygoing and polite. He is calm, collected, and analytical. For a Gemini, passion is closely linked to intellect, to the point that they will try to find an explanation for their actions before carrying them out. But passion cannot be explained, which scares a Gemini, and they begin jumping from one extreme to the other. This is why you will find more bigamists among Geminis than any other sign of the Zodiac. Sometimes, Gemini men even have two families, or divorce and marry several times throughout the course of their lives. This may be because they simply can't let new and interesting experiences pass them by. A Gemini's wife or lover needs to be smart, quick, and always looking ahead. If she isn't, he will find a new object for his affection.

Aquarians, Libras, and Aries make good partners for a Gemini. A Sagittarius can be fascinating for him, but they will not marry before he reaches middle age, as both partners will be fickle while they are younger. A Gemini and Scorpio are likely to be a difficult match, and the Gemini will try to wriggle out of the Scorpio's tight embrace. A Taurus will be an exciting sex partner, but their partnership won't be for long, and the Taurus is often at fault.

CANCER

Cancers tend to be deep, emotional individuals, who are both sensitive and highly sexual. Their charm is almost mystical, and they know how to use it. Cancers may be the most promiscuous sign of the Zodiac, and open to absolutely anything in bed. Younger Cancers look for women who are more mature, as they are skilled lovers. As they age, they look for someone young enough to be their own daughter, and delight in taking on the role of a teacher. Cancers are devoted to building a family and an inviting home, but once they achieve that goal, they are likely to have a wandering eye. They will not seek moral justification, as they sincerely believe it is simply something everyone does. Their charm works in such a way that women are deeply convinced they are the most important love in a Cancer's life, and that circumstances are the only thing preventing them from being together. Remember that a Cancer man is a master manipulator, and will not be yours unless he is sure you have throngs of admirers. He loves feminine curves, and is turned on by exquisite fragrances. Cancers don't end things with old lovers, and often go back for a visit after a breakup. Another type of Cancer is rarer – a faithful friend, and up for anything in order to provide for his wife and children. He is patriotic and a responsible worker.

Scorpios, Pisces, and other Cancers are a good match. A Taurus can make for a lasting relationship, as both signs place great value on family and are able to get along with one another. A Sagittarius will result in fights and blowouts from the very beginning, followed by conflicts and breakups. The Sagittarius will suffer the most. Marriage to an Aries isn't off the table, but it won't last very long.

LEO

A typical Leo is handsome, proud, and vain, with a need to be the center of attention at all times. They often pretend to be virtuous, until they are able to actually master it. They crave flattery, and prefer women who comply and cater to them. Leos demand unconditional obedience, and constant approval. When a Leo is in love, he is fairly sexual, and capable of being devoted and faithful. Cheap love affairs are not his thing, and Leos are highly aware of how expensive it is to divorce. They make excellent fathers. A Leo's partner needs to look polished and well-dressed, and he will not tolerate either frumpiness or nerds.

Aries, Sagittarius, and Gemini make for good matches. Leos are often very beguiling to Libras; this is the most infamous astrological "master-slave" pairing. Leos are also inexplicably drawn to Pisces – this is the only sign capable of taming them. A Leo and Virgo will face a host of problems sooner or later, and they might be material in nature. The Virgo will attempt to conquer him, and if she does, a breakup is inevitable.

VIRGO

Virgo is a highly intellectual sign, who likes to take a step back and spend his time studying the big picture. But love inherently does not lend itself to analysis, and this can leave Virgos feeling perplexed. While Virgo is taking his time, studying the object of his affection, someone else will swoop in and take her away, leaving him bitterly disappointed. Perhaps for that reason, Virgos tend to marry late, but once they are married, they remain true, and hardly ever initiate divorce. In bed, they are modest and reserved, as they see sex as some sort of quirk of nature, designed solely for procreation. Most Virgos have a gifted sense of taste, hearing, and smell. They cannot tolerate pungent odors and can be squeamish; they believe their partners should always take pains to be very clean. Virgos usually hate over-the-top expressions of love, and are immune to sex as a mean s of control. Many Virgos are stingy and more appropriate as husbands than lovers. Male Virgos tend to be monogamous, though if they are unhappy or disappointed with their partner, they may begin to look for comfort elsewhere and often give in to drunkenness.

Taurus, Capricorn, and Scorpio make the best partners for a Virgo. They may feel inexplicable attraction for Aquarians. They will form friendships with Aries, but rarely will this couple make it down the aisle. With Leos, be careful – this sign is best as a lover, not a spouse.

LIBRA

Libra is a very complex, wishy-washy sign. They are constantly seeking perfection, which often leaves them in discord with the reality around them. Libra men are elegant and refined, and expect no less from their partner. Many Libras treat their partners like a beautiful work of art, and have trouble holding onto the object of their affection. They view love itself as a very abstract concept, and can get tired of the physical aspect of their relationship. They are much more drawn to intrigue and the chase- dreams, candlelit evenings, and other symbols of romance. A high percentage of Libra men are gay, and they view sex with other men as the more elite option. Even when Libras are unhappy in their marriages, they never divorce willingly. Their wives might leave them, however, or they might be taken away by a more decisive partner.

Aquarius and Gemini make the best matches for Libras. Libra can also easily control an independent Sagittarius, and can easily fall under the influence of a powerful and determined Leo, before putting all his strength and effort into breaking free. Relationships with Scorpios are difficult; they may become lovers, but will rarely marry.

SCORPIO

Though it is common to perceive Scorpios as incredibly sexual, they are, in fact, very unassuming, and never brag about their exploits. They will, however, be faithful and devoted to the right woman. The Scorpio man is taciturn, and you can't expect any tender words from him, but he will defend those he loves to the very end. Despite his outward control, Scorpio is very emotional; he needs and craves love, and is willing to fight for it. Scorpios are incredible lovers, and rather than leaving them tired, sex leaves them feeling energized. They are always sexy, even if they aren't particularly handsome. They are unconcerned with the ceremony of wooing you, and more focused on the act of love itself.

Expressive Cancers and gentle, amenable Pisces make the best partners. A Scorpio might also fall under the spell of a Virgo, who is adept at taking the lead. Sparks might fly between two Scorpios, or with a Taurus, who is perfect for a Scorpio in bed. Relationships with Libras, Sagittarians, and Aries are difficult.

SAGITTARIUS

Sagittarian men are lucky, curious, and gregarious. Younger Sagittarians are romantic, passionate, and burning with desire to experience every type of love. Sagittarius is a very idealistic sign, and in that search for perfection, they tend to flit from one partner to another, eventually forgetting what they were even looking for in the first place. A negative Sagittarius might have two or three relationships going on at once, assigning each partner a different day of the week. On the other hand, a positive Sagittarius will channel his powerful sexual energy into creativity, and take his career to new heights. Generally speaking, after multiple relationships and divorces, the Sagittarian man will conclude that his ideal marriage is one where his partner is willing to look the other way.

Aries and Leo make the best matches for a Sagittarius. He might fall under the spell of a Cancer, but would not be happy being married to her. Gemini can be very intriguing, but will only make for a happy marriage after middle age, when both partners are older and wiser. Younger Sagittarians often marry Aquarian women, but things quickly fall apart. Scorpios can make for an interesting relationship, but if the Sagittarius fails to comply, divorce is inevitable.

CAPRICORN

Practical, reserved Capricorn is one of the least sexual signs of the Zodiac. He views sex as an idle way to pass the time, and something he can live without, until he wants to start a family. He tends to marry late, and almost never divorces. Young Capricorns are prone to suppressing their sexual desires, and only discover them later in life, when they have already achieved everything a real man needs – a career and money. We'll be frank – Capricorn is not the best lover, but he can compensate by being caring, attentive, and showering you with valuable gifts. Ever cautious, Capricorn loves to schedule his sexual relationships, and this is something partners will just have to accept. Women should understand that Capricorn needs some help relaxing – perhaps with alcohol. They prefer inconspicuous, unassuming women, and run away from a fashion plate.

The best partners for a Capricorn are Virgo, Taurus, or Scorpio. Cancers might catch his attention, and if they marry, it is likely to be for life. Capricorn is able to easily dominate Pisces, and Pisces-Capricorn is a well-known "slave and master" combination. Relationships with Leos tend to be erratic, and they are unlikely to wed. Aries might make for a cozy family at first, but things will cool off quickly, and often, the marriage only lasts as long as Capricorn is unwilling to make a change in his life.

AQUARIUS

Aquarian men are mercurial, and often come off as peculiar, unusual, or aloof, and detached. Aquarians are turned on by anything novel or strange, and they are constantly looking for new and interesting people. They are stimulated by having a variety of sexual partners, but they consider this to simply be normal life, rather than sexually immoral. Aquarians are unique – they are more abstract than realistic, and can be cold and incomprehensible, even in close relationships. Once an Aquarius gets married, he will try to remain within the realm of decency, but often fails. An Aquarian's partners need uncommon patience, as nothing they do can restrain him. Occasionally, one might encounter another kind of Aquarius – a responsible, hard worker, and exemplary family man.

The best matches for an Aquarius are female fellow Aquarians, Libras, and Sagittarians. When Aquarius seeks out yet another affair, he is not choosy, and will be happy with anyone.

PISCES

Pisces is the most eccentric sign of the Zodiac. This is reflected in his romantic tendencies and sex life. Pisces men become very dependent on those with whom they have a close relationship. Paradoxically, they are simultaneously crafty and childlike when it comes to playing games, and they are easily deceived. As a double bodied sign, Pisces rarely marry just once, as they are very sexual, easily fall in love, and are constantly seeking their ideal. Pisces are very warm people, who love to take care of others and are inclined toward "slave-master" relationships, in which they are the submissive partner. But after catering to so many lovers, Pisces will remain elusive. They are impossible to figure out ahead of time – today, they might be declaring their love for you, but tomorrow, they may disappear – possibly forever! To a Pisces, love is a fantasy, illusion, and dream, and they might spend their whole lives in pursuit of it. Pisces who are unhappy in love are vulnerable to alcoholism or drug addiction.

Cancer and Scorpio make the best partners for a Pisces. He is also easily dominated by Capricorn and Libra, but in turn will conquer even a queen-like Leo. Often, they are fascinated by Geminis – if they marry, it will last a long time, but likely not forever. Relationships with Aries and Sagittarians are erratic, though initially, things can seem almost perfect.

Women

ARIES

Aries women are leaders. They are decisive, bold, and very protective. An Aries can take initiative and is not afraid to make the first move. Her ideal man is strong, and someone she can admire. But remember, at the slightest whiff of weakness, she will knock him off his pedestal. She does not like dull, whiny men, and thinks that there is always a way out of any situation. If she loves someone, she will be faithful. Aries women are too honest to try leading a double life. They are possessive, jealous, and not only will they not forgive those who are unfaithful, their revenge may be brutal; they know no limits. If you can handle an Aries, don't try to put her in a cage; it is best to give her a long leash. Periodically give her some space – then she will seek you out herself. She is sexual, and believe that anything goes in bed.

Her best partners are a Sagittarius or Leo. A Libra can make a good match after middle age, once both partners have grown wiser and settled down a bit. Gemini and Aquarius are only good partners during the initial phase, when everything is still new, but soon enough, they will lose interest in each other. Scorpios are good matches in bed, but only suitable as lovers.

TAURUS

Taurean women possess qualities that men often dream about, but rarely find in the flesh – they are soft, charming, practical, and reliable – they are very caring and will support their partner in every way. A Taurus is highly sexual, affectionate, and can show a man how to take pleasure to new heights. She is also strong and intense. If she is in love, she will be faithful. But when love fades away, she might find someone else on the side, though she will still fight to save her marriage, particularly if her husband earns good money. A Taurus will not tolerate a man who is disheveled or disorganized, and anyone dating her needs to always be on his toes. She will expect gifts, and likes being taken to expensive restaurants, concerts, and other events. If you argue, try to make the first peace offering, because a Taurus finds it very hard to do so – she might withdraw and ruminate for a long time. Never air your dirty laundry; solve all your problems one-on-one.

Scorpio, Virgo, Capricorn, and Cancer make the best matches. A relationship with an Aries or Sagittarius would be difficult. There is little attraction between a Taurus and a Leo, and initially Libras can make for a good partner in bed, but things will quickly cool off and fall apart. A Taurus and Aquarius make an interesting match – despite the difference in signs, their relationships are often lasting, and almost lifelong.

GEMINI

Gemini women are social butterflies, outgoing, and they easily make friends, and then break off the friendship, if people do not hold their interest. A Gemini falls in love hard, is very creative, and often fantasizes about the object of her affection. She is uninterested in sex without any attachment, loves to flirt, and, for the most part, is not particularly affectionate. She dreams of a partner who is her friend, lover, and a romantic, all at once. A Gemini has no use for a man who brings nothing to the table intellectually. That is a tall order, so Geminis often divorce and marry several times. Others simply marry later in life. Once you have begun a life together, do not try to keep her inside – she needs to travel, explore, socialize, attend events and go to the theater. She cannot tolerate possessive men, so avoid giving her the third degree, and remember that despite her flirtatious and social nature, she is, in fact, faithful – as long as you keep her interested and she is in love. Astrologists believe that Geminis do not know what they need until age 29 or 30, so it is best to hold off on marriage until then.

Leo and Libra make the best matches. A relationship with a Cancer is likely, though complex, and depends solely on the Cancer's affection. A Gemini and Sagittarius can have an interesting, dynamic relationship, but these are two restless signs, which might only manage to get together after ages 40-45, once they have had enough thrills out of life and learned to be patient. Relationships with a Capricorn are very difficult, and almost never happen. The honeymoon stage can be wonderful with a Scorpio, but each partner will eventually go their own way, before ending things. A Gemini and Pisces union can also be very interesting – they are drawn to each other, and can have a wonderful relationship, but after a while, the cracks start to show and things will fall apart. An Aquarius is also not a bad match, but they may have little sexual chemistry.

CANCER

Cancers can be divided into two opposing groups. The first includes a sweet and gentle creature who is willing to dedicate her life to her husband and children. She is endlessly devoted to her husband, especially if he makes a decent living and remains faithful. She views all men as potential husbands, which means it is dangerous to strike up a relationship with her if your intentions are not serious; she can be anxious and clingy, sensitive and prone to crying. It is better to break things to her gently, rather than directly spitting out the cold, hard truth. She wants a man who can be a provider, though she often earns well herself. She puts money away for a rainy day, and knows how to be thrifty, for the sake of others around her, rather than only for herself. She is an excellent cook and capable of building an inviting home for her loved ones. She is enthusiastic in bed, a wonderful wife, and a caring mother.

The second type of Cancer is neurotic, and capable of creating a living hell for those around her. She believes that the world is her enemy, and manages to constantly find new intrigue and machinations.

Another Cancer, Virgo, Taurus, Scorpio, and Pisces make the best matches. A Cancer can often fall in love with a Gemini, but eventually, things will grow complicated, as she will be exhausted by a Gemini's constant mood swings and cheating. A Cancer and Sagittarius will initially have passionate sex, but things will quickly cool off. A relationship with a Capricorn is a real possibility, but only later in life, as while they are young, they are likely to fight and argue constantly. Cancer can also have a relationship with an Aries, but this will not be easy.

LEO

Leos are usually beautiful or charming, and outwardly sexual. And yet, appearances can be deceiving – they are not actually that interested in sex. Leo women want to be the center of attention and men running after them boosts their self-esteem, but they are more interested in their career, creating something new, and success than sex. They often have high-powered careers and are proud of their own achievements. Their partners need to be strong; if a Leo feels a man is weak, she can carry him herself for a while- before leaving him. It is difficult for her to find a partner for life, as chivalrous knights are a dying breed, and she is not willing to compromise. If you are interested in a Leo, take the initiative, admire her, and remember that even a queen is still a woman. Timid men or tightwads need not apply. Leos like to help others, but they don't need a walking disaster in their life. If they are married and in love, they are usually faithful, and petty gossip isn't their thing. Leo women make excellent mothers, and are ready to give their lives to their children. Their negative traits include vanity and a willingness to lie, in order to make themselves look better.

Sagittarius, Aries, and Libra make the best matches. Leos can also have an interesting relationship with a Virgo, though both partners will weaken each other. Life with a Taurus will lead to endless arguments – both signs are very stubborn, and unwilling to give in. Leos and Pisces are another difficult pair, as she will have to learn to be submissive if she wants to keep him around. A relationship with a Capricorn will work if there is a common denominator, but they will have little sexual chemistry. Life with a Scorpio will be turbulent to say the least, and they will usually break up later in life.

VIRGO

Virgo women are practical, clever, and often duplicitous. Marrying one isn't for everyone. She is a neat freak to the point of annoying those around her. She is also an excellent cook, and strives to ensure her children receive the very best by teaching them everything, and preparing them for a bright future. She is also thrifty – she won't throw money around, and, in fact, won't even give it to her husband. She has no time for rude, macho strongmen, and is suspicious of spendthrifts. She will not be offended if you take her to a cozy and modest café rather than an elegant restaurant. Virgos are masters of intrigue, and manage to outperform every other sign of the Zodiac in this regard. Virgos love to criticize everyone and everything; to listen to them, the entire world is simply a disaster and wrong, and only she is the exception to this rule. Virgos are not believed to be particularly sexual, but there are different variations when it comes to this. Rarely, one finds an open-minded Virgo willing to try anything, and who does it all on a grand scale – but she is rather the exception to this general rule.

The best matches for a Virgo are Cancer, Taurus, and Capricorn. She also can get along well with a Scorpio, but will find conflict with Sagittarius. A Pisces will strike her interest, but they will rarely make it down the aisle. She is often attracted to an Aquarius, but they would drive each other up the wall were they to actually marry. An Aries forces Virgo to see another side of life, but here, she will have to learn to conform and adapt.

LIBRA

Female Libras tend to be beautiful, glamorous, or very charming. They are practical, tactical, rational, though they are adept at hiding these qualities behind their romantic and elegant appearance. Libras are drawn to marriage, and are good at imagining the kind of partner they need. They seek out strong, well-off men and are often more interested in someone's social status and bank account than feelings. The object of their affection needs to be dashing, and have a good reputation in society. Libras love expensive things, jewelry, and finery. If they are feeling down, a beautiful gift will instantly cheer them up. They will not tolerate scandal or conflict, and will spend all their energy trying to keep the peace, or at least the appearance thereof. They do not like to air their dirty laundry, and will only divorce in extreme circumstances. They are always convinced they are right and react to any objections as though they have been insulted. Most Libras are not particularly sexual, except those with Venus or the Moon in Scorpio.

Leos, Geminis, and Aquarians make good matches. Libra women are highly attracted to Aries men – this is a real case of opposites attract. They can get along with a Sagittarius, though he will find that Libras are too proper and calm. Capricorn, Pisces, and Cancer are all difficult matches. Things will begin tumultuously with a Taurus, before each partner goes his or her own way.

SCORPIO

Scorpio women may appear outwardly restrained, but there is much more bubbling below the surface. They are ambitious with high self-esteem, but often wear a mask of unpretentiousness. They are the true power behind the scenes, the one who holds the family together, but never talk about it. Scorpios are strong-willed, resilient, and natural survivors. Often, Scorpios are brutally honest, and expect the same out of those around them. They do not like having to conform, and attempt to get others to adapt to them, as they honestly believe everyone will be better off that way. They are incredibly intuitive, and not easily deceived. They have an excellent memory, and can quickly figure out which of your buttons to push. They are passionate in bed, and their temperament will not diminish with age. When she is sexually frustrated, a Scorpio will throw all of her energy into her career or her loved ones. She is proud, categorical, and "if you don't do it right, don't do it at all" is her motto. Scorpio cannot be fooled, and she will not forgive any cheating. Will she cheat herself? Yes! But it will not break up her family, and she will attempt to keep it a secret. Scorpios are usually attractive to men, even if they are not particularly beautiful. They keep a low profile, though they always figure out their partner, and give them some invisible sign. There is also another, selfish type of Scorpio, who will use others for as long as they need them, before unceremoniously casting them aside.

Taurus is a good match; they will have excellent sexual chemistry and understand each other. Scorpio and Gemini are drawn to each other, but are unlikely to stay together long enough to actually get married. Cancer can be a good partner as well, but Cancers are possessive, while Scorpios do not like others meddling in their affairs, though they can later resolve their arguments in bed. Scorpio and Leo are often found together, but their relationship can also be very complicated. Leos are animated and chipper, while Scorpios, who are much deeper and more stubborn, see Leos as not particularly serious or reliable. One good example of this is Bill (a Leo) and Hillary (a Scorpio) Clinton. Virgo can also make a good partner, but when Scorpio seemingly lacks emotions, he will look for them elsewhere. Relationships with Lira are strange and very rare. Scorpio sees Libra as too insecure, and Libra does not appreciate Scorpio's rigidity. Two Scorpios together make an excellent marriage! Sagittarius and Scorpio are unlikely to get together, as she will think he is shallow and rude. If they do manage to get married, Scorpio's drive and persistence is the only thing that will make the marriage last. Capricorn is also not a bad match, and while Scorpio finds Aquarius attractive, they will rarely get married, as they are simply speaking different languages! Things are alright with a Pisces, as both signs are emotional, and Pisces can let Scorpio take the lead when necessary.

SAGITTARIUS

Sagittarius women are usually charming, bubbly, energetic, and have the gift of gab. They are kind, sincere, and love people. They are also straightforward, fair, and very ambitious, occasionally to the point of irritating those around them. But telling them something is easier than not telling them, and they often manage to win over their enemies. Sagittarius tends to have excellent intuition, and she loves to both learn and teach others. She is a natural leader, and loves taking charge at work and at home. Many Sagittarian women have itchy feet, and prefer all kinds of travel to sitting at home. They are not particularly good housewives – to be frank, cooking and cleaning is simply not for them. Their loved ones must learn to adapt to them, but Sagittarians themselves hate any pressure. They are not easy for men to handle, as Sagittarians want to be in charge. Sagittarius falls in love easily, is very sexual and temperamental, and may marry multiple times. Despite outward appearances, Sagittarius is a very lonely sign. Even after she is married with children, she may continue living as if she were alone; you might say she marches to the beat of her own drum. Younger Sagittarians can be reckless, but as they mature, they can be drawn to religion, philosophy, and the occult.

Aries and Leo make the best matches, as Sagittarius is able to bend to Leo's ways, or at least pretend to. Sagittarians often end up with Aquarians, but their marriages do not tend to be for the long haul. They are attracted to Geminis, but are unlikely to marry one until middle age, when both signs have settled down. Sagittarius and Cancer have incredible sexual chemistry, but an actual relationship between them would be tumultuous and difficult. Capricorn can make a good partner- as long as they are able to respect each other's quirks. Sagittarius rarely ends up with a Virgo, and while she may often meet Pisces, things are unlikely to go very far.

CAPRICORN

Capricorn women are conscientious, reliable, organized, and hard-working. Many believe that life means nothing but work, and live accordingly. They are practical, and not particularly drawn to parties or loud groups of people. But if someone useful will be there, they are sure to make an appearance. Capricorn women are stingy, but not as much as their male counterparts. They are critical of others, but think highly of themselves. Generally, they take a difficult path in life, but thanks to their dedication, perseverance, and willingness to push their own limits, they are able to forge their own path, and by 45 or 50, they can provide themselves with anything they could want. Capricorn women have the peculiarity of looking older than their peers when they are young, and younger than everyone else once they have matured. They are not particularly sexual, and tend to be faithful partners. They rarely divorce, and even will fight until the end, even for a failed marriage. Many Capricorns have a pessimistic outlook of life, and have a tendency to be depressed. They are rarely at the center of any social circle, but are excellent organizers. They have a very rigid view of life and love, and are not interested in a fling, as marriage is the end goal. As a wife, Capricorn is simultaneously difficult and reliable. She is difficult because of her strict nature and difficulty adapting. But she will also take on all the household duties, and her husband can relax, knowing his children are in good hands.

Taurus, Pisces, and Scorpio make good matches. Aries is difficult, once things cool off after the initial honeymoon. When a Capricorn meets another Capricorn, they will be each other's first and last love. Sagittarius isn't a bad match, but they don't always pass the test of time. Aquarius and Capricorn are a difficult match, and rarely found together. Things are too dull with a Virgo, and while Leo can be exciting at first, things will fall apart when he begins showing off. Libra and Aquarius are both difficult partners for Capricorn, and she is rarely found with either of them.

AQUARIUS

A female Aquarius is very different from her male counterparts. She is calm and keeps a cool head, but she is also affectionate and open. She values loyalty above all else, and is unlikely to recover from any infidelity, though she will only divorce if this becomes a chronic trend, and she has truly been stabbed in the back. She is not interested in her partner's money, but rather, his professional success. She is unobtrusive and trusting, and will refrain from listening in on her partner's phone conversations or hacking into his email. With rare exceptions, Aquarian women make terrible housewives. But they are excellent partners in life – they are faithful, never boring, and will not reject a man, even in the most difficult circumstances. Most Aquarians are highly intuitive, and can easily tell the truth from a lie. They themselves only lie in extreme situations, which call for a "white lie" in order to avoid hurting someone's feelings.

Aquarius gets along well with Aries, Gemini, and Libra. She can also have a good relationship with a Sagittarius. Taurus often makes a successful match, though they are emotionally very different; the same goes for Virgo. Aquarius and Scorpio, Capricorn, or Cancer is a difficult match. Pisces can make a good partner as well, as both signs complement each other. Any relationship with a Leo will be tumultuous, but lasting, as Leo is selfish, and Aquarius will therefore have to be very forgiving.

PISCES

Pisces women are very adaptable, musically inclined, and erotic. They possess an innate earthly wisdom, and a good business sense. Pisces often reinvent themselves; they can be emotional, soft, and obstinate, as well as sentimental, at times. Their behavioral changes can be explained by frequent ups and downs. Pisces is charming, caring, and her outward malleability is very attractive to men. She is capable of loving selflessly, as long as the man has something to love. Even if he doesn't, she will try and take care of him until the very end. Pisces' greatest fear is poverty. They are intuitive, vulnerable, and always try to avoid conflict. They love to embellish the truth, and sometimes alcohol helps with this. Rarely, one finds extremely unbalanced, neurotic and dishonest Pisces, who are capable of turning their loved ones' lives into a living Hell!

Taurus, Capricorn, Cancer, and Scorpio make the best matches. She will be greatly attracted to a Virgo, but a lasting relationship is only likely if both partners are highly spiritual. Any union with a Libra is likely to be difficult and full of conflict. Pisces finds Gemini attractive, and they may have a very lively relationship – for a while. Occasionally, Pisces ends up with a Sagittarius, but she will have to fade into the background and entirely submit to him. If she ends up with an Aquarius, expect strong emotional outbursts, and a marriage that revolves around the need to raise their children.

Tatiana Borsch

Printed in Great Britain
by Amazon

56754172R00175